sugar-free
kids

Over **150** Fun & Easy Recipes to Keep the Whole Family **Happy & Healthy**

INTERNATIONAL BESTSELLING AUTHOR

Maria Emmerich
Foreword by Halle Berry

Victory Belt Publishing Inc.

Las Vegas

First published in 2021 by Victory Belt Publishing Inc.

Copyright © 2021 Maria Emmerich

ISBN-13: 978-1-628601-31-2

Front and back cover photos by Hayley Mason and Bill Staley

Cover design by Kat Lannom

Interior design by Crizalie Olimpo and Charisse Reyes

Illustrations by Eli San Juan

Recipe photography by Jenny Ross

Photo on page 5 by Axelle/Bauer-Griffin / FilmMagic / Getty Images

Printed in Canada

TC 0322

Contents

Foreword by Halle Berry / 4

Letter to the Reader / 7

chapter 1: The Science Behind Sugar-Free Eating / 8

chapter 2: The Sugar-Free Kitchen / 54

chapter 3: Breakfast / 80

chapter 4: Appetizers & Snacks / 126

chapter 5: Lunches That Rock! / 172

chapter 6: Classic Kid Meals / 196

chapter 7: Instant Pot & Slow Cooker Recipes / 232

chapter 8: Holiday Fun / 252

chapter 9: Desserts / 290

chapter 10: Chaffles & Waffles / 332

chapter 11: Basics, Sauces & Dips / 362

chapter 12: Babies' First Foods / 390

With Gratitude / 404

Recipe Quick Reference / 406

Index / 415

Foreword

For over thirty years, I've found myself on an eternal health journey. In my twenties, I made the decision to look at my life from a holistic perspective and completely transformed my lifestyle from the ground up, tackling my overall wellness from a place that encompassed mind, body, and spirit. I learned to take food seriously because, to me, the most important factor in staying healthy and in great shape comes down to my diet and what I consume.

While I'm fortunate enough to call Maria Emmerich a friend today, I was a fan of her work long before we formed our bond. After receiving a life-changing diagnosis, I had to change every aspect of my life in order to retain my own sense of well-being—including my diet. I chose to nourish my body by following keto principles, and for me, it just didn't get much better than Maria's recipes. I was—and am continually—impressed by the way Maria effortlessly creates her keto-friendly meals with no shortage of effervescence or flavor.

In my life, I've used my platform to discuss the things that are most important to me, and my health falls within that category. I couldn't just keep Maria to myself—everyone deserves to know who she is and to pick up all of her books (they're bestsellers for a reason!). So one day, I went on Instagram to scream from the virtual rooftops that her incredible recipes had helped me in such a deeply personal way in the hopes that they could make an impact on someone else's health journey.

In a moment that I can only attribute to kismet, I discovered that Maria had written to me in order to thank me for highlighting some of her recipes, and the rest is herstory! We forged a connection rooted in our parallel philosophies on a ketogenic diet and the understanding of the power of nutrition when it comes to health struggles and personal healing.

For years, Maria has helped people like me who value health and nutrition while struggling with disorders that are out of our control. She's an international bestselling author of over sixteen books, with dedicated fans globally who have adopted healthier lifestyles because of her impact.

As parents, so many special moments with our children happen right in the kitchen. Maria has raised her two sons on a sugar-free diet, focusing on the incorporation of healthy protein and fats instead. She's now drawing from her personal success with her children in order to help other parents do the same—without sacrificing any of the fun. Even on days where it feels like there is no time, Maria has found a way to create a book for all families that's chock-full of quick and easy-to-make recipes sans processed sugars that still look and taste delicious to the pickiest eaters. Whether we're eating family dinner or making meals from scratch, I want to instill a love for food in my own children and teach them the transformative practice of nourishing their bodies with the best ingredients.

Maria is a guide for life change no matter where you are in your keto journey. I know she'll help change the lives of so many to come in the next generation of more mindful eaters. Happy cooking!

Actor and Academy Award Winner Halle Berry

Letter to the Reader

Our family is on a mission! We want to teach kids around the world to cook! Cooking seems to be a lost art these days. Many of us don't know where our food comes from, and just as many don't know how to make delicious food.

Our family likes to cook together, and we want to encourage you to do the same for the following reasons:

- It is much healthier. Even if you don't live a sugar-free lifestyle as we do, it is still more nutritious to eat homemade meals that you cook from scratch than to eat processed foods. Whole foods come with more vitamins and minerals than processed foods.

- It is much cheaper. Cooking from scratch is always less expensive than buying premade foods.

- It is fun to spend time together cooking! Many of my best memories as a mother involve making a mess in the kitchen with my boys!

- It builds self-confidence and helps improve moods.

- It teaches the whole family to respect where food comes from.

Cooking at home isn't hard. Plan, plan, plan is the key to success when it comes to our food and our health! We plan for all other aspects of life—college, vacations, weddings, etc. Why would planning our eating be any different?

With all these delicious and family-friendly recipes, we invite your family to join us in our sugar-free lifestyle! If you want to watch the boys cook many of the recipes in this book, check out our YouTube channel.

Many blessings to all of you!

Maria, Craig, Micah, and Kai

Find my blog: KetoMaria.com

Find my website: Keto-Adapted.com

Find my YouTube: youtube.com/mariamindbodyhealth

Find me on Instagram: @mariaemmerich

chapter 1:

the science behind sugar-free eating

It's a typical Monday morning, and the whole family is running late. The school bus is coming, but the kids haven't eaten anything yet. So you pour them a glass of no-sugar-added, "all-natural" grape juice and toss a breakfast bar their way. Then they get on the bus, and no one is late. Whew! Thank goodness for prepackaged "food."

No time for breakfast means no time to pack lunch, either, so the kids have to eat school lunch—chicken nuggets with a side of mashed potatoes from a box, a roll, some fruit cocktail, and chocolate milk. After-school programs and sports keep them at school until 4:30, so they grab a granola bar and a small bottle of Gatorade to keep their energy up. Once all the activities are over, you're tired from driving the kids all over the place, so you throw in a frozen pizza for dinner, followed by a bowl of Lucky Charms with skim milk a few hours later for a bedtime snack.

Does this scenario sound familiar?

Tuesday is a better day. Everyone has time for breakfast at home. The kids have Honey Nut Cheerios (10 teaspoons of sugar) with skim milk (3½ teaspoons of sugar) and a sliced banana on top (6 teaspoons of sugar). You pack a lunch of Lunchables turkey and cheddar (14¾ teaspoons of sugar), Goldfish crackers (5 teaspoons of sugar), and a juice box (6¾ teaspoons of sugar). The after-school snack is yogurt-covered raisins (5 teaspoons of sugar) and Gatorade (3½ teaspoons of sugar). You have time to make dinner, so you cook spaghetti with meat sauce (10¾ teaspoons of sugar), a side of garlic bread (5½ teaspoons of sugar), a salad with fat-free French dressing (2¼ teaspoons of sugar), and skim milk (3½ teaspoons of sugar). Dessert is fat-free frozen yogurt (9½ teaspoons of sugar). When the day is over, you think you've done pretty well. But have you? That comes out to a total of *86 teaspoons of sugar* for the day, or more than 1¾ cups.

Do you know how much sugar is normally present in our blood? One cup? Two cups? No, one *teaspoon* is normal for adults, and even less for babies, children, and teens. Consuming large amounts of sugar raises blood glucose; rising blood glucose significantly increases insulin production; and chronically elevated insulin is toxic to our bodies and cells.

You often hear parents say, "Let them be kids," and have sugary treats and junk foods. Or, "A little sugar won't hurt them." But the average American child is not getting a "little sugar"; they are getting a *ton of it*. According to the National Cancer Institute and the Centers for Disease Control and Prevention National Health and Nutrition Examination Survey, children as young as one to three years of age typically consume around 12 teaspoons (48 grams) of added sugar a day! And that is just *added* sugar; they also get naturally occurring sugar from foods like apples and milk. On top of that, they are getting much *more* sugar from carbohydrates that quickly turn into sugar in the body, in the form of cereals, pasta, pizza, cookies, candy, and other kid-favorite foods. (I'll talk more about how the body processes various fuels a little later in this chapter.)

A 2010 study showed that the top sources of energy (that is, calories) for two- to eighteen-year-olds were grain desserts (138 kcal per day), pizza (136 kcal per day), and soda (118 kcal per day). Sugar-sweetened beverages (soda and fruit drinks combined) provided 173 kcal per day. Nearly 40 percent of their total energy came from these empty calories![1] I'm sure that number is even higher today. Do we really want our kids getting half of their calories from foods and drinks devoid of vitamins, minerals, and complete proteins, all of which are essential for their growth and development?

We all want to spare our kids from the health problems that we may have developed as adults due to years of poor nutrition, such as fatty liver, diabetes, and heart disease. And we want to give them the best chance to succeed later in life. Why would we put them on the same path that has led to the current adult obesity epidemic and expect that when they turn eighteen, they will magically learn how to eat healthy? We need to address the source of these problems and stop inundating our kids with sugar-filled foods.

We spend lots of money and time making sure our kids get the best education, participate in activities like sports, and learn good manners and respect for others. Why aren't we putting the same effort into the most important thing we can do for our kids? We need to teach them about which foods are healthy and why, giving them the tools they need to enjoy good health later in life.

[1] J. Reedy and S. M. Krebs-Smith, "Dietary sources of energy, solid fats, and added sugars among children and adolescents in the United States," *Journal of the American Dietetic Association* 110, no. 10 (2010): 1477–84.

You and a friend are having a picnic by the side of a river. Suddenly, you hear a shout from the water—a person is drowning. Without thinking, you and your friend dive in, grab the drowning person, and swim to shore. Before you can recover, you hear another person crying for help. So you and your friend jump back into the river to rescue her as well. Then another person and another and another. The two of you can barely keep up with the rescue efforts. Suddenly, you see your friend wading out of the water, walking away from you. "Where are you going?" you ask. Your friend answers, "I'm going upstream to find out why all these people are falling in the water."

Where Sugar Hides

When I was a teenager, I would often skip lunch and eat fat-free frozen yogurt instead. I believed the advertisements that said it was a healthy option. In the absence of fat, the frozen yogurt caused my blood sugar to go extra high. It wasn't healthy at all! Like many seemingly healthy foods, it packs a ton of sugar.

Sugar in its various forms hides in many places, both in foods that are obviously sweet, like the frozen yogurt I loved as a teen, and in those that are not sweet and are often considered healthy, even though they are not. Here are some common foods fed to children and the amount of sugar each one contains:

Food	Cubes	Food	Cubes
1 tablespoon Heinz ketchup	1¼ cubes	1 small orange	6 cubes
1 cup skim milk	3½ cubes	2 slices whole-wheat bread	6 cubes
½ cup Campbell's condensed tomato soup	5 cubes	CLIF Kid Zbar chocolate chip snack bar	6 cubes
1 small ear corn on the cob	5 cubes	6 ounces Yoplait lowfat strawberry yogurt	6¾ cubes
1.1 ounces Goldfish crackers (1 serving)	5 cubes	1 cup unsweetened grape juice	9½ cubes
1 cup grapes	6 cubes	1 cup Cheerios with 1 cup skim milk	10¾ cubes
1 cup Minute Maid orange juice	6 cubes	1 large fast-food strawberry milkshake	16½ cubes
1 medium banana	6 cubes	4 dates	16½ cubes
1 small apple	6 cubes		

These savory foods often have sugar added to them. Some of them have both starch and added sugar!

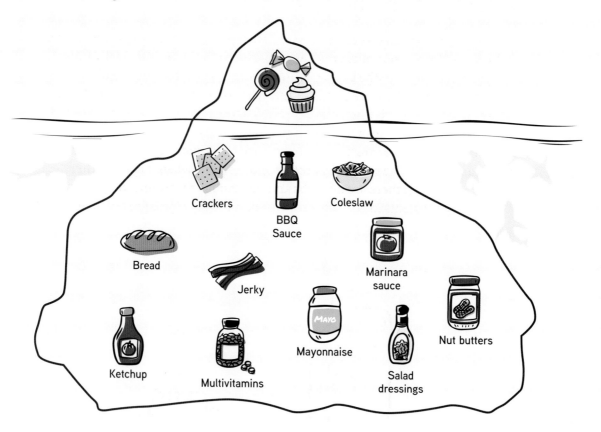

You may not think that you eat sugar, but did you know that a 9-ounce bag of potato chips turns into more sugar in your blood than a milkshake? Yep, the carbohydrates are broken down into glucose (or blood sugar) and sent into your bloodstream. That's what all carbohydrates do; they end up as sugar in your body. Even complex carbohydrates—found in foods like oats, brown rice, bananas, and potatoes—are just long chains of simple sugars. The digestive tract breaks them into sugar as soon as they are digested.

The Three Macronutrients That Make Up the Food We Eat

Let's look at the components of the food we eat and how our bodies process them.

There are three macronutrients: carbohydrate, protein, and fat. Each of them has a specific function in the body, but only one is not necessary in the diet: carbohydrate. While there are essential fatty acids (like omega-3 and omega-6 fats) and essential amino acids (the building blocks of proteins), there are no essential carbohydrates. The body can make any glucose it needs on its own.

Carbohydrate and fat are the body's primary fuels, and protein is used for building and repair. The body uses protein as a fuel only when it has no other choice—that is, when there are no carbs and not enough fat around. So you can think of macronutrients in two categories: building blocks (protein) and fuels (fat and carbs).

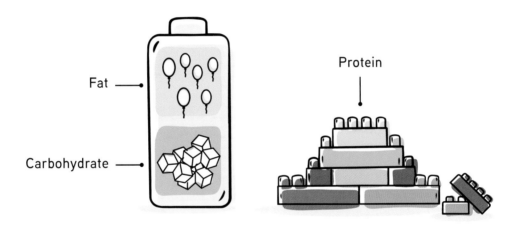

Within each of these three macronutrient categories, there are healthy options and harmful ones.

Carbohydrates

Carbohydrates come predominantly from plant foods—fruits, vegetables, grains, honey, maple syrup, etc. Processed foods are full of them.

Almost all carbohydrates—both complex carbs and simple sugars—are broken down into glucose in the body. The body can use glucose as a fuel, but there is a small storage tank for it. A 75-pound kid can store only about 50 grams of glucose (200 calories' worth) in the liver in the form of glycogen and about 200 grams of glucose (800 calories' worth) in the muscles; a 150-pound adult might store twice as much. The glucose stored in the muscles is locked in there (it can't return to the blood) and gets used only during intense exercise like sprinting or a long run. A brisk one-mile walk will not typically use any of the glucose in the muscles. And unless the rest of the stored glucose is burned as fuel (which is unlikely if the person is sedentary), any excess gets turned into fat to be stored in the body's fat cells.

Starch is a type of carbohydrate. It looks like a string of Christmas tree lights. Once you eat the "string," it's broken down into individual lights, aka sugar. Starch becomes sugar in your blood. So, in my mind, crackers, chips, and noodles are also sugar even though they don't taste sweet.

Too often I hear, "My kids are thin and active! They can eat whatever they want! And they need sugar and carbs for energy!" However, remember that there are no essential carbohydrates. Consider that Zach Bitter, who recently broke the world record time for a 100-mile run on a treadmill in just over twelve hours, eats low-carb/keto. A body like his that taps into stored fat for energy instead of running on sugar is less likely to develop sudden fatigue—what marathoners call "bonking"—during endurance sports.

The sugar-free child athlete

If your kids are into sports or are very active, keep these tips in mind to help them maximize their performance. Remember, kids don't need sugar and carbs for energy, but they do need to get the right balance of electrolytes and focus on other things that will help them perform at their best.

- Try a sugar-free electrolyte drink mix like LMNT or Re-Lyte instead of a sugary sports drink like Gatorade.

- Add more fat to their meals for energy.

- Make sure they eat enough protein to repair and replenish, especially if they get injured. Adding collagen can help with healing and repair.

- Get more sleep! Sleep repairs the body after strenuous activity.

- Add magnesium glycinate, or opt for magnesium foot soaks or baths. Most of us are deficient in magnesium due to our depleted soils and filtered water, so it's good for everyone to supplement.

- Consider adding zinc: As we sweat, we lose a lot of zinc, which is essential for immune health and muscles. Be aware that beef has zinc, but low zinc levels in the body can cause sugar cravings, acne on the face and/or back, and low immunity if your child sweats a lot.

We are sugar-free athletes, too! I love being one of the fastest players on the team. While most of the other kids need breaks and snacks, Kai and I have endless energy! When we refuel, we focus on proteins and healthy fats.

Fruits and vegetables are carbs, too

My mom is a smart woman, but when I told her there are only three macronutrients, she asked, "What about fruits and veggies?" Many people are like my mother. Some even think that since plant foods are full of vitamins and minerals, they are "free foods" that can and should be eaten in abundance. You need to understand that fruits and veggies are carbohydrates.

Millions of years ago, our early ancestors experienced a fat-gaining phenomenon from fruit, which was nature's candy, even though they consumed fructose (the type of sugar found in fruit) in the form of natural fruits rather than massive doses of high-fructose corn syrup as people do today. During the summer, they would consume large amounts of fruit and put on weight to survive the famine during the colder months. This led to a genetic mutation that resulted in a more significant uric acid response to fructose. The more fructose or sugar eaten, the more uric acid the body produces, and the liver and intestines' ability to absorb sugar increases along with it. (That is a bad thing!) Many of my clients have experienced this snowball effect, which leads to a sensitivity to fructose absorption. Once they head down that path, it is almost impossible to stop.

The United States Department of Agriculture's recommendation to eat two to five cups of fruits and vegetables a day needs to be updated for this reason. This suggestion is problematic. A few years ago, I read that most kids actually do get the recommended number of servings of fruits and vegetables. Are you shocked to read this? Yep, they eat french fries, onion rings, and ketchup. It's sad, but these forms of fruits and vegetables do fit the USDA guidelines. Will children reap health benefits from eating these foods? Absolutely not.

Eating three bananas a day isn't a good idea, either. Studies show that today's produce is relatively low in phytonutrients and much higher in sugar than it was in Paleolithic times. Consumers want fruits that taste sweet, so scientists modify them accordingly—to get kids to eat them, if nothing else. The sad part is that we think it's a good thing when kids eat massive amounts of fruit.

Modern Fruits Compared to Ancient Fruits

Wild Peach

1 inch across
and only 64%
edible

Modern Peach

67 times larger
and 90% edible
with 4 times as
much sugar

Wild Banana

Stocky and
hard with large,
tough seeds
throughout

Modern Banana

Nearly seedless,
3 times longer,
and over 21%
sugar

On a visit to the Minnesota Zoo, a zookeeper mentioned to us that even though some of the animals would eat berries in the wild, they could not feed them the hybridized berries that we consume. These sweeter berries would cause them to put on too much weight and develop fatty liver. Interesting!

Sure, many high-sugar fruits contain antioxidants such as vitamins A, C, and E. Antioxidants protect cells against the effects of free radicals, which are molecules produced when the body breaks down food. But you produce little to no free radicals if you stick to low-sugar foods. Interestingly, an orange that is high in vitamin C also packs a lot of sugar. Glucose and vitamin C have similar chemical structures, so what happens when sugar consumption goes up? They compete with one another for entry into the cells. If more glucose is present, less vitamin C will be allowed in. It doesn't take much: a blood glucose level of 120 mg/dl reduces the phagocytic index—which essentially measures the rate at which the immune system can eliminate harmful foreign particles and bacteria—by 75 percent. So, when you eat sugar, whether it's in the form of a candy bar or a piece of fruit, think of your immune system slowing to a crawl. This is why the amount of vitamin C your body needs depends on how many carbs you eat. The fewer carbs you consume, the less vitamin C your body needs!

To help you make the best choices when it comes to fruits and vegetables, I've grouped them according to how much sugar they contain. (Yes, botanically speaking, those non-sweet foods like olives and cucumbers are fruits!) Stick to the green-light produce if you can.

Fruits Highest in Sugar

- Mangoes
- Grapes
- Cherries
- Pears
- Watermelon
- Figs
- Bananas
- Corn

Veggies Highest in Sugar/Carbs

- Potatoes
- Sweet potatoes
- Beets

- Cantaloupe
- Honeydew melon

- Peas
- Butternut squash

Fruits Lowest in Sugar

- Olives
- Cucumbers
- Avocados
- Zucchini
- Chayote squash
- Eggplant
- Tomatoes
- Limes
- Lemons
- Raspberries
- Blueberries
- Blackberries
- Strawberries

Low-Sugar Veggies

- Iceberg lettuce
- Celery
- Jicama
- Button mushrooms
- Bell peppers
- Leafy greens
- Asparagus
- Broccoli
- Cauliflower
- Radishes
- Garlic
- Cabbage
- Bok choy

Protein

As mentioned earlier, protein, in the form of the essential amino acids histidine, isoleucine, leucine, lysine, methionine, phenylalanine, threonine, tryptophan, and valine, serves as the body's building blocks. Our bodies are constantly constructing and rebuilding cells. Protein fuels kids' growth, giving their bodies what they need to become taller and stronger. It also helps shuttle oxygen and nutrients to where they are needed.

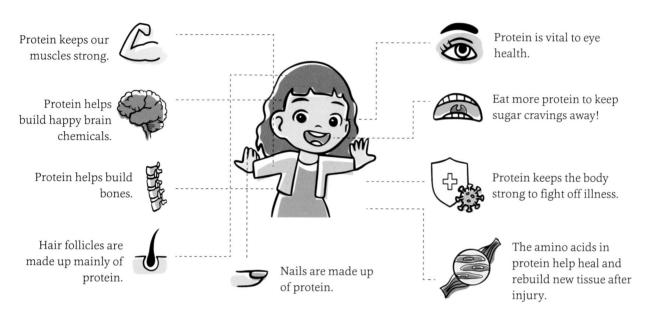

Protein keeps our muscles strong.

Protein helps build happy brain chemicals.

Protein helps build bones.

Hair follicles are made up mainly of protein.

Nails are made up of protein.

Protein is vital to eye health.

Eat more protein to keep sugar cravings away!

Protein keeps the body strong to fight off illness.

The amino acids in protein help heal and rebuild new tissue after injury.

Protein can come from animals or plants. But there's an important difference between the two sources: animal proteins are complete proteins, whereas plant proteins are not. Proteins comprise many different amino acids. The more complete a protein is, the better it is at building muscle and cells.

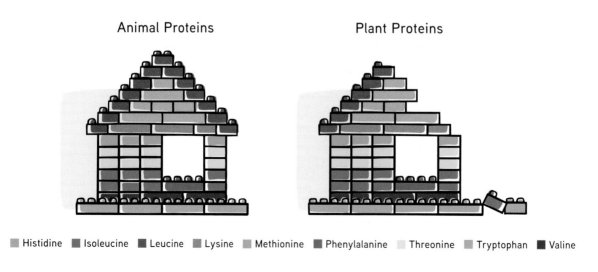

Animal Proteins   Plant Proteins

Histidine Isoleucine Leucine Lysine Methionine Phenylalanine Threonine Tryptophan Valine

How much do you need to eat to get enough complete protein to build muscle? Let's compare broccoli, a significant source of plant protein, to beef. You would have to eat an awful lot of broccoli to get the same amount of the amino acid leucine that you'd get from a very reasonable 7-ounce portion of sirloin steak!

How Much Protein Is Really Needed to Trigger Muscle Building?

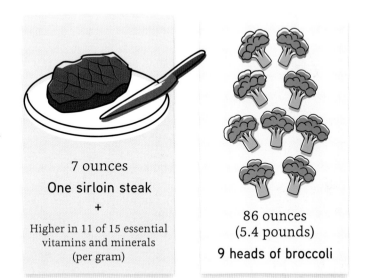

7 ounces
One sirloin steak
+
Higher in 11 of 15 essential
vitamins and minerals
(per gram)

86 ounces
(5.4 pounds)
9 heads of broccoli

(per 100g)	Beef	Broccoli
Calcium	11 mg	47 mg
Magnesium	19 mg	18 mg
Phosphorus	175 mg	66 mg
Potassium	370 mg	316 mg
Iron	3.3 mg	0.7 mg
Zinc	4.5 mg	0.4 mg
Selenium	14.2 mg	2.3 mg
Vitamin A	40 IU	623 IU
Vitamin B6	0.4 mg	0.3 mg
Vitamin B12	2 mcg	0 mcg
Vitamin C	2 mg	89 mg
Vitamin D	7 IU	0 IU
Vitamin E	1.7 mg	0.8 mg
Niacin	4.8 mg	0.6 mg
Folate	6 mcg	61 mcg

Complete proteins are even more critical for kids; they are important to all cells, organs, muscles, tissues, and bones. Making complete proteins the centerpiece of your family's meals is vital for ensuring their bodies get the essential nutrients they need. If you rely on plant foods for protein, your children won't build the muscle they need to grow.

Proteins that have complete amino acids:

- Beef
- Bison
- Pork
- Venison
- Chicken
- Turkey
- Duck
- Pheasant
- Fish
- Seafood
- Eggs
- Dairy

It's helpful to remember that animal proteins are also rich in vitamins and minerals. As you focus on feeding your kids lots of protein, know that they're getting lots of vitamins and minerals, too.

Fats

Fat (or ketones made from fat) is the body's preferred fuel source because the body's tank for storing fat is much larger than its tank for storing sugar from carbohydrates. A lean 75-pound kid with 15 percent body fat has over 5,100 grams of fat stored on their body, which is 45,900 calories of fat—and an obese adult might have over 1 million calories stored as fat! Compare this to the meager 1,000 calories of glucose that this same child can store in their body. This abundance is why fat is the body's preferred fuel.

There are four types of fat:

- **Saturated fats (SFA)** come mainly from animal sources and are more likely to be solid at room temperature.

- **Trans fats** are artificial fats manufactured in a laboratory to make liquid vegetable oils more solid at room temperature. They include margarine, shortening, hydrogenated oils, and partially hydrogenated oils.

- **Monounsaturated fats** are found in avocados, peanut butter, many nuts and seeds, and plant-based oils. They are usually liquid at room temperature but tend to solidify when refrigerated.

- **Polyunsaturated fats (PUFA)** are found in nuts, seeds, soybeans, and plant-based oils and are usually liquid at room temperature. The two types of PUFAs are omega-6 (which includes linoleic acid [LA], arachidonic acid [ARA], gamma linoleic acid [GLA], and conjugated linoleic acid [CLA]) and omega-3 (which includes alpha-linolenic acid [ALA], eicosapentaenoic acid [EPA], and docosahexaenoic acid [DHA]).

Saturated fats and cholesterol

I believe that it's best to focus on saturated fats. They are very stable because they do not oxidize (become rancid) quickly; oxidized oils cause inflammation in our bodies. The higher the saturated fat content in a food, the better.

Here are the healthiest fats based on their saturated and polyunsaturated fat contents:

Coconut oil	1.9% PUFA (92% SFA)
Palm kernel oil	2% PUFA (82% SFA)
Cocoa butter	3% PUFA (60% SFA)
Beef tallow	3.1% PUFA (49.8% SFA)
Butter	3.4% PUFA (50% SFA)
Ghee	4% PUFA (48% SFA)
High-oleic sunflower oil	9% PUFA (8% SFA)
Olive oil	9.9% PUFA (14% SFA)
Macadamia oil	10% PUFA (15% SFA)
Avocado oil	10% PUFA (11% SFA)
Lard	12% PUFA (41% SFA)
Duck fat	13% PUFA (25% SFA)
Hazelnut oil	14% PUFA (10% SFA)
Almond oil	17% PUFA (8.2% SFA)

Saturated fats are not the cause of modern diseases, as many health organizations claim. On the contrary, they play a lot of vital roles in body chemistry. Saturated fatty acids

- Make up at least 50 percent of cell membranes. They maintain our cells' necessary stiffness and integrity.

- Play a vital role in bone health. For calcium to be effectively incorporated into the skeletal structure, at least 50 percent of dietary fats should be saturated.

- Guard the liver against alcohol and other toxins.

- Strengthen the immune system.

- Have antimicrobial properties, which protect us against harmful microorganisms in the digestive tract.

Even the *Journal of the American College of Cardiology,* one of the original pushers of the idea that people should avoid eating saturated fats, recently published a report stating that those recommendations should be reconsidered and that "There is no robust evidence that current population-wide arbitrary upper limits on saturated fat consumption in the United States will prevent [cardiovascular disease] or reduce mortality."[2]

We also need to eat foods containing cholesterol, which is a sterol, or type of lipid (fat). Breast milk is filled with cholesterol because Mother Nature knows that cholesterol fuels a growing brain and helps a baby thrive! The brain contains the most cholesterol in the body.

Cholesterol is not the bad guy that it is made out to be; it is vital for every cell in the body. You cannot live one day without it! I like to refer to cholesterol particles as the firefighters in our bodies; they help stop the "fire," or inflammation.

Cholesterol is so important to the human body that nature has a backup plan in the event that your diet falls short. If you don't get enough cholesterol from the food you eat, your liver steps in to make cholesterol to maintain a baseline level. The large amount of insulin that is released in a low-fat, high-carb diet also triggers the body to tap off leftover blood sugar into the liver to make cholesterol and triglycerides, which are used for energy and fat storage.

In its natural, unstressed state, your liver makes 75 percent of the cholesterol your body needs. The rest comes from some of the foods you eat: meat, shellfish, eggs, butter, and other full-fat dairy products. If you deprive yourself of dietary cholesterol, your liver overproduces cholesterol to compensate and stocks up. This overdrive state can't shut off until you start eating cholesterol again.

Here are some of the key roles that cholesterol plays in our bodies:

- Cholesterol is vital for the production and function of serotonin receptors in the brain. Serotonin is the body's feel-good chemical. Low cholesterol levels have been linked to depression and aggression.

- Mother's milk is high in cholesterol and contains an important enzyme that assists the baby in utilizing this nutrient. Babies and children need foods high in cholesterol to ensure proper development of the brain and nervous system. (We need it as adults, too!)

- Cholesterol acts as a precursor or building block to essential hormones that help us deal with stress and protect our bodies against cancer and heart disease. It is also important to our sex hormones like androgen, testosterone, estrogen, and progesterone. Women trying to get pregnant have more success on a diet high in saturated fats and cholesterol because of this.

---

[2] A. Astrup, F. Magkos, D. M. Bier, et al., "Saturated fats and health: a reassessment and proposal for food-based recommendations: *JACC* State-of-the-Art Review," *JACC Journals* 76, no. 7 (2020): 844–57.

- Cholesterol is necessary for us to utilize fat-soluble vitamins such as A, E, K, and specifically D, which is needed for healthy bones and muscles, proper immune and nervous system function, effective insulin production and mineral metabolism, reproduction, and proper growth.

So don't fear eating saturated fat or cholesterol, but do focus on limiting or avoiding the fats that can have negative effects on long-term health. Let's take a look at those bad fats.

Trans fats

There isn't much to say about trans fats except stay away from them at all costs! Trans fats are so bad for you that they are banned in most countries, but they still pop up sometimes in processed foods in the United States.

Polyunsaturated fats

We know that sugar is terrible for our health, but linoleic acid (an omega-6 PUFA fat) is another scary villain I want you to be aware of. Linoleic acid (LA) is one bad dude that harms cells more than most people realize. Let me put it in a way my boys would understand—they love superheroes!

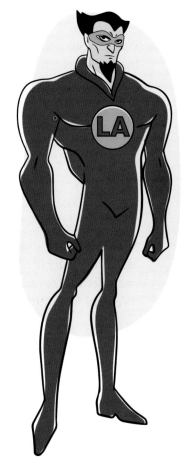

If you are familiar with Batman, you know the Joker and the Penguin are the bad guys. If sugar were a supervillain, it would be the Joker, and vegetable oil (the most common source of LA) would be the Penguin—slimy, globulus, and hard to pin down.

High amounts of PUFAs (especially LA) are harmful because they oxidize quickly and easily. There are many PUFA oils, but here is a short list:

Grapeseed oil	70.6% PUFA
Sunflower oil	68% PUFA
Flaxseed oil	66% PUFA
Safflower oil	65% PUFA
Corn oil	54.6% PUFA
Walnut oil	53.9% PUFA
Cottonseed oil	52.4% PUFA
Vegetable oil (soybean oil)	51.4% PUFA
Sesame oil	42% PUFA
Canola oil	19% PUFA

These harmful vegetable oils are everywhere, and doctors tell us they are healthy. So, mistakenly, too many people have traded healthy saturated fats like coconut oil and butter for vegetable oils. Soybean oil now accounts for 60 percent of all edible oil consumed in the United States. This increase directly mirrors the rise in obesity rates in recent decades.[3]

The following graph shows the alarming rise in the use of these unhealthy oils since the 1960s, and especially in recent years.[4]

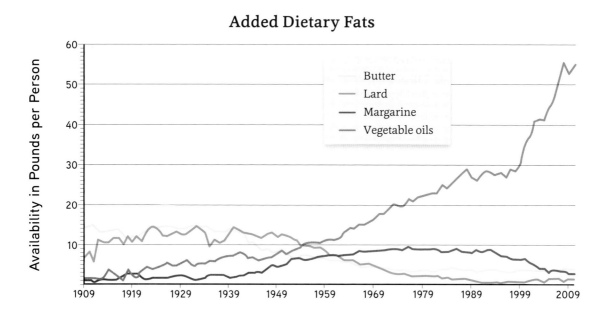

Added Dietary Fats

These oils release toxic chemicals called aldehydes that have been linked to dementia, cancer, and heart disease. If you are concerned about heart disease, you need to understand that vegetable oils can also cause plaque buildup in the arteries, leading to heart disease. Vegetable oils contribute to weight gain as well because they block the enzymes that help break down fat for energy.

[3] University of California–Riverside, "Soybean oil causes more obesity than coconut oil, fructose: scientists found mice on high soybean oil diet showed increased levels of weight gain, diabetes compared to mice on a high fructose diet or high coconut oil diet," ScienceDaily, 22 July 2015, https://www.sciencedaily.com/releases/2015/07/150722144640.htm.

[4] T. L. Blasbalg, J. R. Hibbeln, C. E. Ramsden, et al., "Changes in consumption of omega-3 and omega-6 fatty acids in the United States during the 20th century," *American Journal of Clinical Nutrition* 93, no. 5 (2011): 950–62.

Scientists have been researching the use of these harmful oils for years, and the results of studies such as this[5] are remarkable! The researchers divided mice into four groups:

- Group 1 included coconut oil, which consists primarily of saturated fat.

- Group 2 included half coconut oil and half soybean oil.

- Groups 3 and 4 included added fructose, comparable to the amount consumed by many Americans.

Each group was fed the same number of calories, so you would think that their weight would have stayed about the same. However, the mice on the soybean oil–enriched diet gained almost 25 percent more weight than the mice on the coconut oil diet and 9 percent more weight than those on the fructose-enriched diet.

In the past, I would have thought the fructose groups would have gained the most weight, but in this study, the groups given fructose gained only 12 percent more weight than those on the saturated fat diet. Compared to the coconut oil group, the soybean oil group also had more significant fat deposits, insulin resistance, diabetes, and fatty liver with signs of injury, all of which are hallmarks of metabolic syndrome.

PUFA-Driven Diabetes

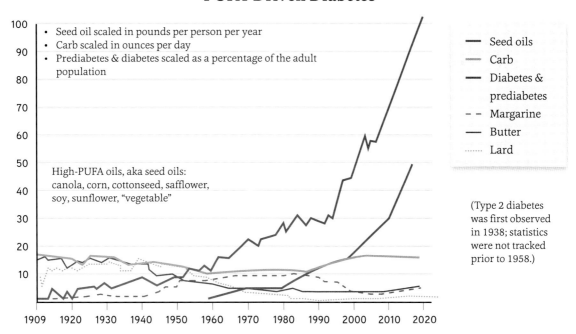

(Type 2 diabetes was first observed in 1938; statistics were not tracked prior to 1958.)

As you can see in this chart, an increase in seed oil consumption directly correlates to a rise in diabetes—even more so than an increase in carbohydrate consumption!

---

[5] P. Deol, J. R. Evans, J. Dhabi, et al., "Soybean oil is more obesogenic and diabetogenic than coconut oil and fructose in mouse: potential role for the liver," *PLOS One*, July 22, 2015.

The researchers found that adding fructose to the diet had less severe metabolic impacts than soybean oil, even though it caused negative effects in the kidneys and a marked increase in prolapsed rectums, a symptom of inflammatory bowel disease. "This was a major surprise for us—that soybean oil is causing more obesity and diabetes than fructose—especially when you see headlines every day about the potential role of sugar consumption in the current obesity epidemic," said Poonamjot Deol, a professor of cell biology and neuroscience, who directed the project.

I am shocked at how often I see vegetable oils added to foods. It's no big surprise that the vast majority of processed foods and boxed snacks contain PUFAs, but I have even seen it in salmon! Here are a few everyday items containing PUFA-heavy vegetable oils that people routinely consume on sugar-free diets:

- Butter substitutes
- Fast-food burgers
- Mayonnaise
- Peanut butter
- Salad dressing
- Scrambled eggs and omelets from restaurants

As mentioned earlier, there are two types of PUFAs: omega-6 and omega-3. Omega-6 fats are generally considered inflammatory, and omega-3 fats are good at fighting that inflammation. That is why it's good to keep these fats in balance. Both types are essential fatty acids; you do not need many of them to be healthy, but you do need some in your diet. There are good and bad omega-6 and omega-3 fats, however. As discussed previously, you want to limit or eliminate the omega-6 fat linoleic acid as much as possible.

Even omega-3 fats, when refined and stored on a shelf, can oxidize, as they aren't as stable as saturated fats. So aim to get your essential omega-3 and omega-6 fats from whole-food animal sources like fish, grass-fed beef, and pasture-raised chicken and eggs.

Makeup of Common Fats and Oils

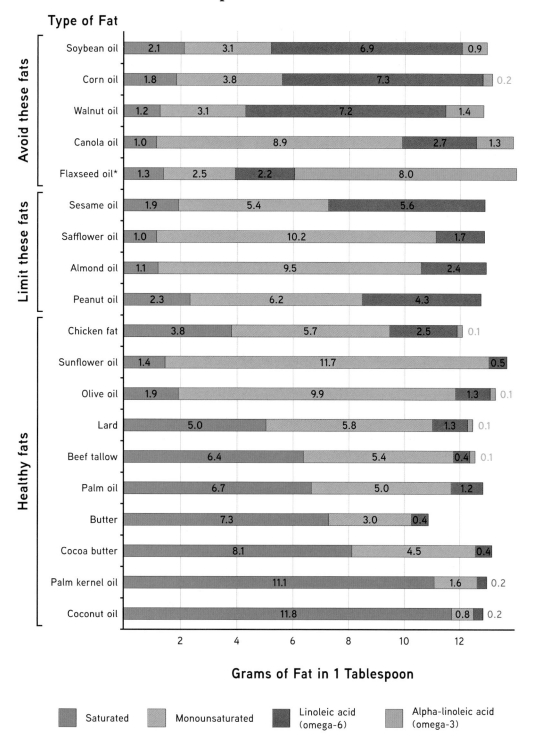

Type of Fat

Avoid these fats

Soybean oil	2.1	3.1	6.9	0.9
Corn oil	1.8	3.8	7.3	0.2
Walnut oil	1.2	3.1	7.2	1.4
Canola oil	1.0	8.9	2.7	1.3
Flaxseed oil*	1.3	2.5	2.2	8.0

Limit these fats

Sesame oil	1.9	5.4	5.6
Safflower oil	1.0	10.2	1.7
Almond oil	1.1	9.5	2.4
Peanut oil	2.3	6.2	4.3

Healthy fats

Chicken fat	3.8	5.7	2.5	0.1
Sunflower oil	1.4	11.7	0.5
Olive oil	1.9	9.9	1.3	0.1
Lard	5.0	5.8	1.3	0.1
Beef tallow	6.4	5.4	0.4	0.1
Palm oil	6.7	5.0	1.2
Butter	7.3	3.0	0.4
Cocoa butter	8.1	4.5	0.4
Palm kernel oil	11.1	1.6	0.2
Coconut oil	11.8	0.8	0.2

Grams of Fat: 2 4 6 8 10 12

Grams of Fat in 1 Tablespoon

- Saturated
- Monounsaturated
- Linoleic acid (omega-6)
- Alpha-linoleic acid (omega-3)

*Flax is a hormone disruptor and very high in phytoestrogens, which raise estrogen levels in the body. We don't recommend it for anyone.

Source: *Nutrition Action Healthletter,* Center for Science in the Public Interest

The Vicious Cycle of Sugar Consumption

Insulin and its counterbalancing hormone, glucagon, control energy metabolism in the body. That is to say, they control how fuels are released into the blood or stored. The word insulin may immediately bring to mind diabetes, and this association is valid because one of insulin's most crucial jobs is to control blood sugar levels. But insulin also handles all the energy (in the form of glucose, fats, and ketones) that is distributed throughout the body in the bloodstream, and the body tightly controls the amount of energy in the blood at any given moment.

Normal blood glucose is 85 mg/dl. That's about 1 teaspoon or 4 grams of sugar in your entire blood volume, which is only 16 calories! If you add up all the fuel in your entire blood volume at rest, you have a total of about 75 calories' worth of energy. You can imagine how your body must go into emergency mode when you consume a sugary drink—a 20-ounce bottle of Mountain Dew with its 77 grams of sugar, for example—that is rapidly absorbed into your bloodstream. This is almost twenty times the amount of glucose the body wants, so it must quickly increase insulin to prevent your blood sugar from reaching dangerous levels, which could seriously harm or even kill you. After this insulin spike, your blood sugar plummets, which means you become hungry again after just a couple of hours, and you find yourself reaching for another sugar-laden snack or drink. This vicious cycle, shown in the illustration below, continues throughout the day. And here is where metabolic damage begins.

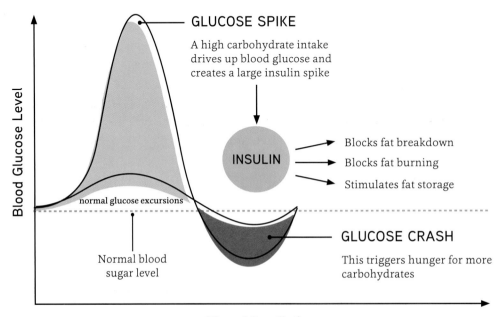

Eating Carbohydrates Leads to More Hunger and More Eating

GLUCOSE SPIKE

A high carbohydrate intake drives up blood glucose and creates a large insulin spike

INSULIN → Blocks fat breakdown
→ Blocks fat burning
→ Stimulates fat storage

Blood Glucose Level

normal glucose excursions

Normal blood sugar level

GLUCOSE CRASH

This triggers hunger for more carbohydrates

Time After Eating

When you eat a big meal with, let's say, 750 calories—that's ten times the fuel normally in the blood—your body knows it needs to get to work in order to protect you. To deal with all this incoming energy, it follows a process called *oxidative priority*, which is a fancy name for the order in which it processes fuels. Since the storage space for glucose is limited whereas the storage space for fat is enormous, your body begins by burning the carbs in your meal.

Meanwhile, the fat in the meal is stored away in your big fat storage tank. This is why you gain weight when you eat lots of sugar and carbs. And when you get the blood sugar crash and go for more carbs, the process begins again. The constant supply of glucose keeps your body from tapping into fat storage for fuel while allowing fat to accumulate.

Over time, this becomes a problem. Your adipose cells are like little balloons in which your body stores fat; you can fill them only so much before they get overstuffed. When these fat cells get too full, they reject insulin and will not allow any more fat to be stored. When many of your fat cells get filled to the point where they reject insulin, you are deemed *insulin resistant*. Your body tells your pancreas to put out more and more insulin because fat is starting to accumulate in your blood—that's when your triglyceride levels go up—but your fat cells won't accept any more fat. When your body has run out of space to store excess energy, a condition called *energy toxicity* develops. Fat starts to get pushed into your organs, like your liver and pancreas, leading to fatty liver disease and type 2 diabetes, respectively.

Constantly spiking insulin causes various other problems: it increases cholesterol production in the liver; thickens artery walls, resulting in high blood pressure; and causes the kidneys to retain salt and fluid.

Childhood prevalence of these issues is on the rise. Type 2 diabetes used to be known as "adult-onset diabetes" because it occurred only in adulthood, But we are seeing a sharp increase in cases in children. As of 2017–2018, 19.3 percent of kids ages two to nineteen in the US were obese. That is about 14.4 million children, and the number is rising every year.[6] This represents an increase of over 400 percent since 1980.[7] As a result, type 2 diabetes rates among kids are also growing. It has hit communities of color especially hard. According to the National Institutes of Health, in 2017, the rate of newly diagnosed cases had risen by 8.5 percent in Asian Americans and Pacific Islanders and 6.3 percent in non-Hispanic Black youths ages ten to nineteen, with smaller increases seen in Hispanic (3.1 percent) and white youths (0.6 percent). The rate for Native American young people was highest (8.9 percent).[8]

Nonalcoholic fatty liver disease (NAFLD) also used to be rare in children. Now it is estimated that 3 to 12 percent of children have NAFLD.[9]

---

[6] "Childhood obesity facts," Centers for Disease Control and Prevention, https://www.cdc.gov/obesity/data/childhood.html, last updated April 5, 2021.

[7] "Obesity rates and trend data," State of Childhood Obesity, https://stateofchildhoodobesity.org/data/

[8] J. Reedy and S. M. Krebs-Smith, "Dietary sources of energy, solid fats, and added sugars among children and adolescents in the United States," *Journal of the American Dietetic Association* 110, no. 10 (2010): 1477–84.

[9] H. Bush, P. Golabi, and Z. M. Younossi, "Pediatric non-alcoholic fatty liver disease," *Children* 4, no. 6 (2017): 48.

The best way to reverse this trend is to limit sugar and carbs, thereby ending the cycle of hunger that results from blood glucose spiking and dropping. When you eat less sugar and carbs, you tend to eat less overall because you aren't as hungry all the time. Your body, then, starts using fat as its primary fuel, lowering the amount of stored fat and reversing energy toxicity and all the damage it does. There's no need to spend huge amounts of money on prescription medications. I have seen time and time again with my clients how proper nutrition is the key to a healthy body. You can pay the doctor or pay the farmer.

Many of us with a family history of heart disease, high cholesterol, diabetes, high blood pressure, and other metabolic diseases inherited these tendencies from our birth parents. This does not mean we are destined to get these diseases no matter what, but we are much more susceptible to them if we follow the same diet and lifestyle. What we feed our children is so important. We want to give kids the tools to make healthy choices and avoid the same health struggles we may have faced. Sure, planning and preparing meals takes time, but we all set priorities. When your kids' attitude and grades improve, and when you lose weight, feel great, and look amazing, you will never regret the time you put into it!

The Harmful Effects of Eating Too Much Sugar

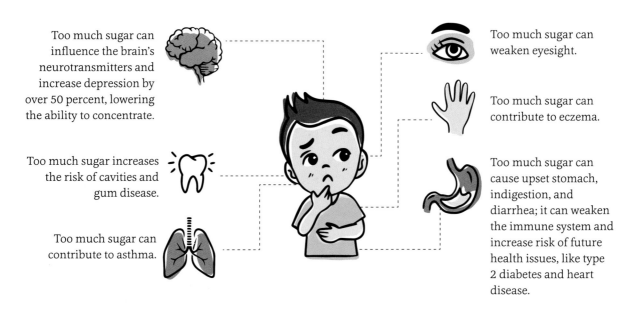

Too much sugar can influence the brain's neurotransmitters and increase depression by over 50 percent, lowering the ability to concentrate.

Too much sugar increases the risk of cavities and gum disease.

Too much sugar can contribute to asthma.

Too much sugar can weaken eyesight.

Too much sugar can contribute to eczema.

Too much sugar can cause upset stomach, indigestion, and diarrhea; it can weaken the immune system and increase risk of future health issues, like type 2 diabetes and heart disease.

Sugar and the Depletion of Micronutrients

In addition to doing metabolic damage, sugar depletes the body of important nutrients. Eating sugar creates a sequence of metabolic pathways that requires the body to use up more of its resources of important vitamins and minerals.

Magnesium

It takes twenty-eight molecules of magnesium to process one molecule of sugar. Having high blood sugar also causes the kidneys to excrete magnesium faster. Because magnesium is essential to stabilize blood sugar, a harmful cycle continues. Deficiencies cause muscle spasms and pain, insomnia, and fatigue. Magnesium assists in maintaining muscle and nerve function, maintains heartbeat, helps our immune system, and keeps bones strong.

Vitamin C

Have you ever noticed kids get sick a lot from Halloween until Valentine's Day? Several holidays during that period focus on candy. Studies show that sugar depresses the immune system, at least temporarily.[10] White blood cells need vitamin C so that they can phagocytize (ingest) viruses and bacteria, both of which can cause illness. The inside of a white blood cell requires a fifty times higher concentration than the outside, so the cells have to accumulate quite a bit of vitamin C. The phagocytic index tells you how rapidly a particular lymphocyte can gobble up a virus, bacteria, or cancer cell.

Sugar and vitamin C have similar chemical structures, so what happens when sugar levels go up? Sugar and vitamin C compete with one another to enter the cells. And the same thing that mediates the entry of glucose into cells mediates the entry of vitamin C into cells. If there is more glucose around, less vitamin C is going to be allowed in.

---

[10] S. Yu, G. Zhang, and L. H. Jin, "A high-sugar diet affects cellular and humoral immune responses in Drosophila," *Experimental Cell Research* 368, no. 2 (2018): 215–24.

Vitamin D

Fructose is a type of sugar. To break down fructose, the body increases the production of 25-hydroxylase, an enzyme that also breaks down vitamin D. This enzyme also hinders the production of another enzyme needed to create vitamin D.

Insufficient vitamin D is harmful in many ways; it weakens the immune system and increases the risk of depression, bone loss, and many other serious issues, including certain cancers.

Chromium

Chromium is important for regulating blood sugar. Low levels of chromium cause decreased glucose tolerance, a precursor to diabetes. High sugar intake causes chromium excretion. Studies have found that a diet consisting of 35 percent sugar increased chromium excretion rates by 300 percent.[11]

The Benefits of Cutting Sugar for Kids

Now that you know about the harmful effects of sugar in the body, let's talk about the benefits of a low-sugar diet for kids.

Our boys have been eating sugar-free and low-carb for over nine years and are thriving. When we adopted them at ages one and two, they barely registered on the growth charts. Within a little over a year, they were around the fiftieth percentile for weight, and now both of them are in the seventy-fifth percentile or above. Ample protein and nutrient-dense foods are fueling their growth. They are very sharp and have great memories. Micah has a nearly photographic memory and never forgets anything.

---

[11] A. S. Kozlovsky, P. B. Moser, S. Reiser, and R. A. Anderson, "Effects of diets high in simple sugars on urinary chromium losses," *Metabolism* 35, no. 6 (1986): 515–8.

Kai's Growth Chart

Birth to 36 months: Boys

Length-for-age and weight-for-age percentiles

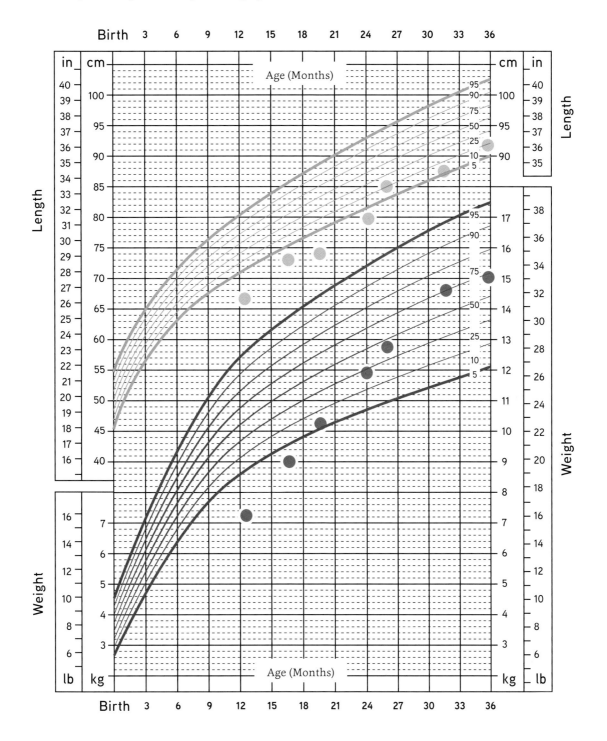

What else can cutting sugar help with? Over the past two decades, I have helped tons of parents get their kids on a sugar-free diet and seen huge improvements in moods, focus, overall health, and much more. Here are a few testimonials from my clients. For starters, I hear many stories from parents about ADHD and eczema, like this one:

> 66 I wish I had pics of my son's skin beforehand. But eating sugar-free has cleared up his eczema, and it has done miracles for his ADHD. I just had a meeting with his teacher this morning, who confirmed that he had been much more even-keeled."
>
> —Stacy

This lifestyle can be excellent for helping kids focus, too. Here is a report from another happy parent:

> 66 We put our ten-year-old son on your diet in November in the hope that it would help his ADHD symptoms. We did not use medication and did not want to, but his gluten-free diet was not enough. In December, his teacher remarked that he seemed more focused in class, especially after snack time, which used to be marked with bursts of energy and a lack of self-control. Although the new diet took more planning on my part and required him to try new foods, my son said he felt better. Well, last night, he got his report card. His grades went up in every subject. The change is remarkable. Thank you."
>
> —Katie

The improvements in moods and focus go beyond ADHD, and I have helped many clients with children on the autism spectrum. Here is one client:

> ❝ We just went on your diet plan, and there was an immediate shift in behavior. I honestly thought that we would have a grieving period over cake pops from Starbucks. In the past, we had an upset little girl every time she saw that dang green mermaid. I honestly think yanking the processed sugar out completely was way bigger for our child. She is four and has an ASD diagnosis. It's mostly speech and language we are dealing with, so explaining the changes to her was not going to help. She's on a whole new protocol, but this diet was the first step. We are very impressed by the removal of sugar. She takes one simple no for an answer now. It's crazy."
>
> — Heather

If you have a child on the autism spectrum, you understand just how powerful it is to be on a whole new level and protocol.

Here is another testimonial showing considerable improvements in moods:

> ❝ I have seen a complete behavior change in my three-year-old after switching to a sugar-free diet—like mind-blowing change. He is no longer angry all the time, and I've heard more I-love-yous since he stopped eating wheat and sugar than I did in the months before. This [diet] really does work! I have seen no change in my daughter, but her behavior was nothing like my son's. Neither of them has lost weight (they didn't need to, but growth was one of my earlier concerns about switching), and I've only seen positive outcomes. Give the body the nutrition it needs to function properly!"
>
> — Nicole

I have hundreds of client testimonials covering improved eczema, seizures, asthma, acid reflux, acne, gestational diabetes, massive weight loss, A1c control for children with type 1 diabetes, GERD, Crohn's, Tourette's, narcolepsy, and immune function. They show that not only is a sugar-free lifestyle not dangerous for kids, but it can be amazing for helping kids thrive and regain health. Yes, a sugar-free diet can be very helpful for the whole family.

> **"** I've lost 99 pounds eating your diet. I'm now weaning off fibromyalgia pain medication because this diet reduces inflammation and helps with my pain more than meds, so why take them? My husband lost 70 pounds, got off his CPAP at night, said goodbye to migraines, cured his acid reflux, and normalized his blood pressure. My oldest daughter lost about 20 pounds. My middle daughter has lost almost 50 pounds and reversed ADHD, oppositional defiant disorder, sleep apnea, migraines, and undiagnosable tummy troubles (her doctor assumed she was lying!). My youngest didn't need to lose any weight, but she no longer gets bloated after eating, and it doesn't take her two full weeks to get better after being sick anymore. Your diet has completely changed our family for the better."
>
> — Amanda

These examples demonstrate just how much a sugar-free, low-carb lifestyle can help kids. There is emerging science to back up these claims as well. A March 2021 study showed a link between sugar consumption and its effects on gut microbiome diversity, finding that "Diet-induced alterations in the gut microbiota may be linked with altered neurocognitive development."[12] Sugar consumption resulted in memory impairment and inflammation in the hippocampus (the part of the brain responsible for learning and memory) of young rats.[13] Another study showed that sugar consumption in early life had long-term negative effects on memory function.[14]

---

[12] E. E. Noble, C. A. Olson, E. Davis, et al., "Gut microbial taxa elevated by dietary sugar disrupt memory function," *Translational Psychiatry* 11, 194 (2021).

[13] T. M. Hsu, V. R. Konanur, L. Taing, et al., "Effects of sucrose and high fructose corn syrup consumption on spatial memory function and hippocampal neuroinflammation in adolescent rats," *Hippocampus* 25, no. 2 (2015): 227–39.

[14] E. E. Noble, T. M. Hsu, J. Liang, and S. E. Kanoski, "Early-life sugar consumption has long-term negative effects on memory function in male rats," *Nutritional Neuroscience* 22, no. 4 (2019): 273–83.

Nine Tips for Cutting Sugar

So you're ready to go sugar-free? Many families prefer to cut out all sugar at once. If going cold turkey seems too overwhelming for you, here are a few ways to gradually get sugar out of your life:

- Rid your pantry of table sugar and other sugars like brown sugar, coconut sugar, corn syrup, honey, maple syrup, and molasses. Keeping it in the house just provides a temptation to use it.

- Replace sodas and sugary drinks with the following:
  - » Water: It's free, and it's refreshing! And you can mix in a product like Everly that adds great flavor without any sugar.
  - » Sparkling water: A home sparkling water maker can help cut costs.
  - » Homemade sodas: We make sugar-free sodas with our soda machine, adding a touch of flavored liquid stevia (we like grape, lime, cola, or root beer) to the soda water.
  - » Herbal tea: Try hibiscus tea; it's fragrant and has a beautiful bright pink color.

- Toss the sugary sports/energy drinks. Kids don't need energy drinks for energy! Try electrolyte drink mixes without sugar, like Re-Lyte, Everly, and LMNT.

- Read labels and avoid products with added sugar.

- Eat a healthy, savory sugar-free breakfast. Starting the day with a bowl of sugary cereal will cause cravings for sugar later in the day.

- Focus on nutrient-dense proteins and brain-building fats. Consuming plenty of healthy fats and proteins will keep sugar cravings at bay.

- Start cutting out natural sugars, such as those found in fruits.

- Use natural sweeteners that are not harmful. See pages 75 and 76 for my suggestions.

- Get enough sleep. Lack of sleep causes the body to crave sugar.

> " Hi Maria! I wanted to give you an update on how you changed my whole family's life! To date, I've lost over 100 pounds (and counting). My husband no longer needs statins, and I am completely off my diabetes meds! My now-five-year-old is better than normal. She reads and writes at the first-grade level! When I changed my diet, all of a sudden, her interest in food changed towards the types of food that I ate. Her favorite is your 'apple' pie waffles."
>
> —Kate

Feeding Babies

For the first six months or so, babies do best on breast milk. We all know that breast milk is ideal, but many people do not realize that about 57 percent of the calories in breast milk are from fat, 38 percent are from carbs, and 5 percent are from protein. Over half of the fat is saturated, and breast milk is also high in cholesterol.

You might have noticed that breast milk has a pretty high carb content. Why is that? The answer is easy if you look at a baby's body proportions.

The brain is the biggest energy hog in the body. Adults' brains make up only about 2 percent of their body weight but consume about 25 percent of total energy. That little bundle of joy has different proportions. A baby's brain makes up about 10 percent of their total body weight, and some estimates put a baby's brain at up to 60 percent of its energy needs![15] So the amount of sugar a baby needs is proportionally higher because the baby's body has to fuel this huge brain.

Additionally, breast milk is designed to help a baby put on weight quickly to ensure survival. A lean baby wouldn't do well in a harsh winter. When fed both high carbs and high fat, a baby will put on body fat quickly. (This is true for adults, too, and is the major problem with the standard American diet.) On average, a baby boy goes from 10 percent body fat at birth to 24 percent at three months, while a baby girl goes from 10 percent to 26 percent.[16]

Babies also need lots of protein to grow. In fact, they need a much higher proportion of protein than at any other stage of life—over 3⅓ times as much as an adult. From their daily average of 750 ml of breast milk, they get about 19 grams (76 calories) of protein along with 22 grams of fat (198 calories) and 45 grams of carbs (180 calories). This is 2.7 times their lean mass in grams of protein per day!

After breastfeeding exclusively for about six months, you might wonder which foods you should transition your baby to. Many parents start supplementing with store-bought baby foods. But how does baby food compare to breast milk in terms of fat, protein, vitamins, and minerals? Here is a comparison of some common commercial baby foods to egg yolks, pureed beef, and beef liver. I have highlighted the first and second place foods for each nutrient with the darker and lighter colors, respectively, but I disqualified baby foods that are fortified with vitamins and minerals. This is the same as adding a multivitamin, which you could just as easily do if you were feeding the baby egg yolks or beef.

---

[15] D. G. Cotter, D. A. d'Avignon, A. E. Wentz, M. L. Weber, and P. A. Crawford, "Obligate role for ketone body oxidation in neonatal metabolic homeostasis," *Journal of Biological Chemistry* 286, no. 9 (2011): 6902–10.

[16] A. E. Carberry, P. B. Colditz, and B. E. Lingwood, "Body composition from birth to 4.5 months in infants born to non-obese women," *Pediatric Research* 68 (2010): 84–8.

Comparing Baby Foods

(per 100g)	Gerber Organics Apples & Peaches	Gerber Organics Pears, Carrots & Peas	Gerber Banana Puffs	Egg Yolks	Beef	Beef Liver
Calcium (mg)	5.1	16.3	171	129	11	11
Magnesium (mg)	4.6	9.9	59	5	19	18
Phosphorus (mg)	8.5	23.3	162	390	175	387
Potassium (mg)	101	151	152	109	370	380
Iron (mg)	0.28	0.4	21	2.7	3.3	8.8
Zinc (mg)	0.06	0.2	1.25	2.3	4.5	4
Selenium (mg)	0.32	0.3	23.5	56	14.2	39.7
Vitamin A (IU)	85.5	3,480	2.3	1,442	40	53,400
Vitamin B6 (mg)	0.03	0.05	0.56	0.35	0.4	1.1
Vitamin B12 (mcg)	0	0	0	2	2	111
Vitamin C (mg)	15.9	15.9	0.28	0	2	27
Vitamin D (IU)	0	0	0	218	7	19
Vitamin E (mg)	0.29	0.33	6.5	2.58	1.7	0.63
Niacin (mg)	0.22	0.36	11.42	0.02	4.8	17
Folate (mcg)	3.75	13.7	15	145	6	145
Fat	0	0	0	26.5	15	5.3
Protein	0	0.9	0	16	30	29
Carbs	14	14	82	0	0	0
Ingredients	Organic apples, organic peaches, **Vitamin C (ascorbic acid)**	Pears, carrots, peas, water, lemon juice concentrate, **Vitamin C (ascorbic acid)**	Rice flour, whole wheat flour, wheat starch, cane sugar, whole grain oat flour, dried apple puree, natural banana flavor, less than 1% of mixed tocopherols (to maintain freshness), sunflower lecithin, caramel color, turmeric extract color, **Vitamins and minerals, iron (electrolytic), Vitamin E (alpha tocopherol acetate)**	Egg yolks	Beef	Beef liver

What's striking to me is the lack of protein and saturated fat in baby foods. As I've said, babies need protein to grow! And, as I have shown, animal proteins are not only complete proteins but come with more vitamins and minerals, too.

If you think about it, most store-bought baby foods are vegetarian: vegetables like carrot, pea, and sweet potato; fruits like apple, banana, and pear; and even worse, grains like oatmeal, rice, and whole wheat. That is kind of shocking. Why are we switching babies from breast milk, which is loaded with healthy saturated fat, cholesterol, and protein, to baby food with no saturated fat, no cholesterol, and little to no protein at a critical time for growth and brain development? Baby food is about the worst thing you can feed to a child transitioning from breast milk.

Why Rice Cereal Is a Terrible Baby Food

Rice cereal is a common first food for babies. Here's why I think it's a bad choice:

- Rice cereal significantly spikes blood sugar and thus insulin levels.

- White rice cereal is 94 percent starch, all of which ends up as sugar in the blood. In other words, a bowl of rice cereal isn't much different from a bowl of sugar.

- Rice cereal has been found to contain arsenic (five times the amount found in oatmeal). Not only is arsenic a carcinogen, but it can also set up kids for health problems later in life.

- The only vitamins and minerals in rice cereal come from the fortification process. So it is nothing more than a bowl of starch (aka sugar) with a multivitamin added. Babies can get the iron and other nutrients they need from foods like red meat—no fortification necessary.

- Starting babies on a starchy diet of rice cereal sets them up for craving processed carbs like bread, cookies, and cakes when they get older.

Babies' First Solid Foods (6–24 months)

Instead of commercial baby food, try the following whole-food options. These foods are loaded with vitamins and minerals and will give your baby the saturated fat, cholesterol, and protein they need to grow and thrive. Plus, they are a lot less expensive than store-bought baby foods!

- Baked salmon or tuna (see the illustration, opposite, for age-appropriate sizes)

- Beef or chicken liver pâté

- Beef or other roasts (see chart for age-appropriate sizes)

- Pork ribs or chicken bones with a little meat left on them
- Bone broth
- Bone marrow
- Egg yolks (hard-boiled and mashed or crumbled into small bits)
- Ground beef or chicken (see chart for age-appropriate sizes)
- Pureed berries or no-churn ice cream for a treat
- Caviar and fish eggs

The size of the pieces you offer to the baby will vary by age. For younger babies (six to nine months), it is best to either puree the meat until there are no chunks or leave it in large pieces that they can't swallow (about the size of two adult fingers held together). This shape is easy for a baby to grab and hold. Babies can also gnaw on bigger pieces of steak or chicken bones. They will mostly be sucking out the juices and acquiring a taste for meat. If a piece breaks off in the baby's mouth, you can either remove it yourself or teach the child to spit it out. But if offering larger pieces, make sure to watch for any chunks that break off.

When babies are nine to twelve months old or so, you can start giving them very finely chopped pieces that they can pick up and easily swallow. Then, at twelve to twenty-four months, you can offer bite-sized pieces that they can start picking up with a fork. You can also begin feeding them foods that the rest of the family eats. Meat and nonstarchy veggies are great.

Age-Appropriate Food Sizes

How to cut meat by baby's age

6–9 months

9–12 months

12 months+

Ways to serve meat to babies

Cut into a finger (to suck juices from)

Bite size

Shredded

Ground, in sauce

Ground

Hamburger finger

A great method is called baby-led weaning (BLW). There have even been studies demonstrating that kids allowed to choose their own food from only nutrient-dense sources will choose what their bodies need for optimal growth and development.[17]

Don't be afraid to offer healthy foods to your baby. Their tastes are still forming, and their palates will be developed by what you feed them. If you give them nothing but sugar and starch, which is what most parents do, their palates will shift to the sweet end of the spectrum, and they are likely to want more and more of that sweet taste. I see too many kids who have been fed only sugars and starches and now eat basically bread and sugar and not much else. Their palates are so limited that they aren't even willing to try other flavors.

Studies have shown that kids need to try a food eight or nine times to develop a taste for it.[18] If your baby (or older child) doesn't like one of these healthy foods the first time you offer it, offer it a few more times before giving up. They just might come to love it—even if you don't!

Carbohydrate Consumption for Kids

An adult whose body is fueled primarily by fat needs about 60 grams of glucose per day for fueling the neurons of the brain, making red blood cells, and other functions that require glucose. Gluconeogenesis is the body's process for turning protein into glucose, and it can easily supply this amount of glucose even if you eat no carbs.

So, if an adult doesn't need any carbohydrates and the body needs only 60 grams of glucose a day, and since breast milk is designed to make babies gain body fat and grow rapidly, 45 to 100 grams of carbs is a good range for carbohydrate intake in kids, depending on their age and size. Kids really shouldn't need more than that to thrive. Can they handle more and be fine? Sure. But they don't *require* more.

And the hope is that little to none of this carbohydrate would come from refined sugars— just the natural carbs that come from foods like tomatoes, berries, and nonstarchy vegetables. If you are relying on whole-food sources for carbohydrates and avoiding veggies and fruits that are higher in starch and sugar, this will be a natural level of carbohydrate consumption. When you ditch the processed foods, fruit juices, and sugary treats and make sure your kids are meeting their daily protein goal, it will be hard to eat too many carbs. They will just be too satiated.

---

[17] S. Strauss, "Clara M. Davis and the wisdom of letting children choose their own diets," *Canadian Medical Association Journal* 175, no. 10 (2006): 1199–1201.

[18] A. Lakkakula, J. Geaghan, M. Zanovec, S. Pierce, and G. Tuuri, "Repeated taste exposure increases liking for vegetables by low-income elementary school children," *Appetite* 55, no. 2 (2010): 226–31.

Protein Needs for Healthy Kids

At this point, you might be wondering how much protein and fat your children should be eating after they leave the baby stage. Many factors contribute to this balance, and in this section, we want to outline some considerations and highlight various developmental stages.

Animal protein is key not only for growth but also for all the vitamins and minerals it contains; it is one of the most nutrient-dense foods. Here's a chart that gives a rough outline of how much protein a person needs over time.[19]

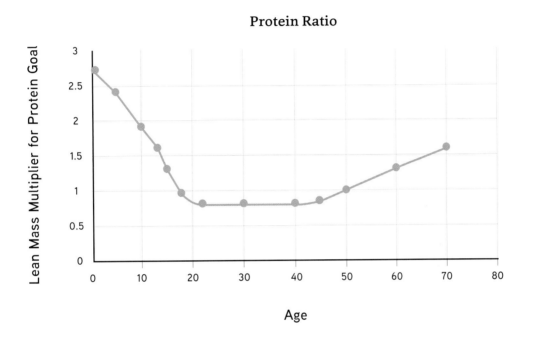

Protein Ratio

Little Kids (2–7 Years)

Beginning at age two, your kids can eat whatever you do.

As for how much to eat, two-year-olds still need **twice their lean mass in grams of protein per day,** or even more. Lean mass is just total weight minus body fat. So if a child weighs 30 pounds and has 25 to 30 percent body fat, their lean mass is 21 to 23 pounds, and they need 42 to 46 grams of protein a day. This goal should not be hard to reach, as just one 6-ounce chicken breast has over 50 grams of protein.

The demand for protein starts to decrease when a child gets closer to age seven. Even then, you still want to make protein the focus of the plate. For example, a 50-pound child would have about 38 pounds of lean mass, so you would want to

[19] L. Breen and S. M. Phillips, "Skeletal muscle protein metabolism in the elderly: interventions to counteract the 'anabolic resistance' of ageing," *Nutrition & Metabolism* 8 (2011): 68.

shoot for about 72 grams of protein per day. This is about 10 ounces of 85 percent lean ground beef. That might sound like a lot, but broken into two or three meals and maybe a snack, it is the equivalent of about 4 ounces per meal. When not filling up on the bun and a side of fries, a kid can eat a quarter-pound hamburger in one sitting with no problem.

One of the great things about sugar-free eating is that you can allow your kids to go by their hunger signals. If you want them to have three traditional mealtimes, that's fine. If they get hungry between meals, add a snack. Just make protein the focus, and make sure to combine the protein with a good amount of healthy fat, especially if it's a leaner protein. If you're serving chicken, for example, you can add some homemade mayonnaise, bone marrow, or other high-fat foods to the meal. Then fill the rest of their calories for the day with fats, low-starch veggies, and some berries or other low-sugar snacks.

Big Kids (8–12 Years)

Kids between ages eight and twelve still need **close to twice their lean mass in grams of protein per day.** A child who weighs 85 pounds with around 65 pounds of lean mass would need about 130 grams of protein a day. This is the equivalent of a little more than a pound of 85 percent lean ground beef. Again, broken up over three meals, this total should not be hard for a growing child to hit.

The body has little to no need for carbs at this age, although your kids can have some low-sugar fruits like berries if they want—and of course, any low-starch veggies, too.

Kids in this age range can go through growth spurts, so let their hunger signals guide you. Craig and I can always tell when our boys are going through a growth spurt because they start asking for another serving of lasagna or for snacks at night.

Teens

Kids in their early teens need **around 1.5 times their lean mass in grams of protein per day.** For a 110-pound child with around 80 pounds of lean mass, that would mean 120 grams of protein.

As teens get closer to their maximum height, that protein number decreases to about 1.0 times their lean mass.

Once they are fully grown, they can follow the adult standard of 0.8 times lean mass for protein grams per day. If your kids are typical teenagers, they should have no problem eating this much protein!

Food Dye Dangers

Processed foods are not only high in sugar but also contain a plethora of artificial dyes and additives. Many of these food dyes have been shown to cause harmful effects.

Artificial food dyes are found in almost all processed foods and even some fresh whole foods; growers are allowed to spray oranges with an artificial red food dye that may be carcinogenic to make them more appealing, for example. We have a natural instinct linking color to freshness, and color is used to entice kids to eat junk. It's not just the hot-pink berries in the Cap'n Crunch cereal that have these harmful dyes; I recently found hot-pink cheese sticks in the grocery store. Vegetable juices and some yogurts also contain food dyes.

Synthetic dye causes hyperactivity because it is an excitotoxin, overstimulating dopamine production, but then the body doesn't produce enough dopamine, which causes a deficiency. Dopamine deficiency has been studied as a possible factor in ADHD.

Becoming quickly bored with routine and having a hard time focusing are classic symptoms of dopamine deficiency. People with these deficiencies tend to start a lot of things yet don't finish them. They work on many tasks at once. Low dopamine levels prevent a child who has ADHD from focusing or attending to anything in the environment, appearing physically hyperactive due to their lack of focus. As dopamine levels in the brain begin to rise, the child becomes excited and energized.

If dopamine gets too high, which usually happens when chemicals like MSG and artificial food dyes are ingested, the body becomes guarded and suspicious from being hyperstimulated. When dopamine levels are low, we can't focus; when they're high, our focus becomes intense to the point of focusing on everything as though it were directly related to our situation. Steering clear of these excitotoxins is the best defense for your family!

Kraft, Coca-Cola, and other manufacturers have already removed artificial dyes from the products they distribute in other countries, but not in the US, including Red 40, Yellow 6, and Blue 1, all of which are banned in Europe. For years, Nutri-Grain bars sold in the US contained these dyes while the bars sold in Europe used beetroot red, annatto, and paprika extracts for color. Thankfully, the US formula has been changed—likely due to public outcry. We need to vote with our dollars and stop buying the products that use these harmful dyes and instead select ones that use natural colorings or no added dyes.

Bone Health and Our Food

Yes, what your kids eat affects their bones, too! Here are some key facts on bones:

- Children build 42 percent of their bone mass between the ages of twelve and eighteen. What are your teens eating? Sodas and sports drinks ruin bones' strength, and people who drink them once a day have a five times higher risk of fracture.[20]

- Bones are alive, and they are either breaking down (osteoclasts) or building up (osteoblasts).

- Bones need collagen! My favorite way to give kids collagen is to serve them bone broth. It is not only excellent for collagen; it is also rich in highly absorbable minerals.

- You may not realize that the cellular wall of bone is made up of fat. And not just any fat; it is mainly made up of the unfairly demonized saturated fat! Yep! If you avoid saturated fat, you are putting your bones at risk.

- Antacids contribute to hip fractures. Tums is calcium carbonate, which is a terrible form of calcium because it is very alkaline. We want more acidic stomachs, not less. Nexium, Prilosec, and other acid blockers increase fractures by 44 percent![21] Doctors in the US prescribe over 100 million of these medications a year, many of them to tiny babies. I had a client whose baby had such terrible acid reflux that when the first acid blocker didn't work, the doctor added another one! This tiny baby was on *two* acid blockers! I helped the mother change the baby's diet, and the acid reflux went away within days.

- Magnesium deficiency is a common cause of calcium not getting into the bones. But don't waste your money on calcium-magnesium supplements; those two minerals are "frenemies." I do not recommend calcium supplements; however, we are all deficient in magnesium, mainly because it was once supplied through drinking water. Without adequate magnesium (along with K2; see below), calcium gets deposited in areas it shouldn't be, causing kidney stones and plaque buildup on teeth and in arteries. Taking a high-quality magnesium supplement, such as magnesium glycinate, at night can also calm you and help with sleep.

---

[20] G. Wyshak, "Teenaged girls, carbonated beverage consumption, and bone fractures," *Archives of Pediatrics and Adolescent Medicine* 154, no. 6 (2000): 610–3.

[21] C. Vangala, J. Niu, C. R. Lenihan, et al., "Proton pump inhibitors, histamine-2 receptor antagonists, and hip fracture risk among patients on hemodialysis," *Clinical Journal of the American Society of Nephrology* 13, no. 10 (2018): 1534–41; B. K. S. Thong, S. Ima-Nirwana, and K. Chin, "Proton pump inhibitors and fracture risk: a review of current evidence and mechanisms involved," *International Journal of Environmental Research and Public Health* 16, no. 9 (2019): 1571.

- The most crucial bone-building supplement, in my opinion, is vitamin K2, which is found in organ meats. How often do your kids eat organ meats? Yep, that's what I thought—never, or at best rarely. This is why even my kids take a vitamin K2 supplement. I also suggest adding a serving of beef liver, which is one of the most nutrient-dense foods there is, every week or twice a month to kick up your nutrient density. If your kids don't like liver, you'll have to be creative about how you serve it. I make a dish that has a spicy flavor profile, like Sloppy Kai Dogs (page 190), Touchdown Tacos (page 192), or Taco Meatballs (page 272), and replace one-fifth of the ground beef with ground liver. My boys don't even know there's liver in there!

- Listen up, moms: Having low progesterone causes bone loss. You don't need to be in menopause to be lacking in progesterone. If you find yourself waking up at 2 or 3 a.m. and can't get back to sleep, or if you have high anxiety, I suggest getting your progesterone level checked.

- Low vitamin D is a common cause of bone loss. Do your kids have levels that are not as high as they should be? They *must* get sunlight without the filter of sunscreen. How much vitamin D do they need? Well, when we are in the sun without sunscreen, we make 20,000 to 30,000 IU per hour; that is 5,000 to 7,500 IU in only fifteen minutes! Adults and kids alike need 1,000 IU per 25 pounds of body weight per day. If getting direct sun isn't possible, consider vitamin D supplements. Because they are fat-soluble, they *must* be taken with food. I also recommend taking vitamin D in the morning because it increases serotonin and lowers melatonin (the hormone that helps you sleep). If you take it before bed, it can cause sleep issues.

When we brought our boys home from Ethiopia, we were required to get a full range of tests done on them in the US to check for deficiencies, one of which was vitamin D. Even though they had been living on the equator, their vitamin D levels were only in the thirties—way too low! They have very dark skin, which is a natural sunscreen. Children with dark skin need to take even more care about getting good sun exposure and supplementing when D levels fall below 50 ng/mL or so.

Immune Health and Our Food

What do you crave when you're sick? Your body doesn't always tell you what you need!

As I described in the "Sugar and the Depletion of Micronutrients" section earlier in this chapter, sugar consumption reduces the phagocytic index by 75 percent. This means the immune system slows to a crawl. The more sugar your kids eat, the more likely they are to get sick, and the more severe the illness is likely to be.

When I was sick as a little girl, I remember eating saltine crackers with canned chicken noodle soup full of trans fats and sugar—nothing healing! I cringe when I think of all the harmful ingredients in these foods and how I often see them being fed to little children.

So what should you do when your kids get sick? Or, better yet, what can you do to prevent them from getting sick in the first place? Supporting kids' immune health can reduce the time they are sick, and a healthy gut is connected to many health benefits, including improvements in mental health.[22] A healthy microbiome (the population of bacteria in the gut that help keep our immune system and digestion strong) plays an important role in overall health. The first and most important thing you can do to enable this is to keep their sugar consumption low. This keeps their phagocytic index high and their immune function strong.

People typically talk about supporting the gut microbiome with plant fiber. But many animal sources feed the gut microbiome as well, and in many cases, those animal foods do an even better job at it than plants. Glucosamine and collagen in meats feed the gut microbiome better than fiber does. Butyric acid in butter and other dairy can also feed the gut microbiome.

Other great gut microbiome–boosting foods are organ meats and naturally fermented veggies like sauerkraut and pickles. But they need to be naturally fermented, which you can do at home or buy a quality brand like Bubbies. Low-sugar yogurt is also a good source of probiotics. Bone broth, which is rich in collagen and nutrients, is another great food for gut health and healing. (Find my delicious bone broth recipe on page 392.)

When my boys were just one and two years old, I started them drinking homemade bone broth, which is one of the most nourishing foods there is. Given that they came from another country (Ethiopia), you would think that they would have been sick often being exposed to new viruses and illnesses here in the United States. But they were never ill! I know it was mainly because of what they were

---

[22] S. Zhu, Y. Jiang, K. Xu, et al., "The progress of gut microbiome research related to brain disorders," *Journal of Neuroinflammation* 17 (2020), https://jneuroinflammation.biomedcentral.com/articles/10.1186/s12974-020-1705-z.

eating—healthy sugar-free food, lots of good-quality protein, and daily bone broth. I even have a video of baby Kai begging for a bottle of bone broth!

If your child isn't a big fan of bone broth, organ meats, or naturally fermented veggies, then adding a quality probiotic supplement is a great option to ensure they have a strong and healthy gut. Our whole family takes Just Thrive Probiotic.

Sleep and Mental Health

When I consult with clients, one of the questions I ask is, "Do you sleep well?" However, I had to change my question to, "How long do you sleep?" Clients often responded to the first question with a "yes," but when I would ask them how long they slept, the answer was often five or six hours. Of course you slept well; you are sleep-deprived!

Children tend to do a little better than adults when it comes to sleep, but it's still an important subject. Sleep is as critical as what we feed our kids. Children's brain health suffers with lack of sleep—not to mention their emotional health! Studies have shown that lack of sleep in kids can lead to reduced cognitive performance,[23] moods,[24] vocabulary acquisition,[25] and learning and memory.[26] Believe me; no one wants to hang out with a sleep-deprived kid, no matter how cute they are. My boys love being smart and excelling at their schoolwork. I always tell them that their brains grow as they sleep!

I am shocked that my boys are rarely sick. It could be that they do not eat sugar, but I know it also has a lot to do with the fact that they get proper sleep. Most kids I know are not getting nearly enough!

As you can see in the chart on the following page, children need a lot of sleep. Micah is eleven and Kai is ten at the time we are writing this book. For proper growth and health, they need ten to eleven hours of sleep a night. Some need more than the average. Micah thrives on eleven to twelve hours of sleep.

---

[23] E. J. Paavonen, K. Räikkönen, A. Pesonen, et al., "Sleep quality and cognitive performance in 8-year-old children," *Sleep Medicine* 11, no. 4 (2010): 386–92.

[24] K. Maasalo, T. Fontell, J. Wessman, and E. T. Aronen, "Sleep and behavioural problems associate with low mood in Finnish children aged 4–12 years: an epidemiological study," *Child and Adolescent Psychiatry and Mental Health* 6 (2016): 37.

[25] K. Horváth and K. Plunkett, "Frequent daytime naps predict vocabulary growth in early childhood," *Journal of Child Psychology and Psychiatry, and Allied Disciplines* 57, no. 9 (2016): 1008–17.

[26] J. F. Dewald, A. M. Meijer, F. J. Oort, et al., "The influence of sleep quality, sleep duration and sleepiness on school performance in children and adolescents: A meta-analytic review," *Sleep Medicine Reviews* 14, no. 3 (2010): 179–89.

Sleep Recommendations for Kids

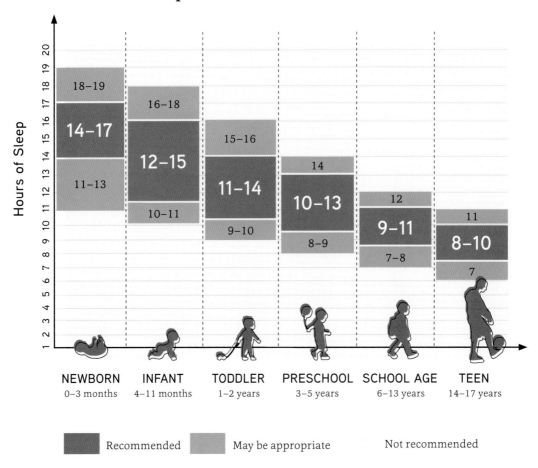

Hours of Sleep

	NEWBORN	INFANT	TODDLER	PRESCHOOL	SCHOOL AGE	TEEN
Not recommended	18–19	16–18	15–16	14	12	11
Recommended	14–17	12–15	11–14	10–13	9–11	8–10
May be appropriate	11–13	10–11	9–10	8–9	7–8	7

NEWBORN	INFANT	TODDLER	PRESCHOOL	SCHOOL AGE	TEEN
0–3 months	4–11 months	1–2 years	3–5 years	6–13 years	14–17 years

■ Recommended   ■ May be appropriate   Not recommended

Not only does sleep impact weight, cravings, and mood, but it also has a significant impact on immune health. It is true that "sleep helps healing." Having a strong immune system is more important than ever, and sleep can be a huge contributor to improved immune function. Studies have shown that sleep allows brain cells to "take out the trash" each night, flushing out disease-causing toxins. Sleep also helps T cells (a type of immune cell that fights viruses) fight off infection. Studies have found that adults who got less than seven hours of sleep a night were 294 percent more likely to get a cold than those who got eight or more hours![27]

Another study showed that adults who got only six hours of sleep a night were 420 percent more likely to catch a cold when exposed to it versus those who got more than seven hours.[28] Chronic lack of sleep has also been shown to make the flu vaccine less effective by reducing the body's ability to respond.

---

[27] S. Cohen, W. J. Doyle, C. M. Alper, et al., "Sleep habits and susceptibility to the common cold," *Archives of Internal Medicine* 169, no. 1 (2009): 62–7.

[28] A. A. Prather, D. Janicki-Deverts, M. H. Hall, and S. Cohen, "Behaviorally assessed sleep and susceptibility to the common cold," *Sleep* 38, no. 9 (2015): 1353–9.

Immune Health and Sleep

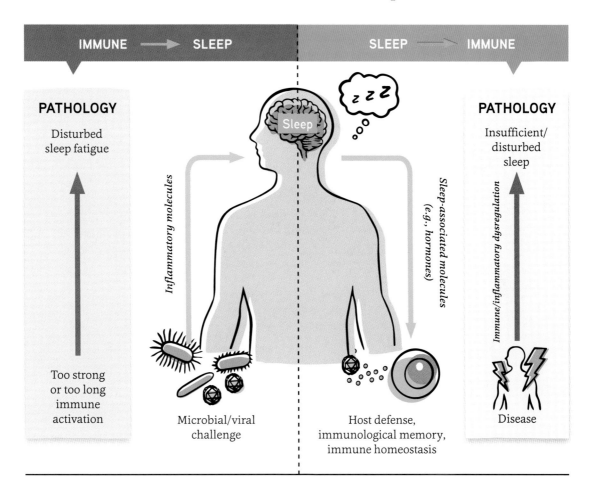

During sleep, our bodies produce proteins known as cytokines, which help fight illness, infection, inflammation, and stress. When you have the flu or a cold, you often get exhausted, which is your body's way of forcing you to rest, which aids the body's ability to heal. Without adequate sleep, your body makes fewer cytokines, causing big problems.

Another way that lack of sleep impacts immune health relates to the stress hormones adrenaline and noradrenaline (also known as epinephrine and norepinephrine). When stress hormones are high, they inhibit the "stickiness" of adhesion molecules called integrins. While you are sleeping, your levels of adrenaline, noradrenaline, and prostaglandins (compounds that control processes such as inflammation and blood flow) are low, which makes the integrins stickier. This stickiness is vital because, for T cells to kill virus-infected or cancerous cells, they need to get in direct contact with them, and the integrins' stickiness promotes this contact.

The scariest news from the scientific research is how quickly kids fall into the danger zone. The repercussions of sleep deprivation happen after only four nights of one less hour of sleep per night!

Tips for Better Sleep

The following tips can help kids and adults alike get better-quality sleep at night:

- Cut sugar intake to stabilize blood sugar and avoid a drop in the middle of the night, which will wake you up.

- Take magnesium glycinate supplements or use topical magnesium; magnesium is calming and often helps with sleep. An Epsom salt bath or foot soak is another way to absorb magnesium through the skin.

- Make sure your bedroom is cool; it helps promote sleep.

- Wear blue and green light–blocking glasses at night to block out light from TVs, computers, tablets, and smartphones, which can hinder the production of the sleep hormone melatonin. Especially in winter, when it's darker longer, we are all exposed to more artificial light, making it extra important to support a natural sleep cycle and circadian rhythm. Blocking blue light (along with certain green light wavelengths) allows the body to generate melatonin naturally.

- Use lavender essential oil on the big toe. Kai called it his "magic potion" when he struggled with sleep.

Getting good sleep helps not only with blood sugar regulation and immune function but also with moods and mental health.

I have had the opportunity to work with mental health hospitals, which are now being outfitted with kitchens to help patients with depression and anxiety. It's no secret that sugar is terrible for our physical health, but it is also detrimental to our mental health.

Too often, when we feel sad or anxious, we want to eat our feelings. I remember drowning my sorrows in a pint of Ben & Jerry's ice cream, and it never made me feel better. Consuming a large amount of sugar can actually increase sadness and irritability.

Sugar causes depression because insulin rises rapidly after you eat it, leading to a neurotransmitter imbalance and a reduction of serotonin, gamma-aminobutyric acid (GABA), dopamine, and acetylcholine. A sugar-free diet stimulates the energetic output of our mitochondria, reduces the production of damaging free radicals, and promotes GABA production.

A sugar-free diet also reduces the toxic effects of the excitatory pathways in our brains, which naturally lowers depression. And when I say sugar, I also mean carbs. A cracker may not taste sweet, but once ingested, the cracker has one fate: it turns into sugar in the blood, causing insulin to rise.

Eating healthy food helps boost our moods, and sharing delicious food with family and friends has a powerful effect on our minds.

The Importance of Planning

As a busy working mom, I understand that some days the last thing you want to do is make dinner. This is why I am always one step ahead! I plan, plan, plan so meals are easy and fast. We plan so much for our children's future in every other way: we research the best schools, help them with their homework, encourage them to participate in sports and other activities, and encourage them to prepare for college, among so many other things. Why would what we feed them be any different? In fact, I feel that planning our meals is even more important since they fuel my children's brains!

Putting effort into planning and making meals for our children is gratifying. One evening as we sat down to dinner, my son Kai said, "Mom, this is the best pizza ever made in history!" Two years have passed since then, but I still remember that moment vividly, and my heart still bursts with joy when I think about what Kai said. Moments like this can't and won't happen if you're serving food that comes in a box or bringing home takeout.

As a parent, I know it's hard to do it all. As I sat down to write this, Kai asked for lunch. So I got up to make him taco wraps (page 192), his favorite (I made extra taco meat, so later, all I'd have to do is heat up the meat and put it in lettuce cups with salsa, cheese, and sour cream). As I was making lunch, the dishwasher finished. So I unloaded it. Then as I was about to sit back down to resume writing, I heard the dryer running and knew that I'd have to get up to do laundry soon.

Craig and I homeschool the boys, which throws another wrench into things. But a sugar-free diet keeps us healthy and energetic so we can keep going and accomplish everything we need to do in a day. I remember my sugar-filled past when I barely had enough energy to make it through each day before crashing on the couch to watch television. Cutting out sugar has made my life more fulfilling, and it will do the same for you and your family!

Inflammation is the root of all disease, and sugar is one of the leading causes of inflammation. Starting your children on a sugar-free lifestyle at a young age will help them thrive! I hope the recipes that follow provide lots of inspiration and show you just how fun and delicious sugar-free eating can be.

chapter 2:
the sugar-free kitchen

Now that you've got a handle on why cutting sugar is a smart idea, it's time to get into the kitchen! This chapter outlines some handy cooking tips, helps you plan healthy meals and snacks for your family, and introduces you to some useful tools and ingredients for sugar-free cooking and baking.

Getting Comfortable in the Kitchen

Many families come to rely on sugar-filled processed foods, fast food, and takeout because they are intimidated by the idea of cooking meals from scratch, thinking they don't have the skills or the time to be successful. And of course, kids are notorious for being picky eaters, and the last thing we want is to put effort into cooking only to find that our kids refuse to eat the healthy food we make for them!

Tips for New Cooks

If you're new to cooking, keep these tips in mind to set yourself up for success:

- Read the entire recipe before you start cooking. This helps you understand how the recipe is laid out and prepared and prevents you from overlooking key information about timing. If a dish needs to be chilled for an hour before you can eat it, for example, it's good to know that in advance!

- Before you begin a recipe, set out all the ingredients and do the prep work noted in the ingredient list. If you have everything ready, you avoid panic, and you won't burn foods in the middle of cooking when you step away to track down an ingredient.

- When flipping foods such as pancakes, burgers, and fish, always flip them away from you. That way, if grease splatters, it won't land on you and burn your skin.

- Remember that you can always add, but you can't take away. Taste and season as you cook.

- Don't just season at the end; otherwise, your food will taste like it has salt sitting on top of it instead of *in* it.

- *Advanced tip:* Finish with a fresh, lively flavor like lemon or lime juice, which brightens up any dish.

Tips for Getting Your Kids to Help You Cook

I encourage you to invite your kids to help you prepare meals, both to build lifelong skills and to get them to try a broader range of foods. Here are some ways to entice them:

- **Start with the basics.** Don't begin with a complicated recipe. You'll see that I've marked the recipes in this book by difficulty level: easy, medium, and hard. When cooking with kids, especially very young ones, start with the easy recipes.

- **Get a slow cooker.** Slow-cooking is the ultimate easy way to teach children about combining flavors to create a meal the whole family can enjoy! It is also a foolproof cooking method, which will boost their confidence. Here are our favorite slow cooker recipes:

  » Sloppy Kai Dogs (page 190)

  » Cheeseburger Lettuce Wraps (page 238)

  » Spaghetti Bolognese (page 240)

  » Epic Cheesy Beef Nachos (page 242)

- **Be forgiving!** Don't worry about perfection. Many times, even I forget to add an ingredient. For example, while filming a YouTube video in which we made a BBQ meatloaf, I forgot to add the mushrooms. Guess what? The meatloaf still turned out great! This tip extends to messes, too. Most kids make a big mess when they do a task. Instead of worrying about the cleanup, focus on the fact that they are learning essential skills—one of which is how to clean up their messes!

- **Let them guide you.** Too often, we are telling children what to do. Let *them* be the leaders in the kitchen. Let them pick out recipes to try. Taking charge is fun for them! Allowing your kids to assume leadership will help foster their interest in cooking and help them become strong leaders in other areas.

Cooking Is a Great Homeschool Project or Learning Opportunity

- It puts to use reading and math skills.
- It teaches kids to follow directions.
- It's a fun way to bond with your children.
- It teaches practical life skills.
- It boosts self-confidence.
- Letting kids experiment with flavors and spices teaches creativity.
- Bonus: You end up with a delicious meal!

Tips for Busy Families

Are you upset that your family always seems to be too busy in the evenings to eat dinner together? Don't stress! It isn't the act of eating together that matters; it's the act of *spending time* together. Craig, the boys, and I don't always have our evening meal at the same time; however, we find opportunities during the day to take walks and bike rides together, play games together, and talk. The saying "families that eat together, stay together" is more about the fact that eating is often the only time a family gathers in one place. If you can't eat dinner together, just make sure to find time for special moments with your children.

That being said, there are ways to save time in the kitchen that might free up more time for you to eat as a family. Here are my top time-saving tips:

- **Get a slow cooker.** I *love* my slow cooker. I have three of them, and sometimes they are all going simultaneously. Slow-cooking is great for busy families because individual family members can eat whenever they have time. When Mom or Dad is going to get home late from work, or when the kids are participating in sports or other activities at different times in the evening, there will be a hot and delicious meal waiting for them as soon as they get home. Some of our favorite slow cooker recipes are noted above, where I talk about how a slow cooker is also a great way to encourage kids to help cook.

- **Get an Instant Pot.** If you forgot to fill the slow cooker and dinner needs to be served, get out the Instant Pot! It will make dinner while you help your kids with homework. Our favorite Instant Pot recipe is Spaghetti Bolognese (page 240).

- **Batch cook.** I make quadruple batches of my boys' favorite foods, like my Touchdown Tacos (page 192). Leftovers are my lifesaver, and we think leftovers taste better because the flavors have had time to meld. I suggest finding five recipes that your family loves and making large batches for easy leftovers when life gets busy and you need food fast. I've included notes in the recipes about which ones can be doubled, tripled, or quadrupled.

- **Plan, plan, plan.** I always am one step ahead when it comes to planning meals. The day before I plan to serve something, I take the meat out of the freezer and make sure the other components are ready, such as prepping all the taco fixings for taco night and storing them in ramekins in the fridge. That way, meals come together in no time.

- **Divide and conquer.** Most superheroes have a sidekick who helps them tackle the tough jobs. Why take on all the responsibility alone? Divide the work! Teach your children to cook. Sure, the first time you make a recipe together, it will take longer, but eventually, they can be in charge of a few recipes. If your children are not old enough to cook, put them in charge of cleanup.

As I write this book, I often have to stop to make meals for my family. Sometimes my life is so busy that if I stopped to think about everything I need to accomplish, I probably would have a panic attack. I need to finish writing this book before leaving in only a few weeks for Costa Rica, where a TV show in which I am the keto chef will be filmed. I have another manuscript due one month after I get back from Costa Rica. I had five new clients sign up for phone consultations yesterday. I am teaching my keto college students. And earlier this week, I recorded cooking videos with Halle Berry. My plate is *full.* However, I make sure that I have healthy food on the table for all of our meals. I also make sure to get outside and exercise in the fresh air daily.

I just had to set my writing aside to make breakfast for my boys. I often get up a few hours before anyone else so I have quiet time to write. Now that the boys are awake, I want to make them a quick breakfast. I have batter for my Blender Pancakes (page 102) in the fridge from two days ago. I also have pureed strawberries from a video that I did. So I quickly heated up a pan and made a bunch of pancakes, which will make nice leftovers for the boys to reheat for breakfast tomorrow. They love to top them with the strawberry puree.

I know that we all get overwhelmed by life. Having tricks like this up my sleeve keeps me grounded, and eating healthy helps me accomplish everything on my plate!

My Favorite Time-Saving Food Products

I like to make our food from scratch whenever I can, but I get busy like anyone else. For those times when from-scratch cooking just isn't an option, I rely on these products, which I know I can trust to be low in sugar and healthy for my family:

- **Folios Cheese Wraps:** Sandwich wraps made from one ingredient: cheese! They work great to make a cold sandwich, or you can heat them up for a crispy taco shell.

- **The Good Chocolate:** When I make The BEST Chocolate Chip Cookies (page 312), I often chop up a Good Chocolate bar and use that instead of chocolate chips.

- **Just Made Keto cupcakes and sugar-free frostings:** You can make sugar-free cupcakes from scratch (see my Baseball Blender Cupcakes on page 302), but this company sells ready-made cupcakes and frostings.

- **Kettle & Fire bone broth:** I used this product in many recipes while writing this book! I encourage you to make your own bone broth following my recipe on page 392, but this brand is a handy alternative.

- **Moon Cheese:** A crispy snack that is 100 percent cheese

- **Pork panko:** I like to use store-bought pork panko for breading things like chicken tenders and fish sticks. You can make your own by crushing whole pork rinds in a blender, but it's convenient to have a container already crushed. I purchase mine online.

- **Primal Kitchen mayonnaise, salad dressings, marinara sauce, and pizza sauce:** I used Primal Kitchen sauces in many recipes while writing this book, such as my Pizza Eggs (page 84), Meaty Lasagna Bowls (page 220), Pizza Dog Casserole (page 236), and Spaghetti Bolognese (page 240).

- **ROAM Snack Sticks:** When life is too busy to make your own jerky (see pages 148 and 156), you can buy these pasture-raised pork snack sticks.

- **Teton Waters Ranch Mini Hot Dogs** (for Pigs in a Blanket, page 142)

- **Whisps Cheese Crisps:** Another crispy cheese snack

Ten Recipes in Ten Minutes or Less

Some days get busy, your kids are hungry, and you need a meal in a snap. I've been there! Here are some of our favorite meals that can be ready in minutes:

- English Muffin Pizzas (page 178)
- Better Than School Lunch Chicken Patties (page 184)
- Meat Cookies (page 188)
- Cheese Quesadillas (page 194)
- Cheeseburger Lettuce Wraps made in an Instant Pot (page 238)
- Egg Roll in a Bowl made in an Instant Pot (page 250)
- Chaffle Sub Sandwich (page 334)
- Chaffle Breakfast Sammie (page 338)
- Drive-Thru Chaffle Burger (page 346)
- Crispy Taco Chaffles (page 348)

Twelve Recipes That Freeze Well

When I go through the trouble of getting out all the ingredients to cook our favorite recipes, I often make quadruple batches and store the extras in the freezer. That way, all I have to do is take them out of the freezer and heat them up—just like easy frozen meals at the grocery store, but much healthier! Here are my top recipes that freeze well:

- Blender Pancakes (page 102)
- Pigs in a Blanket (page 142)
- Chicken Protein Noodle Soup (page 180)
- Better Than School Lunch Chicken Patties (page 184)
- Sloppy Kai Dogs (page 190)
- Touchdown Tacos (page 192)
- Dinosaur Droppings (aka Meatballs) (page 198)
- Bon Vie Chicken Tenders (page 200)
- Protein Noodle Taco Lasagna (page 202)
- Fish Fingers (page 204)
- Mama Maria's Pizza Chicken Balls (page 208)
- Pizza Party (page 224)—You can freeze both the pizzas and the cheese sticks

Having these basics in the freezer makes my life so much easier. When I prepare one of these recipes, I make extras so the boys can make easy meals with them later:

- Pizza Crust (page 225)
- Easy Blender Waffles (page 336)
- Soft Tortillas (page 382)
- Sandwich Buns (page 384)
- Easy English Muffins (page 386)

Planning Sugar-Free Meals

"What's for dinner?" (or lunch, or breakfast) is one of the most common questions to come out of kids' mouths. As you transition to a sugar-free lifestyle, you may be unsure of what to feed your kids in place of the sugar-filled convenience foods you are probably used to. This section outlines some great options for every meal!

Breakfast on the Go

We all have hectic mornings! Here are my top ideas for breakfasts that you can pull together in minutes or make ahead for quick meals throughout the week:

- Strawberry Breakfast Parfait (page 86)—I prefer Two Good brand yogurt.
- Easy Baked Bacon and Sausages (page 90)
- Chocolate Minute Muffins (page 98)
- Chocolate Protein Shake (page 100)—A super fast and easy recipe!
- Blender Pancakes (page 102)
- Strawberry Pudding (page 146)
- Basic Savory Chaffles or Paffles (page 334)
- Deli turkey or ham and cheese roll-ups—You don't always need traditional breakfast foods in the morning. Think outside the box!

- Sweet 'n' Sour Turkey Jerky (page 148) or Salmon Jerky Fingers (page 156)
- Chicken Protein Noodle Soup (page 180)—Soup is a breakfast staple in many cultures. My boys love this soup at any time of the day!

Packed Lunches from the Deli

My clients often tell me that their kids love this way of eating, but once they start school, they're bombarded with pizza parties, donut parties, candy jars—and the week of Halloween candy! I get a little nauseated just thinking about all the candy I used to eat after trick-or-treating.

So what's a parent to do? It's hard; I know. I do my best to educate my boys on what foods make them strong and what foods will cause their bellies to hurt. Too bad the nutrition classes taught in middle school still preach about eating whole grains and drinking skim milk.

We homeschool the boys, and I've found that sitting inside on beautiful days is really hard on kids. I can often be found teaching lessons to my boys while hiking, which brings up the same difficulties you might have with kids who attend school away from home. I need to prepare and pack for our hikes, and sometimes I am without a kitchen to prepare meals. So what do I do? We have a lesson at the grocery store that morning and pick out healthy lunches that will keep us strong and full of energy for our hike!

Here are some tasty lunch items that you can buy from a deli and pack for school, work, or a hiking trip:

- Beef sticks (Choose a high-quality sugar-free brand like Thousand Hills, Mission Meats, or Epic.)

- Cheese sticks or cheeses

- Guacamole and/or salsa with pork rinds, celery sticks, or cucumber slices for dipping

- Hard-boiled eggs

- Jerky (Check the labels, as many brands contain sugar—or make your own using my recipes on pages 148 and 156.)

- Mini pickles

- Olives

- Organic ham and pickle roll-ups (I buy these premade from the deli section of my grocery store.)

- Pork rinds (Choose a high-quality brand like Bacon's Heir.)

- Sardines (Don't laugh! Some kids love them!)

- Smoked oysters (Seriously tasty!)

- Smoked salmon

- Tuna or salmon in a packet and a jar of organic mayo (I mix them together on the trail and wrap the salad in Boston leaf lettuce for a little "unwich.")

Easy Lunches at Home or on the Go

Sometimes when lunchtime rolls around, we don't want to make a big meal; we want something simple to eat. I love that my boys enjoy these quick-and-easy foods:

- **Bologna:** Kai loves US Wellness Meats bologna, which is sugar-free. He could eat it every day for lunch with mustard. I love that he likes it because it is a super simple meal.

- **Hot dogs:** Hot dogs get a bad rap because people think they are made from the organ "scraps," but organ meat is the most nutrient-dense food without antinutrients. I prefer organic sugar-free hot dogs from ButcherBox, US Wellness Meats, Pederson Farms, Applegate, and Teton Waters Ranch.

- **Premade meatballs:** I love ordering healthy foods like the premade meatballs from US Wellness Meats for easy lunches that my boys can reheat on their own.

- **Leftovers:** I always make extras. Leftovers are a lifesaver! I love just reheating meals and having lunch ready in minutes. Here are some of our favorite leftover lunches:

  » Pigs in a Blanket (page 142)

  » Touchdown Tacos (page 192)

  » Dinosaur Droppings (aka Meatballs) (page 198)

  » The Easiest Mac 'n' Cheese (page 210)

  » Pizza Party (page 224)

- **"Unwich" wraps:** I wrap sugar-free ham, rotisserie chicken, turkey, salami, sliced tomatoes, sliced onions, mustard, and mayo inside romaine or Boston leaf lettuce, rolling it tightly like a burrito. You can add cheese if your kids eat dairy. You can also make wraps using Folios Cheese Wraps (see page 59) instead of lettuce.

Bento Box Ideas

If you are looking for healthy lunches to send to school with your children, you'll find some of our favorite combinations on the following pages.

Micah's Egg Muffin Sandwich (page 110), berries, No-Bake Chocolate-Topped Energy Bar (page 150), Red Velvet Truffle (page 330)

English Muffin Pizza (page 178), Sweet 'n' Sour Turkey Jerky (page 148), Blueberry Cheesecake Muffin (page 122), melon cutouts, Cookie Dough Truffles (page 331)

Better Than School Lunch Chicken Patties (page 184), Sugar-Free Ketchup (page 369), cheese cutouts, blueberries, Strawberry Cheesecake Truffle (page 328), Red Velvet Truffle (page 330)

Salmon Jerky Fingers (page 156), cheese and bell pepper cutouts, Veggie Dill Dip (page 366) with broccoli

Sandwich on a Stick (page 174), Veggie and Savory Fruit Flowers (page 130), Fruit Flower Bouquet (page 152)

Soft Tortilla (page 382) rolled up with ham and cheese/nut butter and jam and sliced into sushi, baby dill pickles, Cookie Dough Dip (page 166), berries, No-Bake Chocolate-Topped Energy Bar (page 150)

Ham and cheese roll-ups, cheese crisps, green olives, raspberries, Holiday Jigglers (page 280), Red Velvet Truffles (page 330)

Valentine's Day theme: ham cut into hearts, Heart-Shaped Eggs (page 264), strawberries cut into hearts, Strawberry Cheesecake Truffle (page 328), Red Velvet Truffle (page 330)

Halloween theme: Spooky Breadstick Fingers (page 274), roast beef and cheese roll-ups, black olives, baby dill pickles, Pumpkin Pie Gummies (page 286)

Winter theme: meatball snowman with string cheese hat, eyes, and buttons, Pizza Chaffle (page 334), melon cutouts, Shamrock Shake Gummies (page 284)

The Healthiest Snacks for Kids

Honestly, my boys rarely snack. Hunger happens when blood sugar starts to fall, and when you stop eating sugar, blood sugar remains more stable. Constant snacking also keeps kids from being hungry for meals. I read a book called *French Kids Eat Everything*, which talks about the eating habits of French children. A key point is that they never snack; they have meals. The book also discusses how French children will eat things that most American children won't, including pâté.

I do see Micah and Kai go through growth spurts, however, and during these times, they are extra hungry and sometimes ask for snacks. These are some of the snack foods that we often reach for:

- **Beef sticks:** Look for sugar-free options.
- **Carnivore Crisps:** These have only two ingredients—meat and salt—and they work great as nacho chips.
- **Cute Mouse Eggs** (page 144): Fun foods are always a hit!
- **The Cutest Deviled Eggs Ever** (page 136): My whole family loves deviled eggs, whether or not I turn them into spiders, flowers, or pumpkins.
- **Homemade jerky:** I have recipes in this book for both turkey and salmon jerky (pages 148 and 156, respectively).
- **Plain yogurt:** Check the carbs; I prefer Two Good brand. You can top it with a few fresh berries if you like.
- **Sardines:** Can you believe Micah snacked on sardines when he was only three years old? Yep! I don't even like sardines! But starting kids on savory foods at an early age can influence their palates. *You* are in control.

My favorite is when we are hiking or at the beach and Mom brings cheese curds or Moon Cheese (cheese crisps).

Sugar-Free Holidays and Birthdays

Staying sugar-free isn't hard during the holidays because there are so many delicious recipes to celebrate with!

My birthday is close to Halloween. I like it when my mom makes Halloween-themed foods for my parties. Last year, she made Spider Deviled Eggs (page 138), Pumpkin Deviled Eggs (page 138), Holiday Jigglers (page 280) cut into Halloween shapes, Spooky Breadstick Fingers (page 274), and her yummy Extreme Chocolate Blender Birthday Cake (page 300). I also had a piñata filled with stickers, little toys like Silly Putty, temporary superhero tattoos, and mini beef snack sticks rather than candy.

My birthday is in July, and I like to have my party at the beach. My mom always makes great sugar-free foods that my friends really like, even though they don't eat sugar-free. She has made Fruit Flower Bouquet (page 152), Antipasto on a Stick (page 176), Bombdiggity Pops (page 282), and Baseball Blender Cupcakes (page 302). I like to show my friends that eating sugar-free is delicious!

I usually throw birthday parties from 1 to 3 p.m. so I don't have to serve a meal. For Valentine's Day, instead of sugar-filled chocolates from the store, I make my Sugar-Free Chocolate (page 310) into heart shapes. I also make heart-shaped chaffles (page 350) and Heart-Shaped Eggs (page 264). For lots more ideas on how to celebrate without sugar, check out the holiday recipe chapter, which starts on page 252.

Picky Eaters: How to Get Children to Try New Foods

So many parents struggle to get their kids to eat more than buttered noodles and chocolate chip cookies. The most important thing to remember is that you *decide* what they are going to eat. If you are persistent about offering healthy options instead of junk, their palates will adapt over time.

That said, sometimes picky eating isn't just a matter of disliking the taste of certain foods. The health of the digestive tract plays a role as well.

The Role of Gut Bacteria and Probiotics

I was the pickiest eater when I was a child. I had ear infections, which meant a lot of antibiotics. Then, as a teenager, I was put on tetracycline, another antibiotic, for my acne. I had extremely low levels of good gut bacteria from years of taking antibiotics. Having low gut bacteria caused me to crave sugar and limited my palate.

Do you have a picky eater who only likes bland foods? They are likely low in healthy gut bacteria. Trillions of bacteria live in the digestive tract, and they make up a significant part of a person's immune system. A healthy lower intestine should have about 85 percent good bacteria to prevent colonization by disease-causing organisms like salmonella and E. coli.

The first two years of life are crucial for long-term immune responses. Bacterial colonization patterns form in the early years and continue to grow throughout our lifetime. The medications and foods that we give to our kids affect this delicate balance.

Taking an antibiotic, eating a diet high in refined carbohydrates, having a bout of diarrhea, or suffering from stress can deplete a healthy intestinal flora. Acne is also an indicator of low good bacteria. If your child has been on an antibiotic, it is extremely important to replenish the beneficial bacteria lost by giving them a quality probiotic supplement as well as supporting their health with a sugar-free diet. Probiotics stop the growth of harmful bacteria, which causes digestive problems. They also improve a person's ability to digest and absorb vitamins and enhance the immune system.

Probiotic supplements promote health in infants, babies, and young children, preventing eczema, diarrhea, diaper rash, and cradle cap and decreasing anemia and asthma. They also lower the chances of food allergies and eliminate thrush. In older children, probiotics have been found to reduce the severity and frequency of respiratory infections and prevent irritable bowel syndrome, diarrhea, and constipation. Kids with allergies, eczema, ADHD, celiac disease, diabetes, chronic bad breath, and leaky gut syndrome and those on the autism spectrum can all benefit from healthy doses of probiotics.

I once had a client, Kate, who had a five-year-old with autism. The boy was underweight, and his doctor had often pressured Kate to have him gain weight.

Kate understood that her son needed to be on a gluten-free diet to reduce his symptoms, but the only three things he would eat were gluten-free waffles, gluten-free chicken nuggets, and chocolate pudding—washed down with skim milk. All of these foods are full of sugar and contain very few nutrients. Kate begged me to help her son put on weight and try new foods.

I knew I needed to strongly encourage her to make some serious changes. You see, her son didn't have a car or money to keep buying these foods. It was Kate who allowed this behavior to continue.

I told Kate to serve him my homemade waffles, chicken nuggets, and chocolate pudding. I also had her mix some unsweetened almond milk into the skim milk to help wean him off dairy and the sugar in it. I had her add a few supplements such as probiotics, magnesium, and zinc, which help reduce sugar cravings.

He did notice a slight shift in the flavor of the foods, and on some days things were difficult. However, the boy's palate eventually opened up, and Kate continued to make the foods I suggested for him to try. Her son is now thirteen and thriving!

What Makes Food Delicious?

Some people think fast food and packaged food tastes better than home-cooked food, but if you learn to season properly, your food will taste better than anything you could order from a restaurant or eat out of a box! I like to incorporate these elements into my recipes to make them extra yummy:

- **Salt** is a flavor enhancer—don't fear it! If you add salt to a recipe, you can reduce the amount of sweetener because it enhances sweetness, too!

- **Fat** (butter, ghee, coconut oil, bacon fat, lard, tallow, avocado oil) adds flavor and texture.

- **Acid** (vinegar, lime juice, lemon juice, tomato sauce) rounds out the flavors of your cooking.

- **Umami** (Parmesan cheese, beef broth, fish sauce) is the fifth taste on your tongue, in addition to bitter, sour, sweet, and salty. It is what makes food so delicious. Adding an umami element to a dish can take it to a whole new level.

- **Fresh herbs and spices** are preferable to dried—especially ginger root, which has a much more intense flavor than its powdered counterpart.

Tips for Getting Your Children to Try New Foods

You know that having healthy gut bacteria is important, and you know the elements that make food taste good. So how do you get those tasty, healthy foods into your kids' mouths? Here are my secrets for encouraging kids to widen their palates and sample what may be unfamiliar or unappealing, at least initially:

- **Have them help you make it!** See page 56 for tips on getting your kids to assist you in the kitchen.

I didn't think I would like scallops, but when my mom had me make them all by myself, I thought they were great. Then I made a video of myself making chicken wings, and they were the best wings I ever had!

- **Put it on a stick!** I love taking my boys to the Minnesota State Fair in August. It is a family tradition that we look forward to every year. However, in 2020, state fairs were canceled. I decided to devise a celebration at home featuring different sugar-free foods on sticks. This fun food craft showed me just how much more open kids are to eating food if it is on a stick! To be honest, so am I, even as an adult. Food on a stick is darn fun to eat! Here are some easy recipes to help your kids eat sugar-free like we do:

  » Breakfast Kabobs (page 92)

  » Veggie and Savory Fruit Flowers (page 130)

  » Fruit Flower Bouquet (page 152)

  » Sandwich on a Stick (page 174)

  » Antipasto on a Stick (page 176)

We always have ice pops in the freezer! I like to experiment with different flavors. If you need a delicious idea, turn the Strawberry Pudding (page 146) into ice pops! Homemade ice pops can be really healthy, and they're easy for kids to make.

- **Make the food cute!** I like to use cookie cutters to cut vegetables and cheeses into fun shapes, like hearts and stars.

- **Go fishing!** Our boys never liked fish until we ate the fish they caught. Now, salmon is one of Micah's favorite foods.

- **Keep trying!** Offer healthy foods more often—at least ten times. Eventually, their palates will change and they will enjoy those foods.

Cooking Tools and Gadgets

For the most part, the recipes in this book require tools that are part of a basic kitchen setup: standard pots, pans, baking sheets, and so on. However, some of the recipes require specialized equipment, and there are some tools that will simply make your life in the kitchen easier.

Large Nonstick Skillet

For: Flourless Protein Pizza Crêpes (page 88),
Fluffy Bunny Scrambled Eggs (page 254)
Does such a thing as a nontoxic nonstick pan exist? Nonstick cookware can be convenient when cooking crêpes, omelets, or pancakes. But most nonstick pans use Teflon and other chemicals that we want to avoid. Instead, you can use a well-seasoned cast-iron skillet or a stainless-steel skillet coated with lots of oil.

I've also found that the glazed ceramic pans from Ceramcor have a great chemical-free nonstick surface. They can be cleaned as you would any other pan—the surface is very hard to scratch. They are super durable and heavy-duty. However, there is a slight learning curve with these pans. Because they are ceramic, they take longer to heat up. For omelets, I turn my burner to low heat to warm the pan for two to three minutes, and then I add my cooking fat; I cook the eggs and turn off the heat when I flip the omelet (it holds heat longer, like a cast-iron pan). The omelet slides right out!

High-Powered Blender

For: pureeing; making pudding (page 146), shakes, sauces, dips
High-powered blenders, such as those from Blendtec and Vitamix, have better performance, durability, and speed—but they're also more expensive. Instead of purchasing a new blender every other year when the previous one wears out, I suggest investing in a quality blender that will last for decades.

Immersion Blender

For: pureeing and blending
I can't believe I went so long without an immersion blender. I'm not a gadget person like my husband is—I like simplicity, and I'm not a fan of clutter—so when Craig first asked if I wanted an immersion blender, I politely said, "No, thank you." But I have to tell you, when I started using one, I was immediately hooked! It is so easy to operate, and I can't believe the power behind this little tool. I love it for making pureed soups, homemade mayonnaise, sauces, and salad dressings, as well as shakes.

Tip: Kids love using immersion blenders! It is a great way to get them to help out in the kitchen.

Waffle Maker

For: waffles (see Chapter 10)
I love to keep sugar-free waffles in the freezer for easy breakfasts. My advice is to spend the money on a quality waffle maker. I adore my Waring Pro double Belgian waffle maker. It can make two waffles at once!

Mini Waffle Maker

For: chaffles (see Chapter 10)
A mini waffle maker costs about $10. We love making chaffles so much that we often have three going at once! Mini waffle makers are helpful for families because children who are old enough can make a quick meal in minutes. You can even buy them in cute shapes, like a heart or a pumpkin.

Slow Cooker (6 Quarts)

For: slow cooking on low heat for several hours (see Chapter 7)
If you don't have a lot of time for hands-on cooking, a slow cooker can save you time and effort. You can prep the ingredients the night before, turn the slow cooker on before you leave for work in the morning, and come home to a wonderful hot meal.

Instant Pot (6 Quarts)

For: Instant Pot recipes (see Chapter 7)
Did you forget to plan something for dinner? No problem! An Instant Pot can make dinner in minutes. If you have a larger family, I suggest an 8-quart Instant Pot. I also like the 8-quart size so I can make extras for leftovers.

Ice Pop Molds

For: freezing liquids into individual treats, such as Bombdiggity Pops (page 282) and Raspberries and Cream Ice Pops (page 298)

Gummy Molds

For: molding gummies into shapes (pages 284 and 286)

Spiral Slicer

For: cutting vegetables into noodles, especially zoodles
People often ask me what my favorite spiral slicer is. My answer is that it depends on the thickness of the noodle you want. For a thicker noodle, I love the Veggetti Pro Tabletop Spiralizer. If you prefer a thin, angel hair–sized noodle, I recommend the Joyce Chen Saladacco Spiral Slicer.

Sugar-Free Ingredients

When it comes to cooking and baking without sugar, a few ingredients merit some extra discussion.

Fish Sauce

Fish sauce is a special ingredient that makes good food fantastic. It is a staple that every cook should have in the fridge. Fish sauce, along with mushrooms and aged cheeses, have something called "umami," a pleasant savory taste that occurs naturally in many foods. Umami is subtle and not generally identified by people when they encounter it, but it blends well with other flavors, intensifying and enhancing them.

Psyllium Husk Powder

Be aware that some brands of psyllium husk powder can give breads and other baked goods a purple hue. Don't be alarmed; they will still taste great! Make sure to choose a fine powder, and do not attempt to substitute for the psyllium in any recipe that calls for it.

Natural Sweeteners

"Sugar-free" doesn't have to mean "not at all sweet"! I simply use natural sweeteners in my recipes. Just as sugarcane and honey are found in nature, so are erythritol and the stevia herb. However, I prefer not to use sweeteners such as honey, maple syrup, and agave. The reason is that even though they're natural, they raise blood sugar, which causes inflammation and illness.

Fructose is particularly problematic. More than glucose, it promotes a chemical reaction called glycation, which results in advanced glycation end products (AGEs). AGEs form a crust around cells that has been linked to a wide range of diseases, from diabetes and heart disease to asthma, polycystic ovary syndrome, and Alzheimer's. Fructose also contributes to nonalcoholic fatty liver disease. For these reasons, I avoid sweeteners that are high in fructose: table sugar, high-fructose corn syrup, honey, agave, and some fruits.

The following are the natural sweeteners that I recommend, all of which have little effect on blood sugar:

- **Erythritol:** This sugar alcohol is found naturally in some fruits and fermented foods. Erythritol is generally available in granulated form, though sometimes you can find it powdered. I prefer the powdered (confectioners'-style) form because it gives food a smooth texture. If you purchase a granulated product, I recommend grinding it to a powder before using it.

- **Allulose:** Allulose works great for ice cream and cookies. It keeps ice cream soft, whereas erythritol doesn't melt and keeps ice cream very hard. Allulose also caramelizes, so it works well in recipes for chewy cookies.

- **Swerve and other blended sweeteners:** These products combine two zero-calorie natural sweeteners, usually erythritol (see above) and oligosaccharides found in many plants. They do not affect blood sugar and measure cup for cup just like table sugar. I use the powdered form of Swerve (the one labeled "confectioners") because it dissolves particularly well. Other blends I recommend are Pyure (erythritol and stevia), Norbu (erythritol and monk fruit), Natvia (erythritol and stevia), Lakanto (erythritol and monk fruit), and Zsweet (erythritol and stevia).

- **Stevia:** Stevia is available as a powder and as a liquid. Because stevia is so concentrated, many companies add bulking agents like maltodextrin to the powdered form to make it easier to use in baking. You want to stay away from those products. Instead, look for products that contain only stevia or stevia combined with monk fruit.

- **Stevia glycerite:** A thick liquid form of stevia that is similar in consistency to honey. Do not confuse it with liquid stevia, which is much more concentrated. Stevia glycerite is about twice as sweet as sugar, making it a bit less sweet than liquid or powdered stevia. I prefer stevia glycerite because, unlike powdered and liquid stevia, it has no bitter aftertaste. Stevia glycerite is excellent for cooking because it maintains its flavor when heated. However, it doesn't caramelize or create bulk, so most baking recipes call for combining it with another sweetener. When making my no-churn ice cream (see pages 317 to 323), sometimes the divine taste of heavy cream is enough, and all you need to add is a teaspoon of stevia glycerite.

- **Monk fruit:** Also known as lo han go, monk fruit comes in pure liquid and powdered forms. Because it is 300 times sweeter than sugar, the powdered form is typically bulked up with another sweetener so that it measures cup for cup like sugar. Check the ingredients for maltodextrin and other harmful additives.

- **Xylitol:** A naturally occurring low-calorie sweetener found in fruits and vegetables, xylitol has a minimal effect on blood sugar and insulin.

If you're just starting out on your sugar-free lifestyle, the recipes in this book should have just the right amount of sweetness for your family. But as you continue eating this way, you may find that food naturally begins to taste sweeter, and you may want to reduce the amount of sweetener used in these recipes.

Tip: Slowly add natural sweetener to a recipe, taste, and adjust the sweetness to your liking. Note that some of the sweet taste will bake off in baked-goods recipes, resulting in the finished products being less sweet.

Using Sweeteners in the Recipes in This Book

My go-to choice for sweetening recipes is the powdered (confectioners'-style) form of erythritol because it gives a smoother finished product and better overall results than other sweeteners. That said, you can always pulverize a granular form of erythritol in a blender or clean coffee grinder to get a powdered texture.

If a recipe calls for a specific type of sweetener (such as powdered or liquid), do not substitute any other sweetener; these recipes rely on these particular sweeteners. For example, in a recipe where the sweetener has to melt, some products won't work—so it's important to use exactly what's called for.

If a sweetener in an ingredient list is followed by "or equivalent," such as "¼ cup confectioners'-style erythritol or equivalent amount of liquid or powdered sweetener," you are free to use any sugar-free natural sweetener you like, liquid or powdered. For example, you could use allulose, liquid stevia, monk fruit, stevia glycerite, or xylitol.

If you prefer to use a sweetener other than erythritol, here are the conversions:

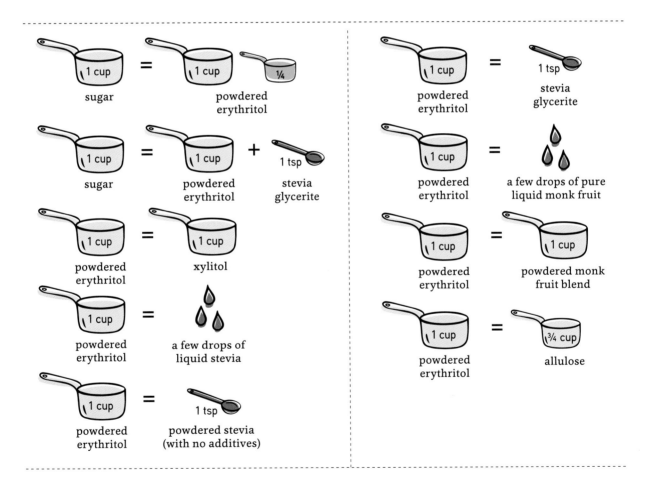

1 cup sugar = 1 cup powdered erythritol + ¼	1 cup powdered erythritol = 1 tsp stevia glycerite
1 cup sugar = 1 cup powdered erythritol + 1 tsp stevia glycerite	1 cup powdered erythritol = a few drops of pure liquid monk fruit
1 cup powdered erythritol = 1 cup xylitol	1 cup powdered erythritol = 1 cup powdered monk fruit blend
1 cup powdered erythritol = a few drops of liquid stevia	1 cup powdered erythritol = ¾ cup allulose
1 cup powdered erythritol = 1 tsp powdered stevia (with no additives)	

Blending Sweeteners for the Tastiest Sugar-Free Treats

For newcomers to the sugar-free lifestyle, I try to keep my recipes as simple as possible and limit the number of ingredients used. For example, in recipes that are sweetened, I usually just call for erythritol or an equivalent. But the truth is, you'll get better results if you use a blend of natural sweeteners.

For example, if a recipe calls for 1 cup of confectioners'-style erythritol, I use this combination:

- ½ cup confectioners'-style erythritol

- 1 teaspoon stevia glycerite

- 10 to 15 drops liquid monk fruit

Adding a pinch of salt will also increase the sweetness because salt is a flavor enhancer.

How to Use the Recipes in This Book

The rest of this book is packed with kid-friendly recipes that the whole family will love, from sugar-free breakfasts to easy dinners and snacks. I have worked hard to make these foods visually appealing, especially in the holiday chapter, which features fun foods for celebrations throughout the year.

My books always include a bonus chapter, and here, it's sweet and savory grain-free waffles and chaffles (which are waffles made from cheese!) that you can serve for breakfast or use to make yummy sandwiches. You will also find a chapter of babies' first foods.

Because kids who eat sugar-free often snack less and therefore are hungry for larger portions at mealtime, the serving sizes are typical for adults and big kids alike. If you have younger children, they might prefer smaller portions. Use their hunger signals as your guide.

There are many types of cooks with a wide range of skill levels. To help you find the recipes that are well suited to your cooking abilities and time constraints, I've marked each recipe with a difficulty level:

EASY   MEDIUM   HARD

I also recognize that many families are dealing with food sensitivities, food allergies, and special diets, so I've used icons to denote which recipes are free of dairy, eggs, and/or nuts and which ones are vegetarian. If the word *option* appears below an icon, that recipe can be modified to make it free of that allergen or make it vegetarian.

DAIRY-FREE   EGG-FREE   NUT-FREE   VEGETARIAN

I encourage you to try plenty of these recipes and see which ones become favorites in your family. Let your kids help you in the kitchen, too, so they learn not only to eat well, but to make healthy, tasty food for themselves!

chapter 3:

breakfast

Protein-Packed Blue Milk / 82

Pizza Eggs / 84

Strawberry Breakfast Parfait / 86

Flourless Protein Pizza Crêpes / 88

Easy Baked Bacon and Sausages / 90

Breakfast Kabobs / 92

Ham 'n' Cheese Cupcakes / 94

French Toast Porridge / 96

Chocolate Minute Muffins / 98

Chocolate Protein Shake / 100

Blender Pancake Snowmen / 102

Easy Blender Chocolate Donuts / 104

Dippy Eggs with Toast Fingers / 106

Green Eggs and Ham / 108

Micah's Egg Muffin Sandwiches / 110

Crunch Berry Cereal / 112

Cheeseburger Breakfast Casserole / 114

Cinnamon Rolls / 116

Sugar-Free Toaster Pastries
(aka Gilmore Girls Breakfast) / 118

Pizza Breakfast Pie / 120

Blueberry Cheesecake Muffins / 122

Monkey Bread / 124

Protein-Packed
Blue Milk

EASY   option   option option

yield: 4 servings • prep time: 5 minutes

My family loves Disney, and we love Star Wars. There is a popular drink sold at Disney's theme parks called Galaxy's Edge Blue Milk. It is a frothy, fruity beverage that represents Bantha Milk in the movie *Star Wars*—the blue-colored drink that Sentients drank. I like to add collagen to our blue milk for an extra punch of protein.

½ cup unsweetened almond milk (or coconut milk for nut-free)

½ cup plain low-carb yogurt or heavy cream (or coconut cream for dairy-free) (see note)

½ cup ice cubes

2 tablespoons confectioners'-style erythritol or equivalent amount of liquid or powdered sweetener (see page 77)

2 tablespoons vanilla-flavored collagen powder (optional; omit for vegetarian)

¼ teaspoon vanilla extract

¼ teaspoon raspberry, cherry, or strawberry extract

¼ teaspoon fine sea salt

¼ teaspoon blue spirulina, or ¼ cup frozen blueberries (optional, for natural blue coloring)

Place all the ingredients in a blender and puree until smooth. Taste and adjust the sweetness to your liking. Pour into glasses and enjoy! Best served fresh.

note:

You can use heavy cream in place of yogurt in this recipe to make the milk extra delicious; however, yogurt (I use Two Good brand) increases the healthy protein while keeping the sugar low.

(per serving):
calories **170** • fat **13g** • protein **10g** • carbs **2g** • fiber **0.3g**

Pizza
Eggs

EASY   option

yield: 2 servings • prep time: 5 minutes • cook time: 6 minutes

This is my absolute favorite breakfast. It has so much flavor, it is like having pizza for breakfast that is healthy! My mom really likes this breakfast because it is so easy for her to make.

1 cup sugar-free pizza sauce, homemade (page 370) or store-bought (see note)

4 large eggs, room temperature

½ teaspoon fine sea salt

¼ teaspoon Italian seasoning

FOR GARNISH (OPTIONAL)

Fresh basil leaves

Freshly grated Parmesan cheese (omit for dairy-free)

Pour the pizza sauce into an 8-inch skillet. Crack the eggs into the sauce, spacing them evenly around the pan, and season the eggs with the salt and Italian seasoning. Cook over medium heat for 6 minutes, or until the whites are set and the yolks are cooked to your liking (6 minutes will give you yolks that are over medium). Remove from the heat and serve garnished with the basil leaves and cheese, if desired. Best served fresh.

note:

If using store-bought pizza sauce, check for added sugars; I buy Rao's brand.

(per serving):
calories **188** • fat **13g** • protein **14g** • carbs **4g** • fiber **1g**

Strawberry Breakfast Parfait

EASY   option   option

yield: 4 servings • prep time: 5 minutes, plus time to make cereal if using

 I love this recipe for breakfast, and I love it for a snack, too! It is creamy with a crunchy top and sweet strawberries. It's so easy, I make it all by myself!

4 cups plain low-carb yogurt (use dairy-free yogurt for dairy-free)

¼ cup vanilla- or strawberry-flavored collagen powder (optional; omit for vegetarian)

2 cups sliced strawberries

½ cup Crunch Berry Cereal (page 112) or sliced or crushed almonds or macadamia nuts

Put the yogurt in a large bowl and stir in the collagen. Place ⅓ cup of the yogurt mixture in a serving dish, top with a layer of sliced strawberries, followed by ⅓ cup of yogurt, then another layer of strawberries, then yogurt, then strawberries. Top the parfait with 2 tablespoons of cereal or crushed nuts. Repeat with the remaining ingredients to make 4 parfaits. Store extras covered in the refrigerator for up to 4 days.

> *note:*
>
> *If you prefer a sweeter parfait, you can sweeten the yogurt with a few tablespoons of powdered sweetener or a few drops of liquid stevia. You can also use strawberry-flavored stevia if desired.*

(per serving):
calories **292** • fat **16g** • protein **26g** • carbs **15g** • fiber **5g**

Flourless Protein
Pizza Crêpes

EASY   option   option

yield: 4 crêpes (2 per serving) • prep time: 3 minutes (not including time to boil eggs) • cook time: 16 minutes

If you love eating pizza for breakfast, you must try this protein-packed breakfast! I make the crêpe batter the night before and store it in the blender jar in the fridge. All I have to do in the morning is heat up the skillet, and breakfast is ready in minutes!

PROTEIN CRÊPES

2 large eggs

2 hard-boiled eggs, peeled

2 tablespoons unsweetened almond milk (or unsweetened hemp milk for nut-free)

¼ teaspoon fine sea salt

¼ teaspoon baking powder

Coconut oil, for the skillet

PIZZA FILLING

¼ cup shredded mozzarella or Parmesan cheese (omit for dairy-free)

¼ cup pepperoni slices or chopped sugar-free breakfast sausage

¼ cup sugar-free pizza sauce, homemade (page 370) or store-bought, warmed, for serving

1. Make the crêpe batter: Place all the ingredients, except the coconut oil, in a blender and blend until very smooth.

2. Heat 1½ teaspoons of coconut oil in a large nonstick skillet over medium heat. Once hot, pour one-quarter of the batter into the skillet. Tilt and swirl the pan to make a very thin crêpe. Cook until golden brown, about 2 minutes, then flip and cook the other side until browned, another 1 to 2 minutes. Remove from the skillet and repeat with additional coconut oil and batter, making a total of 4 crêpes.

3. Fill the crêpes with the cheese (if using), pepperoni, and pizza sauce. Store extra crêpes, unfilled, in an airtight container in the refrigerator for up to 4 days, or freeze for up to a month. To reheat, place in a greased skillet over medium heat for 1 minute per side, or until warmed through.

(per serving):
calories **272** • fat **21g** • protein **19g** • carbs **3g** • fiber **1g**

Easy Baked
Bacon and Sausages

EASY

yield: 2 servings • prep time: 2 minutes • cook time: 17 minutes

One of my sons loves bacon, and the other loves sausage. When I'm in a rush in the morning, the boys know this method well. All they have to do is put as many bacon slices and/or sausage links as they want on a rimmed baking sheet and put it in the toaster oven on their own. Baking the meat instead of frying it means that I don't have to worry about the kids burning themselves or their breakfast!

4 slices bacon (pork or beef)

4 sugar-free breakfast sausage links

1. Preheat a toaster oven or oven to 400°F. Line a rimmed baking sheet with parchment paper.

2. Place the bacon and sausages in a single layer on the prepared baking sheet and place in the oven (no need for the oven to be fully preheated).

3. Bake for 8 to 17 minutes, or until cooked to your liking. (The sausages I buy are fully cooked, so they take only a few minutes to brown.)

4. Best served fresh.

(per serving):
calories **191** • fat **17g** • protein **10g** • carbs **0g** • fiber **0g**

Breakfast Kabobs

EASY option option

yield: 8 kabobs (2 per serving) • prep time: 8 minutes (not including time to make waffles) • cook time: 2 minutes

Kids love eating foods on a stick. Even grown-ups do! These breakfast kabobs are delicious and easy to make. You can serve them with whipped cream, whipped coconut cream, softened cream cheese (regular or the dairy-free Kite Hill version), or my Sugar-Free Strawberry Jam (page 378).

4 Easy Blender Waffles (page 336), cut into 1½-inch squares

1 (8-ounce) ham steak (¾ inch thick), cut into 1-inch pieces (omit for vegetarian)

8 strawberries, stemmed and sliced in half

Whipped cream or whipped coconut cream, for serving (optional)

SPECIAL EQUIPMENT:

8 (4-inch) wooden skewers

1. Soak the skewers in water for 8 to 10 minutes. Preheat the oven to 350°F.

2. Thread a piece of waffle onto a skewer and slide it down to about ½ inch from the end. Thread on a piece of ham, then a strawberry half. Repeat with another piece of waffle, piece of ham, and strawberry. Repeat with the remaining skewers and ingredients.

3. Place the kabobs on a rimmed baking sheet. Bake for 2 to 5 minutes, until warmed to your liking. Remove from the oven and serve with whipped cream for dipping, if desired.

4. Store extras in an airtight container in the refrigerator for up to 4 days. To reheat, place in a 350°F oven for 2 to 5 minutes, or until heated to your liking.

(per serving):
calories **207** • fat **15g** • protein **17g** • carbs **1g** • fiber **0g**

Ham 'n' Cheese Cupcakes

EASY   option

yield: 12 cupcakes (2 per serving) • prep time: 5 minutes • cook time: 20 minutes

My boys love these savory cupcakes for breakfast. They really love that they are called cupcakes because it makes them seem extra special and somehow tastier than ham 'n' cheese scrambled eggs. Everyone loves cupcakes, even if they are savory!

Coconut oil or unsalted butter, for the pan

1 cup diced ham

8 large eggs

1 cup shredded cheddar cheese (omit for dairy-free)

2 tablespoons chopped green onions (optional)

½ teaspoon fine sea salt

¼ teaspoon ground black pepper

1. Preheat the oven to 350°F. Lightly grease a standard-size 12-well muffin pan (or two 6-well pans) with coconut oil or butter, or use silicone liners.

2. Place the eggs in a medium bowl and beat lightly, then add the remaining ingredients and mix to combine. Divide the egg mixture evenly among the prepared wells of the muffin pan, filling them about two-thirds full. Bake for 15 minutes, or until set.

3. Store extras in an airtight container in the refrigerator for up to 4 days. To reheat, place on a rimmed baking sheet in a 350°F oven for a few minutes, until warmed through.

(per serving):
calories **231** • fat **17g** • protein **18g** • carbs **1g** • fiber **0.1g**

French Toast
Porridge

EASY option option   yield: 2 servings • prep time: 2 minutes • cook time: 4 minutes

I grew up on Malt-O-Meal hot cereal. It was little pieces of grains thickened in milk. This porridge reminds me of that cereal. For a chocolate version, add a few tablespoons of unsweetened cocoa powder and use vanilla extract in place of maple!

4 large eggs

⅔ cup unsweetened almond milk or heavy cream, plus ½ cup more, divided, for serving if desired

2 tablespoons confectioners'-style erythritol or equivalent amount of liquid or powdered sweetener (see page 77)

1 tablespoon plus 1 teaspoon maple or vanilla extract

½ teaspoon fine sea salt

1 tablespoon coconut oil or unsalted butter

Ground cinnamon, for sprinkling

1. In a small bowl, whisk together the eggs, almond milk, sweetener, extract, and salt.

2. In a medium saucepan, melt the coconut oil over medium heat. Add the egg mixture and cook, scraping the bottom with a wooden spoon, until the mixture thickens and starts to curdle, about 4 minutes. Use a whisk to separate the curds.

3. Once the curds have formed and the porridge has thickened, remove the pan from the heat and transfer the porridge to serving bowls. Sprinkle with cinnamon and serve with ¼ cup of almond milk, if desired. Best served fresh.

(per serving):
calories **207** • fat **17g** • protein **13g** • carbs **1g** • fiber **0g**

Chocolate Minute Muffins

EASY option option

yield: 5 muffins (1 per serving) • prep time: 3 minutes • cook time: 8 to 12 minutes, depending on method

If you prefer more of a frosting rather than a glaze for these muffins, you can use the frosting from the Sugar-Free Toaster Pastries recipe on page 118.

½ cup coconut flour

¼ cup confectioners'-style erythritol or equivalent amount of powdered sweetener (see page 77)

3 tablespoons unsweetened cocoa powder

1 teaspoon baking soda

Pinch of fine sea salt

4 large eggs, lightly beaten

¼ cup coconut oil or unsalted butter, melted but not hot

½ cup unsweetened almond milk or heavy cream

1 teaspoon vanilla extract

GLAZE (OPTIONAL)

3 tablespoons coconut oil or unsalted butter, melted

3 tablespoons confectioners'-style erythritol or equivalent amount of powdered sweetener (see page 77)

¾ teaspoon vanilla extract

1. If using the oven, preheat the oven to 350°F. Grease five 4-ounce microwave-safe cups or ramekins (use ramekins if baking the muffins in the oven).

2. In a medium bowl, whisk together the coconut flour, sweetener, cocoa powder, baking soda, and salt. Stir in the eggs, melted coconut oil, almond milk, and vanilla. Divide the batter among the greased cups or ramekins, filling each about three-quarters full.

3. If using the microwave, place one cup or ramekin in the microwave at a time and cook on high for about 1 minute 30 seconds, until a toothpick inserted in the middle comes out clean. If using the oven, bake all 5 ramekins at once for 8 to 12 minutes, until a toothpick inserted in the middle of a muffin comes out clean.

4. Meanwhile, stir together the ingredients for the glaze, if using.

5. Remove the muffins from the microwave or oven and top each with 1 tablespoon of glaze, if desired. Eat warm right out of the cup or ramekin. Best consumed fresh.

busy family tip:
Fill the cups or ramekins with the batter and store covered in the refrigerator for easy on-the-go breakfasts that can be baked as needed. The batter will keep in the refrigerator for up to 3 days.

(per serving):
calories **289** • fat **26g** • protein **7g** • carbs **8g** • fiber **5g**

Chocolate
Protein Shake

EASY   option   yield: 4 servings • prep time: 5 minutes, plus time to chill overnight

In this shake, I use canned coconut milk. If you'd like to lower the calories, you can use boxed coconut milk or more unsweetened almond or cashew milk. The flavor of this shake is best after it is chilled.

This recipe became popular using hard-boiled eggs, but over time, I found that scrambled eggs work just as well, and you don't have to peel the eggs. I also find that the shake has less of a sulfuric odor when using scrambled eggs. Either way, this recipe is sure to become a family favorite!

4 large eggs, hard-boiled and peeled or scrambled

1 cup unsweetened almond or cashew milk

1 cup unsweetened coconut milk

½ cup confectioner's-style erythritol or equivalent amount of liquid or powdered sweetener (see page 77)

¼ cup unsweetened cocoa powder, or more to taste

2 teaspoons banana or vanilla extract

⅛ teaspoon fine sea salt

¼ cup vanilla- or chocolate-flavored collagen powder (optional; omit for vegetarian)

1. Place the eggs in a high-powered blender. Add the rest of the ingredients and puree until very smooth. Taste and adjust the sweetness to your liking. Add more cocoa powder, if desired.

2. Place the shake mixture in the refrigerator overnight to chill before serving, or store for up to 4 days. (I simply cover the blender jar and put it right in the fridge, but you can transfer the shake to a clean airtight container(s) if you prefer.)

tip:
Any leftover shake can be made into ice pops by pouring the shake into ice pop molds and freezing overnight.

(per serving):
calories **224** • fat **15g** • protein **17g** • carbs **3g** • fiber **1g**

Blender Pancake
Snowmen

EASY option option option

yield: 2 snowmen (1 per serving) • prep time: 3 minutes (not including time to boil eggs or cook sausage) • cook time: 4 minutes

I grew up in north central Wisconsin, where dairy month was a big deal. Every Saturday in June, families would gather at one of the local farms for a huge pancake breakfast. I love this sugar-free pancake recipe—it is made of eggs! Eggs are one of the most affordable perfect foods.

PANCAKES

4 large eggs

4 hard-boiled eggs, peeled

½ cup blanched almond flour, or 2 tablespoons coconut flour

¼ cup vanilla-flavored collagen powder (optional; omit for vegetarian)

2 tablespoons confectioners'-style erythritol or equivalent amount of liquid or powdered sweetener (see page 77)

2 teaspoons vanilla extract

½ teaspoon baking powder

¼ teaspoon fine sea salt

Coconut oil, for the skillet

DECORATION

¼ cup heavy cream (see tips) or whipped coconut cream

1 tablespoon confectioners'-style erythritol or equivalent amount of liquid or powdered sweetener (see page 77)

6 raspberries

1 strawberry, stemmed and cut in half lengthwise

2 sugar-free breakfast sausage links, cooked (see page 90; omit for vegetarian)

1 tablespoon melted sugar-free chocolate, homemade (page 310) or store-bought

1. Place all the ingredients for the pancakes, except the coconut oil, in a blender and blend until very smooth.

2. Heat 1½ teaspoons of coconut oil in a large skillet over medium heat. Once hot, pour three different-sized pancakes for a snowman: 1½ tablespoons, 3 tablespoons, and ¼ cup. Cook until golden brown, about 2 minutes, then flip and cook until golden brown on the other side, another 1 to 2 minutes. Remove from the skillet and repeat with the remaining batter, adding more oil to the skillet if needed.

3. Place the pancakes on 2 large plates with the largest pancake on the bottom, followed by the medium pancake and then the smallest pancake on top, overlapping them by about 1 inch.

4. Put the heavy cream in a whipped cream canister (see tips) or in a large bowl and whip with a hand mixer on high speed until soft peaks form. Add the sweetener and whip until stiff peaks form. Dollop mounds of whipped cream at the bottom of each snowman to replicate snow.

5. Place 3 raspberries down the center of the middle pancake for jacket buttons. Place a strawberry half at the top of the snowman for a hat. Slice the sausages in half lengthwise and place cut side down on either side of the middle pancake for arms.

6. Place the melted chocolate in a small resealable plastic bag. Cut a tiny hole in one corner of the bag and use the chocolate to draw the eyes, triangle nose, and dots for the mouth.

7. Store extra pancakes, undecorated, in an airtight container in the refrigerator for up to 4 days, or freeze for up to a month. To reheat, place in a greased skillet over medium heat for 1 minute per side, or until warmed through.

(per serving):
calories **618** • fat **39g** • protein **49g** • carbs **10g** • fiber **3g**

busy family tips:

I always make the batter the night before so all I have to do in the morning is cook the pancakes. This saves me so much time! I also make extra pancakes so my boys can reheat them for an easy breakfast. I use a turkey baster to make neat pancake shapes.

To make the whipped cream snow, I use a whipped cream dispenser. All you have to do is place the cream in the dispenser with a few drops of sweetener, then seal, shake, and pump!

Easy Blender Chocolate Donuts

EASY   option

yield: 12 donuts (1 per serving) • prep time: 15 minutes • cook time: 15 minutes

Everything tastes better when it's shaped like a donut! A silicone donut pan helps prevent sticking. If you don't have a donut pan, you can use a muffin pan.

1½ cups confectioners'-style erythritol or equivalent amount of liquid or powdered sweetener (see page 77)

½ cup unsweetened almond or cashew milk

½ cup (1 stick) unsalted butter (or coconut oil for dairy-free), melted but not hot

2 large eggs

1 teaspoon vanilla extract

2 cups blanched almond flour

¾ cup unsweetened cocoa powder

¼ cup coconut flour

2 teaspoons baking powder

1 teaspoon baking soda

½ teaspoon fine sea salt

½ cup very hot water

CHOCOLATE GLAZE

½ cup plus 2 tablespoons heavy cream (or full-fat coconut milk for dairy-free)

4 tablespoons (½ stick) unsalted butter (or coconut oil for dairy-free)

2 ounces unsweetened chocolate, finely chopped

½ cup confectioners'-style erythritol or equivalent amount of liquid or powdered sweetener (see page 77)

2 teaspoons vanilla extract

1. Preheat the oven to 350°F and grease a 12-well donut pan really well with butter or avocado or coconut oil spray.

2. Put the sweetener, milk, melted butter, eggs, and vanilla in a blender and pulse until well blended and smooth. Add the almond flour, cocoa powder, coconut flour, baking powder, baking soda, and salt. Pour the hot water over the top; it will start to bubble as it hits the baking powder and soda. Pulse, scraping down the sides of the blender once or twice, until the batter is smooth.

3. Pour the batter into the prepared donut pan, filling each well about two-thirds full. Bake for 13 to 15 minutes, until a toothpick inserted in the center of a donut comes out clean. Remove from the oven and allow to cool in the pan for about 10 minutes, then turn out onto a wire rack to cool completely before glazing.

4. While the donuts are cooling, make the glaze: Place the heavy cream and butter in a small saucepan over medium-high heat. Once the mixture reaches a simmer, remove from the heat and add the chopped chocolate and sweetener; stir well until the chocolate is melted. Add the vanilla and stir until the glaze is smooth and thick.

5. Dunk the top of each donut into the glaze. Set the donuts upright on the wire rack or a serving platter to set.

6. Store extras in an airtight container in the refrigerator for up to 4 days, or freeze for up to a month. Allow to come to room temperature before serving.

(per serving):
calories **330** • fat **30g** • protein **7g** • carbs **9g** • fiber **5g**

Dippy Eggs
with Toast Fingers

MEDIUM **option**   yield: 2 servings • prep time: 7 minutes (not including time to make muffins) • cook time: 10 minutes

I love to serve dippy eggs (also known as soft-boiled eggs) with my Easy English Muffins cut into "fingers." You can make the English muffins in square shapes rather than round if you want fingers that are all the same length.

4 large eggs

2 Easy English Muffins (page 386)

2 tablespoons unsalted butter (or coconut oil for dairy-free)

Fine sea salt and ground black pepper

1. Make the soft-boiled eggs: Fill a medium saucepan about halfway with water and bring just to a simmer. Gently place the eggs one at a time in the simmering water. Cook for 5 to 6 minutes, depending on how runny you prefer the yolks: 5 minutes will give you runny yolks and 6 minutes will give you yolks that are just set. Make sure to hold the water at a simmer; don't let it come to a boil. Remove the eggs and run under cold water for 30 seconds.

2. Meanwhile, make the fingers: Heat a skillet over medium heat. Spread the butter on both sides of the English muffins. Place the muffins in the hot skillet and fry for 2 minutes, or until golden brown, then flip and fry for another 2 minutes, until golden brown on the other side. Remove from the skillet and slice into ¾-inch-wide fingers for dipping.

3. To serve, use a knife to take the cap off the tip of each egg and poke each of the warm yolks. Sprinkle with salt and pepper and enjoy straight from the eggshell with the fingers.

4. The eggs and fingers are best served fresh; however, leftover fingers can be stored in an airtight container in the refrigerator for up to 3 days. To reheat, place the fingers on a rimmed baking sheet in a preheated 400°F oven for 4 minutes, or until warmed through. Make the soft-boiled eggs just before serving or the yolks will harden in the refrigerator.

(per serving):
calories **366** • fat **29g** • protein **23g** • carbs **3g** • fiber **1g**

Green Eggs
and Ham

MEDIUM option

yield: 2 servings • prep time: 5 minutes • cook time: 7 minutes

There are a couple of running themes in my books: I like to include a bonus chapter, and I like to include a special new recipe for green eggs and ham! Every year on Dr. Seuss's birthday, I make green eggs and ham for my family. Dr. Seuss was an integral part of one of my favorite summer memories: When I was in college, I worked at Camp St. Croix, an environmental camp for kids, and every year we would put on a puppet show of *The Lorax* to teach the kids about Earth-friendly practices. I loved that job and all the special people I worked with there. This recipe is in honor of all my amazing camp memories.

2 tablespoons coconut oil or unsalted butter

6 large eggs

¼ cup guacamole (page 376)

½ teaspoon fine sea salt

4 ounces thinly sliced deli ham

Fresh cilantro leaves or sliced green onions, for garnish (optional)

1. Melt the oil in a small saucepan over medium-low heat.

2. In a large bowl, whisk the eggs with a fork. Pour the eggs into the saucepan and cook, whisking constantly, until the eggs are almost set but still a little loose, about 4 minutes.

3. Add the guacamole and salt, mixing well to turn the eggs green. Cook until the eggs are set to your liking.

4. Serve the green eggs alongside the slices of ham, or divide the eggs among the ham slices and wrap up like burritos. Garnish with cilantro leaves or sliced green onions, if desired. Best served fresh.

(per serving):
calories **537** • fat **43g** • protein **32g** • carbs **4g** • fiber **2g**

Micah's
Egg Muffin Sandwiches

MEDIUM   option

yield: 2 servings • prep time: 4 minutes (not including time to make muffins) • cook time: 5 minutes

 I've never had McDonald's food, but everyone tells me that my mom's recipe for egg muffin sandwiches is better than a McDonald's Egg McMuffin. I love to help make these easy sandwiches for an on-the-go breakfast. After we make them, I wrap one in parchment paper and take it with me for a portable meal! My mom often has her Easy English Muffins in the freezer for quick breakfast sandwiches like this.

1 teaspoon bacon fat

2 large eggs

¼ teaspoon fine sea salt

2 Easy English Muffins (page 386)

Unsalted butter or coconut oil

4 ounces shaved ham or turkey

2 (1-ounce) slices cheddar cheese (omit for dairy-free)

1. Heat the fat in a medium cast-iron skillet over medium heat. Place 2 mason jar rings facedown in the skillet. Crack an egg into each ring to form perfect circles. Season the eggs with the salt. Use a fork to scramble the eggs a little inside the rings and break up the yolks. Cover and cook until the eggs are cooked through, about 4 minutes. Remove the eggs from the skillet and set aside on a plate.

2. Slice the English muffins in half and spread butter or coconut oil on the cut sides. Place the muffin halves buttered side down in the hot skillet to toast for 1 minute. Warm the slices of ham in the skillet, topped with the cheese (if using), for about 1 minute.

3. Remove the muffins and ham from the skillet. Place a toasted English muffin half buttered side up on a plate, then top with an egg and a slice of cheese-topped ham. Top with another muffin half, buttered side down. Repeat with the remaining ingredients to make the second sandwich. Wrap in parchment paper or foil if desired for an easy breakfast on-the-go! Best served fresh.

(per serving):
calories **457** • fat **34g** • protein **36g** • carbs **2g** • fiber **1g**

Crunch Berry Cereal

EASY   option

yield: 6 servings • prep time: 5 minutes • cook time: 20 minutes

This cereal reminds me of Cap'n Crunch, but without the sugar bomb! It is filled with healthy protein and fats to fuel children right. It also makes a great snack and can be packed in lunch boxes.

1 cup blanched almond flour

1 cup strawberry- or vanilla-flavored whey protein powder (or egg white protein powder for dairy-free) (see note)

⅓ cup confectioners'-style erythritol or equivalent amount of liquid or powdered sweetener (see page 77)

¼ teaspoon fine sea salt

½ cup (1 stick) unsalted butter (or coconut oil for dairy-free), softened

2 tablespoons water

1 teaspoon cherry or strawberry extract

1 teaspoon natural red food coloring (optional)

Unsweetened almond milk or coconut milk, for serving (optional)

1. Preheat the oven to 300°F. Line a rimmed baking sheet with parchment paper.

2. Put the almond flour, protein powder, sweetener, and salt in a food processor or blender and pulse to combine. Add the butter and pulse to combine. Pour the water into a small bowl and add the extract and food coloring. Stir, then add to the food processor and pulse until small pebbles form.

3. Spread the pebbles on the prepared baking sheet. Bake for 12 to 20 minutes, until golden brown. Remove from the oven and stir to break up any large clumps while the cereal is still hot. Allow to cool completely on the baking sheet, then break the pieces apart. Enjoy with almond milk, if desired.

note:

When choosing a protein powder for this recipe, check for added sugars. I always choose brands that are sweetened with stevia. If you can't find strawberry-flavored protein powder, you can use vanilla and add extra cherry or strawberry extract for flavor.

(per serving):
calories **297** • fat **25g** • protein **17g** • carbs **5g** • fiber **4g**

Cheeseburger
Breakfast Casserole

MEDIUM   yield: 8 servings • prep time: 10 minutes • cook time: 20 minutes

My recipe testers loved this simple breakfast casserole! The special sauce tastes just like the sauce on a McDonald's Big Mac and makes the casserole extra delicious.

Avocado or coconut oil spray

1 pound ground beef

½ cup chopped onions

1 clove garlic, minced

2 teaspoons fine sea salt, divided

¼ cup sugar-free ketchup, homemade (page 369) or store-bought

8 large eggs, beaten

¾ cup shredded cheddar cheese

2 tablespoons mayonnaise, homemade (page 365) or store-bought

2 teaspoons prepared yellow mustard

¼ teaspoon ground black pepper

SPECIAL SAUCE

½ cup mayonnaise, homemade (page 365) or store-bought

¼ cup chopped dill pickles

3 tablespoons sugar-free ketchup, homemade (page 369) or store-bought

2 tablespoons confectioners'-style erythritol or equivalent amount of liquid or powdered sweetener (see page 77)

⅛ teaspoon fine sea salt

⅛ teaspoon fish sauce (optional)

FOR GARNISH (OPTIONAL)

2 tablespoons toasted sesame seeds

12 dill pickle slices

6 grape or cherry tomatoes, halved

1. Preheat the oven to 350°F. Grease a 9-inch square baking dish with avocado or coconut oil spray.

2. In a large oven-safe skillet over medium heat, combine the ground beef, onions, and garlic and season with 1½ teaspoons of the salt. Cook while crumbling with a wooden spoon until the beef is browned and the onions are translucent, about 7 minutes. Add the ketchup and stir well to combine.

3. Meanwhile, in a large bowl, mix together the eggs, cheese, mayo, and mustard. Stir in the remaining ½ teaspoon of salt and the pepper. Add the cooked beef mixture to the egg mixture and stir to combine.

4. Pour into the greased casserole dish. Bake for 25 minutes, or until the eggs are cooked through in the center.

5. While the casserole is in the oven, make the sauce: Place all the ingredients in a small bowl and stir well to combine. Taste and adjust the sweetness to your liking.

6. Remove the casserole from the oven and let rest for 10 minutes. Serve drizzled with the sauce. If desired, garnish with the toasted sesame seeds, pickles, and tomatoes. Store extras in an airtight container in the refrigerator for up to 3 days. To reheat, place in a 350°F oven for 3 minutes or in the microwave for 30 seconds, or until heated through.

(per serving):
calories **388** • fat **32g** • protein **21g** • carbs **4g** • fiber **1g**

busy family tip:

If you want to shorten the baking time, you can bake this as muffins. Grease a 12-well muffin pan and follow the recipe as written through Step 3. Then transfer the mixture to the greased muffin pan, filling each well about two-thirds full. Bake for 10 to 13 minutes, until golden and puffed. Allow to cool slightly in the pan, then transfer the muffins to a platter and serve warm. Makes 12 muffins (2 per serving).

Cinnamon Rolls

MEDIUM   option   option

yield: 8 servings • prep time: 10 minutes • cook time: 20 minutes

When it comes to baking, measurements are very precise—especially for this recipe. If you're having an issue with bubbles forming in the middle of your rolls, or if they have a gummy wet texture, try weighing the ingredients. Also, do not let the dough sit too long or it will start to harden too much; it will firm up sufficiently after 10 minutes.

Here is a cute email from Leisa, one of my testers, about this recipe: *"Hi Maria! I got up early and made the cinnamon rolls to bring to the office. In retrospect, I should probably try a recipe a few times before I test it on my staff. LOL. Anyway, I toted my sweet treats in this morning, still piping hot, and forewarned them that even I hadn't tried them yet, so I wasn't sure how they had turned out. Not that your recipes ever fail to impress, but I wasn't sure if I got the cooking time or the dough consistency right. But they were a huge hit!"*

DOUGH

1½ cups blanched almond flour (140g), or ½ cup coconut flour (70g)

5 tablespoons psyllium husk powder (45g)

2 teaspoons baking powder

1 teaspoon fine sea salt

1 cup confectioners'-style erythritol, or 1 cup erythritol plus 1 teaspoon stevia glycerite

3 large egg whites (use 8 egg whites if using coconut flour)

1 ounce apple cider vinegar

7 ounces boiling water

Avocado or coconut oil spray

FILLING

2 tablespoons ground cinnamon

2 tablespoons confectioner's-style erythritol

1. Preheat the oven to 325°F. Lightly grease an 8-inch round baking dish.

2. In a medium bowl, combine the flour, psyllium powder, baking powder, salt, and sweetener. Add the egg whites and vinegar and stir to combine into a thick dough. Pour in the boiling water and mix until well combined. The dough will be very sticky right after you add the water, but after you mix it for a couple minutes, it will firm up.

3. Grease a large piece of parchment paper with avocado or coconut oil spray and spread the dough into a 12 by 24-inch rectangle, pressing with your fingers. You can spray some more oil on top of the dough to help keep it from sticking to your fingers. Sprinkle the cinnamon and sweetener evenly over the dough and press them into the dough with your hands.

4. Use a sharp knife to slice the dough into twelve 2-inch strips. Starting at one end of a strip, roll it up tightly until you have a spiral. Repeat with the remaining strips to form 12 rolls.

5. Place the rolls in the greased baking dish. Bake for 20 minutes, or until a toothpick inserted in the center comes out clean. Let cool completely in the pan before frosting.

(per serving):
calories **518** • fat **46g** • protein **14g** • carbs **16g** • fiber **10g**

FROSTING

3 ounces cream cheese (6 tablespoons), softened (or Kite Hill brand cream cheese–style spread for dairy-free)

3 tablespoons unsalted butter (or coconut oil for dairy-free), softened

2 tablespoons confectioners'-style erythritol, or 2 tablespoons erythritol plus ¼ teaspoon stevia glycerite

2 tablespoons unsweetened almond milk (to thin the frosting, if needed)

6. Meanwhile, make the frosting: Place all the ingredients in a medium bowl and stir until smooth. If the frosting is too thick, stir in the milk. Spread the frosting over the cooled rolls.

7. Store extra rolls and frosting in separate airtight containers in the refrigerator for up to 4 days, or freeze for up to a month.

variation:

Turkey Cinnamon Rolls. *To make Thanksgiving turkeys, you'll need 15 slices of cooked bacon, 12 blueberries, and 6 pecan halves. Slice the bacon in half crosswise. Place 5 half-strips of bacon on one side of each cinnamon roll facing up and the cut end of the bacon at the bottom of the roll, spread like feathers. Place 2 blueberries on the front of the cinnamon roll where the eyeballs would be, pressing them into the frosting to hold them in place. Place a pecan half facedown for the turkey neck.*

Sugar-Free Toaster Pastries (aka Gilmore Girls Breakfast)

HARD

yield: 4 pastries (1 per serving) • prep time: 12 minutes, plus 10 minutes to chill dough • cook time: 12 minutes

People often ask me where I get my recipe ideas. Many times, they come from foods I grew up on—like Pop Tarts! This recipe came about when the boys and I were watching *Gilmore Girls*. Lorelei Gilmore *loves* Pop Tarts, and she "makes" them for her daughter for breakfast often. The boys asked what a Pop Tart was, so I said, "Let me show you!" I dashed into the kitchen to create a sugar-free homemade version. They were a huge hit! This recipe is a bit more challenging than most of my recipes, but it is really a showstopper. These healthy pastries taste way better than the cardboard ones from the store. I suggest making a triple batch and keeping some unbaked in the freezer for when cravings strike.

DOUGH

1¾ cups shredded mozzarella cheese

2 tablespoons cream cheese

¾ cup blanched almond flour

1 large egg

FILLING

½ cup raspberries

2 ounces cream cheese (¼ cup), softened

2 to 4 tablespoons confectioners'-style erythritol or equivalent amount of liquid or powdered sweetener (see page 77)

FROSTING

2 ounces cream cheese (¼ cup), softened

¼ cup confectioners'-style erythritol or equivalent amount of liquid or powdered sweetener (see page 77)

2 to 3 tablespoons unsweetened almond milk or heavy cream

A few drops of natural pink food coloring (optional)

1. Preheat the oven to 350°F. Line a rimmed baking sheet with parchment paper and grease the paper well with avocado or coconut oil spray.

2. Make the dough: Place the mozzarella and cream cheese in a heat-safe bowl and microwave for 1 to 2 minutes, until the cheese is entirely melted. Stir well. Add the almond flour and egg and, using a hand mixer, combine well. Place in the freezer to chill for 10 minutes.

3. Divide the chilled dough into 8 equal portions. Place one portion of dough on the greased parchment paper and pat out with your hands to make a small rectangle, about 2 inches by 3 inches. Repeat with the remaining portions of dough.

4. Make the filling: Place the raspberries, cream cheese, and sweetener in a food processor and pulse to combine well. Taste and adjust the sweetness to your liking.

5. Place the mixture in the center of 4 rectangles, trying to cover as much dough as possible but leaving a ½-inch border. Top with the 4 unfilled rectangles of dough and use a fork to seal the edges shut.

(per serving):
calories **379** • fat **31g** • protein **19g** • carbs **9g** • fiber **3g**

6. Place the sealed pastries on the prepared baking sheet. Bake for 8 minutes. If desired, remove from the oven and use a fork to score the edges again to make it look like a Pop Tart. Bake for another 2 minutes, or until the pastries are golden brown and the dough is fully cooked. Remove from the oven and allow to cool on the pan for 10 minutes.

7. While the pastries are cooling, make the frosting: Place the cream cheese and sweetener in a small bowl and stir to loosen the cream cheese. Add just enough almond milk to make it spreadable. If it gets too thin, add a tablespoon of sweetener; if it is too thick, add a splash of milk. Stir in the food coloring, if using. Once the pastries are cool, place the frosting in a piping bag or small plastic bag. Cut off a tiny corner of the plastic bag and pipe the frosting over each pastry.

8. Store extras in an airtight container in the refrigerator for up to 5 days, or freeze for up to a month.

Pizza
Breakfast Pie

MEDIUM

yield: 6 servings • prep time: 8 minutes • cook time: 35 minutes

What's better than pizza for breakfast? The special spice blend that goes on top of this easy pie tastes just like the spice mix used on Pizza Hut's breadsticks. To save time, I brown the meat, combine the ingredients, and place them in the skillet the night before. In the morning, all I have to do is pop the skillet in the oven for an easy breakfast or brunch. This dish makes great leftovers, too!

8 ounces ground pork or ground beef

¼ cup chopped onions

2 tablespoons Italian seasoning

¼ cup tomato sauce

8 large eggs, beaten

¼ cup beef broth

¾ cup shredded mozzarella cheese

2 tablespoons cream cheese

1 teaspoon minced garlic, or ½ head roasted garlic (page 374)

1 teaspoon fine sea salt

SPICE BLEND

3 tablespoons powdered Parmesan cheese (see tip)

2 teaspoons garlic powder

1 teaspoon onion powder

1 teaspoon dried oregano leaves

Sugar-free pizza sauce, homemade (page 370) or store-bought, warmed, for serving (optional)

1. Preheat the oven to 350°F.

2. In a large oven-safe skillet over medium heat, cook the ground pork, onions, and Italian seasoning until the meat is cooked all the way through and the onions are translucent, about 7 minutes. Add the tomato sauce and stir well to combine.

3. Meanwhile, in a large bowl, mix together the eggs, broth, cheeses, garlic, and salt.

4. Add the egg mixture to the pork mixture in the skillet and stir to combine. Cook over medium heat, stirring continuously, for 3 minutes, or until the eggs are just slightly set.

5. Meanwhile, make the spice blend: Place all the ingredients in a small dish and stir well to combine. Sprinkle the spice mix over the top of the breakfast pie.

6. Place the skillet in the oven and bake for 27 minutes, or until the eggs are cooked through in the center. Remove from the oven and let rest for 3 minutes, then slice and serve. If desired, serve with warm pizza sauce.

7. Store extras in an airtight container in the refrigerator for up to 3 days. To reheat, place in a 350°F oven for 3 minutes or in the microwave for 30 seconds, or until heated through.

tip:

To make powdered Parmesan cheese, place grated Parmesan in a food processor or spice grinder and pulse until it is light, fluffy, and powdery. You can also buy fresh pregrated Parmesan from the supermarket cheese counter.

(per serving):
calories **262** • fat **19g** • protein **23g** • carbs **3g** • fiber **0.3g**

busy family tip:

To shorten the baking time, you can bake this as muffins. Grease a 12-well muffin pan and follow the recipe as written through Step 4. Then transfer the mixture to the prepared muffin pan, filling each well about two-thirds full. Bake for 10 to 13 minutes, until golden and puffed. Allow to cool slightly in the pan, then transfer to a serving platter and serve warm. Makes 12 muffins (2 per serving).

Blueberry Cheesecake Muffins

MEDIUM option

yield: 12 muffins (1 per serving) • prep time: 7 minutes • cook time: 40 minutes

I grew up working at a coffee shop called Uncommon Ground. Before school, I would make the muffins, scones, and cinnamon rolls. I loved this job, and my favorite after-school treat was a blueberry cheesecake muffin. It makes me happy to have a sugar-free option for my boys to enjoy!

1½ cups blanched almond flour

1 teaspoon ground cinnamon

½ teaspoon baking soda

¼ teaspoon fine sea salt

½ cup confectioners'-style erythritol or equivalent amount of liquid or powdered sweetener (see page 77)

3 large eggs

2 tablespoons unsalted butter (or coconut oil for dairy-free), softened

1 teaspoon vanilla extract

1 cup fresh or frozen blueberries, thawed if frozen

CREAM CHEESE FILLING

1 (8-ounce) package cream cheese (or Kite Hill brand cream cheese–style spread for dairy-free), softened

¼ cup confectioners'-style erythritol or equivalent amount of liquid or powdered sweetener (see page 77)

1 large egg yolk

2 teaspoons vanilla extract

1. Preheat the oven to 325°F. Grease a standard-size 12-well muffin pan, or line the wells with paper liners.

2. In a large bowl, whisk together the almond flour, cinnamon, baking soda, and salt until well combined. In another bowl, use a hand mixer on medium speed to mix together the sweetener, eggs, butter, and vanilla until smooth. Stir the wet ingredients into the dry. Gently stir in the blueberries. Spoon the batter into the prepared muffin cups, filling each about two-thirds full.

3. Make the filling: Using a hand mixer, beat the cream cheese in a medium bowl until smooth. Add the sweetener, egg yolk, and vanilla and beat until well combined. Top each muffin with about 1 tablespoon of the filling and use a toothpick to swirl it into the batter.

4. Bake for 30 to 40 minutes, until the muffins are golden brown and a toothpick inserted in the center of a muffin comes out clean. Allow to cool completely before removing from the pan. Store extras in an airtight container in the refrigerator for up to 3 days.

(per serving):
calories **197** • fat **17g** • protein **6g** • carbs **6g** • fiber **2g**

Monkey Bread

HARD option option

yield: 14 servings • prep time: 15 minutes, plus time to cool • cook time: 70 minutes

This delicious sweet bread is perfect for a special morning. When it comes to baking, measurements are very precise—especially for this recipe. If you're having an issue with a gummy wet texture or bubbles, try weighing your ingredients. Also, do not let the dough sit too long or it will start to harden too much; it will firm up sufficiently after 10 minutes.

3 cups blanched almond flour (280g), or 1 cup coconut flour (140g)

1 cup plus 2 tablespoons confectioners'-style erythritol or equivalent amount of powdered sweetener (see page 77), divided

½ cup plus 2 tablespoons psyllium husk powder (90g)

1 tablespoon plus 1 teaspoon baking powder

2 teaspoons fine sea salt

8 large egg whites (or 16 egg whites if using coconut flour)

2 ounces apple cider vinegar

14 ounces boiling water

1 (8-ounce) package cream cheese (or Kite Hill brand cream cheese–style spread for dairy-free)

1 tablespoon ground cinnamon

TOPPING

½ cup (1 stick) unsalted butter or coconut oil

1 tablespoon ground cinnamon

½ cup confectioners'-style erythritol or equivalent amount of powdered sweetener (see page 77)

1. Preheat the oven to 375°F. Grease a Bundt pan.

2. In a large bowl, whisk together the flour, 1 cup of the sweetener, the psyllium husk powder, baking powder, and salt. Add the egg whites and vinegar and combine into a thick dough. Pour in the boiling water and mix until well combined. When you add the water, the dough will be very sticky, but after being mixed for a couple minutes, it will firm up.

3. Divide the dough into 20 equal portions and shape each portion into a disc. You can spray the dough with avocado or coconut oil spray to help keep it from sticking to your fingers.

4. Cut the cream cheese into 20 cubes. Place a cube on top of each dough disc and wrap the dough around the sides of the cream cheese.

5. Place 10 of the wrapped cream cheese cubes in the greased Bundt pan with the cream cheese facing up. Sprinkle the cinnamon and the remaining 2 tablespoons of sweetener on top. Then put the remaining 10 cubes on top of the first 10, cream cheese side down. Bake for 55 minutes.

6. Meanwhile, make the topping: Place all the ingredients in a medium bowl and whisk until smooth.

7. After the bread has baked for 55 minutes, remove the pan from the oven and quickly spread the topping over the bread. Bake for 15 more minutes, until a toothpick inserted in the center comes out clean. Allow to cool for 20 to 30 minutes before inverting the pan to release the bread and serving.

8. Store extras in an airtight container in the refrigerator for up to 5 days. To reheat, place in a 350°F oven for 5 minutes, or until heated to your liking.

(per serving): calories 317 • fat 27g • protein 10g • carbs 12g • fiber 8g

chapter 4:
appetizers & snacks

Eggplant Fries / **128**

Veggie and Savory Fruit Flowers / **130**

Kai's Chicken Wings / **132**

Pizza Rolls / **134**

The Cutest Deviled Eggs Ever / **136**

Pigs in a Blanket / **142**

Cute Mouse Eggs / **144**

Strawberry Pudding / **146**

Sweet 'n' Sour Turkey Jerky / **148**

No-Bake Chocolate-Topped Energy Bars / **150**

Fruit Flower Bouquet / **152**

Sticks and Dip / **154**

Salmon Jerky Fingers / **156**

Just Like "Apples" and Dip / **158**

Graham Crackers / **160**

Swedish Fish (or Gummy Bears) / **162**

Little Piggy Eggs / **164**

Cookie Dough Dip / **166**

No-Bake Peanut Butter Lover's Bars / **168**

Iced Animal Crackers / **170**

Eggplant Fries

MEDIUM option option   yield: 8 servings • prep time: 10 minutes • cook time: 15 minutes

I have never been a fan of eggplant, and neither have my children; however, transforming eggplant into french fries makes it extra delicious! These fries are soft on the inside and crispy on the outside. You can dip them in ketchup, as shown, or in ranch dressing or mustard.

1 medium eggplant

2 cups powdered Parmesan cheese (see tip, page 120) (or pork panko for dairy-free)

2 large eggs

Avocado or coconut oil spray

Sugar-free ketchup, homemade (page 369) or store-bought, for serving

1. Preheat the oven to 400°F. Line a rimmed baking sheet with parchment paper.

2. Peel the eggplant and cut it into french-fry shapes about 2½ by ¼ by ¼ inches.

3. Place the powdered Parmesan in a shallow bowl. Beat the eggs in a separate shallow bowl until frothy.

4. Dip the eggplant pieces into the eggs, then into the Parmesan. Use your hands to adhere the coating to the eggplant if needed. Spray the coated eggplant with avocado oil spray.

5. Place the fries on the prepared baking sheet in a single layer and bake for 12 to 15 minutes, until crispy and browned. Serve with ketchup.

6. Store extras in an airtight container in the refrigerator for up to 5 days, or freeze for up to a month. To reheat, place in a 375°F oven for 5 minutes, or until heated through.

(per serving): calories **119** • fat **7g** • protein **10g** • carbs **5g** • fiber **2g**

Veggie and Savory Fruit Flowers

EASY   option   option   option

yield: 12 servings • prep time: 15 minutes (not including time to make dips)

Want your kids to eat their veggies? Put the veggies on a stick! Children love food on a stick, and when you turn it into a bouquet of flowers, they will gobble it up. This pretty presentation is great for a party. If you don't want to make a full bouquet, you can put smaller quantities of veggies on skewers and serve them with just one or two dips.

1 cucumber, peeled

1 medium jicama

1 cup cherry tomatoes

8 medium radishes

4 watermelon radishes (optional)

1 small head cauliflower (purple or white)

½ cup pitted black olives

6 baby dill pickles

6 green onions

4 or 5 sprigs fresh basil

3 large bell peppers (any color), for the dip bowls

1 batch Veggie Dill Dip (page 366; omit for egg-free)

1 batch Protein-Packed Ranch Dip (page 367; omit for egg-free)

1 batch guacamole (page 376)

SPECIAL EQUIPMENT:

24 (12-inch) skewers

Flower-shaped cookie cutters

Toothpicks, cut in half

1. Make the cucumber flowers: Slice the cucumber into ¼-inch-thick rounds. Using a small flower-shaped cookie cutter, cut a flower out of each cucumber slice. Push a skewer from the bottom to the top of each cucumber flower. Place the cucumber flowers in a vase.

2. Make the jicama flowers: Peel the jicama and slice it into ¼-inch-thick rounds. Using a larger flower-shaped cookie cutter, cut a flower out of each jicama round. Cut half of the tomatoes in half and place one half in the center of each jicama flower, securing with half a toothpick (insert the toothpick through the back of the flower). Push a skewer into the bottom of each flower and arrange the flowers in the vase.

3. Make the radish tulips: Cut the tops of the radishes using a zigzag cut to resemble the petals of a tulip. Trim the root off the bottom of each radish and pierce with a skewer. Arrange the radish flowers in the vase.

4. Separate the cauliflower into bite-sized florets, place a skewer in the bottom of each floret, and arrange in the vase.

5. Place the remaining whole tomatoes, the olives, and pickles on skewers and arrange in the vase. Add the green onions and basil leaves to the vase.

6. Make the serving bowls for the dips: Cut each bell pepper in half horizontally and remove the ribs and seeds from the bottom half (reserve the tops for another use). Cut the edges of each bottom half in a zigzag shape. Spoon the dips into the hollowed-out peppers.

7. Store extra skewers and dips in separate airtight containers in the refrigerator for up to 4 days.

(per serving): calories **305** • fat **26g** • protein **7g** • carbs **14g** • fiber **6g**

Kai's
Chicken Wings

MEDIUM   option   option

yield: 4 servings • prep time: 7 minutes • cook time: 32 minutes

Chicken wings cooked in the oven are so delicious; you will never miss oil-fried wings! The tricks are to start at a lower oven temperature and to flip the wings over halfway through baking. The lower temperature allows the fat under the skin to gradually break apart. After that happens, you increase the temperature to 400°F and cook the wings for another 6 to 7 minutes to give them that delicious crispy skin. You end up with a tender inside and a crunchy outside.

I love chicken wings, and when my mom taught me how easy they are to make, I was excited to cook them. Chicken wings was my first recipe that I made all by myself! I even put a video of me making these wings on our YouTube channel. I was only five years old at the time!

2 teaspoons dried parsley

1 teaspoon garlic powder

1 teaspoon onion powder

1 teaspoon fine sea salt

½ teaspoon ground black pepper

½ teaspoon dried chives

½ teaspoon dried dill weed

1 pound chicken wings, separated into flats and drumettes

Ranch dressing, homemade (page 367 or 368) or store-bought, for serving (optional)

1. Preheat the oven to 375°F. Line a rimmed baking sheet with parchment paper.

2. Put the parsley, garlic powder, onion powder, salt, pepper, chives, and dill in a small bowl and stir to combine well. Season the chicken wings on all sides with this mixture. Place the seasoned wings on the prepared baking sheet in a single layer.

3. Bake for 25 minutes, flipping the wings over after 15 minutes. After 25 minutes, increase the oven temperature to 400°F and bake the wings for 6 to 7 more minutes, until the skin is browned and crispy. Serve the wings with ranch, if desired.

4. Store extras in an airtight container in the refrigerator for up to 4 days. To reheat, place the wings in a 350°F oven for 5 minutes, then increase the temperature to 400°F and cook for 3 to 5 more minutes, until the wings are crispy and warmed to your liking.

(per serving):
calories **329** • fat **22g** • protein **30g** • carbs **1g** • fiber **0.2g**

Pizza Rolls

MEDIUM option option option

yield: 8 rolls (1 per serving) • prep time: 10 minutes • cook time: 20 minutes

The texture and flavor of these pizza rolls will remind you of traditional buns. Note that you must use psyllium husk powder for this recipe to work.

1¼ cups plus 3 tablespoons blanched almond flour, or ¾ cup coconut flour

3½ tablespoons psyllium husk powder

1 teaspoon fine sea salt

2 large eggs (or 4 eggs if using coconut flour)

1 cup boiling water or beef broth

Avocado or coconut oil spray

FILLINGS

1 cup shredded mozzarella cheese (omit for dairy-free)

1 cup pepperoni slices (omit for vegetarian)

Additional pizza toppings of choice, such as sliced black olives, sliced mushrooms, and/ or diced onions

1 cup sugar-free pizza sauce, homemade (page 370) or store-bought, for serving

1. Preheat the oven to 325°F. Line a rimmed baking sheet with parchment paper.

2. In a medium bowl, combine the flour, psyllium husk powder, and salt. Stir in the eggs until a thick dough forms. Add the water and mix until well combined. Let the dough sit for 1 to 2 minutes, until it firms up.

3. Grease a large piece of parchment paper with avocado oil spray and spread the dough into a rectangle about 12 inches by 16 inches and ¼ inch thick, pressing it flat with your fingers. You can spray some more oil on top of the dough to help keep it from sticking to your fingers.

4. Sprinkle the dough with the mozzarella, if using. Top the cheese with the pepperoni and any other pizza toppings you like.

5. Starting at a long edge of the rectangle, roll the dough up tightly until you have a cylinder that is 16 inches long. Use a sharp knife to slice the cylinder into eight 2-inch rolls. Place the rolls on the prepared baking sheet.

6. Bake for 20 to 25 minutes, until the rolls are cooked through in the center. Serve with the pizza sauce.

7. Store extra rolls in an airtight container in the refrigerator for up to 4 days, or freeze for up to a month. To reheat, place in a 325°F oven for 5 minutes, or until heated through and the cheese is melted.

(per serving):
calories **307** • fat **25g** • protein **13g** • carbs **9g** • fiber **5g**

The Cutest
Deviled Eggs Ever

MEDIUM   **option**   yield: 24 egg halves (4 per serving) • prep time: 10 minutes • cook time: 11 minutes

There are so many delicious ways to enjoy deviled eggs. You can keep them classic or let your creative juices flow and make them extra cute with decorations! During football season, my boys love football deviled eggs. In the fall, I also like to make owl and pumpkin deviled eggs. In the spring, I make a flower spread using green onions for the stems. You could even use guacamole in place of the mayonnaise and mustard to turn the filling green. Also check out my Valentine's Day–themed deviled eggs on page 266.

Basic Deviled Eggs

12 large eggs

½ cup mayonnaise, homemade (page 365) or store-bought

2 teaspoons prepared yellow mustard

½ teaspoon fine sea salt

1. Place the eggs in a large saucepan and cover with cold water. Bring to a boil, then immediately cover the pan and remove it from the heat. Allow the eggs to cook in the hot water for 11 minutes. After 11 minutes, drain the water and rinse the eggs with very cold water for a minute or two to stop the cooking process. Peel the boiled eggs and cut them in half lengthwise.

2. Remove the egg yolks and place them in a bowl. Mash the yolks with a fork until they have the texture of very fine crumbles. Add the mayonnaise, mustard, and salt and mix until evenly combined. Note: If making Pumpkin Deviled Eggs or Deviled Egg Flowers, see the modifications on pages 138 and 139, respectively.

3. Fill the egg white halves with the yolk mixture.

4. Store extras in an airtight container in the refrigerator for up to 3 days.

(per serving):
calories **213** • fat **17g** • protein **13g** • carbs **1g** • fiber **0g**

Football Deviled Eggs

1 batch Basic Deviled Eggs
(page 136)

3 slices bacon (pork or beef),
cooked and crumbled (about
¼ cup)

1 tablespoon mayonnaise,
homemade (page 365) or store-
bought

Cover the deviled eggs entirely with the crumbled bacon. Place
the mayo into a small plastic bag and cut a tiny hole in one corner.
Pipe football laces on top of the bacon on each egg, making one
stripe lengthwise, then 4 short lines crossing the long stripe.

(per serving):
calories **301** • fat **27g** • protein **14g** • carbs **1g** • fiber **0g**

Pumpkin Deviled Eggs

1 batch Basic Deviled Eggs
(page 136)

2 teaspoons paprika, or more
if needed

1 teaspoon hot sauce (such as
Frank's RedHot)

1 green onion, sliced into
½-inch pieces

Add the paprika and hot sauce to the yolk mixture before filling
the egg white halves. Add more paprika if needed to achieve a
pumpkin-orange color.

Fill the egg white halves with the orange filling. Using the tip of
a knife, score 4 lines, running lengthwise, in the filling to make a
pumpkin design. Place a piece of green onion at the top of each
pumpkin for the stem.

(per serving):
calories **270** • fat **23g** • protein **13g** • carbs **1g** • fiber **0.2g**

Spider Deviled Eggs

1 batch Basic Deviled Eggs
(page 136)

24 pitted black olives

Cut the olives in half and place one half in the middle of each
deviled egg for the body of the spider. Slice the other olive halves
into thin strips for the legs. Place 4 legs on either side of the body.

(per serving):
calories **280** • fat **24g** • protein **13g** • carbs **1g** • fiber **0.3g**

Deviled Egg Flowers

1 batch Basic Deviled Eggs (page 136)

3 green onions, or more as desired for decorating the platter

Paprika, for the middle deviled egg

Fresh flowers, for decorating the platter

Arrange the deviled eggs on a serving platter with 6 eggs in a circle as flower petals and one egg in the center, making a total of 3 flowers. (You will have 3 pieces left over.) I cut a sliver off the bottom of each egg to keep them from sliding. Garnish the center egg with paprika. (In the photo, the paprika has been mixed into the yolk mixture as in the pumpkin variation above, but doing it this way is much easier!) Arrange the green onions as stems to the flowers. Arrange the fresh flowers around the edges of the platter, using more green onions if desired.

(per serving):
calories **274** • fat **23g** • protein **13g** • carbs **2g** • fiber **1g**

Owl Deviled Eggs

1 batch Basic Deviled Eggs (page 136)

24 sliced black olives

12 small sprigs fresh dill

Orange bell pepper (or yellow cheese) sliced into small triangles

24 sliced almonds or small basil leaves

Place 2 olive slices on top of each deviled egg for eyes. Place a sprig of dill at the top of the egg for feathers, then place the bell pepper triangle in the center with the point facing downward for the nose. Place a sliced almond on either side of the egg for wings.

(per serving):
calories **273** • fat **24g** • protein **13g** • carbs **1g** • fiber **0.1g**

Pigs
in a Blanket

MEDIUM

yield: 16 servings as a snack, or 8 as a meal • prep time: 10 minutes • cook time: 25 minutes

What's not to love about smoked cocktail sausages? They are cute and delicious! Be aware that most brands contain added sugar and binders. I prefer Teton Waters Ranch brand. My small local grocery store carries them, but if yours doesn't, ask the manager to stock them. Grocery stores want to know which products you like; they want to please their customers.

This recipe makes a lot of mini pigs in a blanket. My suggestion is to bake them and then freeze them for easy after-school snacks. You can also cut the recipe in half if you prefer.

1½ cups blanched almond flour

5 tablespoons psyllium husk powder

2 teaspoons baking powder

1 teaspoon fine sea salt

2½ tablespoons apple cider vinegar

3 large egg whites

1 cup boiling water

2 (9½-ounce) packages smoked cocktail sausages

Prepared yellow mustard, for serving (optional)

1. Preheat the oven to 325°F. Line a rimmed baking sheet with parchment paper.

2. In a medium bowl, whisk together the almond flour, psyllium husk powder, baking powder, and salt. Stir in the vinegar and egg whites until a thick dough forms. Add the boiling water and mix until well combined. Let the dough sit until it firms up, 1 to 2 minutes.

3. Take 1 tablespoon of the dough, roll it between your hands into a 2-inch ropelike piece (the dough will expand, so the skinnier the dough, the better), and wrap it around a cocktail sausage. Repeat until all the sausages are wrapped.

4. Place the wrapped sausages on the prepared baking sheet, spacing them about 1 inch apart. Bake for 20 to 25 minutes, until the dough is puffed and cooked through. Serve with mustard for dipping, if desired.

5. Store extras in an airtight container in the refrigerator for up to 5 days, or freeze for up to a month. To reheat, place in a 350°F oven for 5 minutes, or until heated through.

(per snack-size serving): calories **153** • fat **11g** • protein **8g** • carbs **5g** • fiber **3g**

Cute
Mouse Eggs

EASY

yield: 2 servings • prep time: 10 minutes (not including time to boil eggs)

You can decorate plain hard-boiled eggs in so many creative ways. This snack is so easy to make, yet so cute! If you don't want to boil your own eggs, you can purchase premade peeled hard-boiled eggs.

4 hard-boiled eggs, peeled and sliced in half lengthwise

½ radish

16 black peppercorns

2 fresh chives

4 ounces cheddar or Swiss cheese

1. Place the hard-boiled eggs cut side down around the edge of a serving platter, with the tips pointing toward the center of the platter. Cut the radish very thinly into 16 slices and push 2 slices into each egg for ears, positioning the ears about one-third of the way down the length of the egg. Push 2 peppercorns into the fronts of the eggs for eyes. Cut the chives into eight 2-inch pieces and insert a piece into the back of each egg for the tail.

2. Slice the cheese into small wedges and place in the center of the platter. Serve.

3. Store extras in an airtight container in the refrigerator for up to 4 days.

(per serving): calories **259** • fat **19g** • protein **20g** • carbs **1g** • fiber **0.1g**

Strawberry Pudding

EASY   option   option

yield: 4 servings • prep time: 5 minutes, plus overnight to chill (not including time to cook eggs)

This amazing pudding is filled with the healthy protein and fat that children need to thrive! The flavor is best after it sits in the fridge overnight. If using hard-boiled eggs, follow this tip from Jacques Pépin, the French chef: put the eggs into ice water immediately after cooking and leave them there for 30 minutes to prevent the sulfuric odor.

10 large eggs, hard-boiled and peeled or scrambled

2 cups unsweetened coconut milk or heavy cream

½ cup confectioners'-style erythritol or equivalent amount of liquid or powdered sweetener (see page 77)

2 teaspoons strawberry extract

A few drops of strawberry-flavored liquid stevia

⅛ teaspoon fine sea salt

OPTIONAL ADDITIONS

¼ cup strawberry- or vanilla-flavored collagen powder (omit for vegetarian)

¼ cup sliced strawberries, plus more for garnish

1. Put all of the ingredients, including the collagen and/or sliced strawberries, if using, in a blender and puree until very smooth. Taste and adjust the sweetness to your liking. Transfer the pudding to an airtight container and place in the refrigerator to chill overnight before serving.

2. Transfer the pudding to 4 serving dishes and garnish with strawberries, if desired.

3. Store extra pudding in an airtight container in the refrigerator for up to 4 days.

tip:
The leftover pudding can be made into ice pops. Simply spoon it into ice pop molds and freeze overnight.

(per serving):
calories **402** • fat **30g** • protein **26g** • carbs **3g** • fiber **0.1g**

Sweet 'n' Sour
Turkey Jerky

EASY

yield: 8 servings • prep time: 5 minutes, plus 1 hour to freeze and 2 hours to marinate turkey • cook time: 1 hour

I love taking my boys camping. One thing that we always pack is jerky! It is a perfect snack for hiking, but I always make my own because most store-bought jerky includes gluten and sugar. Making jerky is very simple; it just takes time.

2 pounds boneless, skinless turkey or chicken breasts

Salt and pepper

MARINADE

½ cup wheat-free tamari

3 tablespoons apple cider vinegar

3 tablespoons olive oil or avocado oil

2 tablespoons confectioners'-style erythritol or equivalent amount of liquid or powdered sweetener (see page 77)

1 tablespoon freshly grated ginger

1 teaspoon minced garlic, or ½ head roasted garlic (page 374)

1 teaspoon ground black pepper

1. Place the turkey in the freezer for 1 hour to make it easier to slice cleanly. Slice the turkey across the grain into long strips, 1 inch wide and ⅛ inch thick.

2. Combine the marinade ingredients in a large shallow bowl. Submerge the strips of turkey in the marinade, cover, and place in the refrigerator to marinate for at least 2 hours or overnight.

3. Preheat the oven to 180°F. Line a rimmed baking sheet with parchment paper.

4. Remove the turkey strips from the marinade and season on all sides with salt and pepper. Lay the strips on the prepared baking sheet in a single layer. Bake for about 1 hour, flipping the strips over after 30 minutes, until cooked through and chewy to your liking; the longer you bake it, the chewier it gets.

5. Store extras in an airtight container in the refrigerator for up to 10 days, or freeze for up to a month.

(per serving):
calories **142** • fat **4g** • protein **25g** • carbs **0.1g** • fiber **0g**

No-Bake Chocolate-Topped Energy Bars

EASY   option

yield: 18 bars (1 per serving) • prep time: 7 minutes, plus 35 minutes to chill • cook time: 2 minutes

These no-bake energy bars have been a family favorite for years. They are dairy-free (assuming you use coconut oil in the topping) and egg-free and perfect for traveling.

BASE

1½ cups shelled sunflower seeds, divided

1 cup raw pecans

¾ cup almond butter or Sugar-Free Chocolate Hazelnut Spread (page 380)

¼ cup coconut oil, melted

¼ cup confectioners'-style erythritol or equivalent amount of liquid or powdered sweetener (see page 77)

1 tablespoon vanilla extract

CHOCOLATE TOPPING

¼ cup coconut oil or unsalted butter

½ cup unsweetened cocoa powder

3 tablespoons confectioners'-style erythritol or equivalent amount of liquid or powdered sweetener (see page 77)

1 cup sugar-free chocolate chips, homemade (page 310) or store-bought (optional)

1. Make the base layer: Place 1 cup of the sunflower seeds, the pecans, almond butter, coconut oil, sweetener, and vanilla in a food processor and pulse until you have small pieces. Stir in the remaining ½ cup of sunflower seeds until well combined. Taste and adjust the sweetness to your liking. Transfer to an 8-inch square baking dish and press the mixture down firmly.

2. Make the chocolate topping: In a small saucepan, melt the coconut oil over low heat. (Alternatively, place the oil in a microwave-safe bowl and microwave for about 20 seconds.) Stir in the cocoa powder and sweetener until thickened.

3. Pour the chocolate topping over the base layer and sprinkle with the chocolate chips, if desired. Refrigerate for 25 to 35 minutes, until firm. Slice into bars and enjoy.

4. Store extras in an airtight container in the refrigerator for up to 12 days, or freeze for up to a month.

(per serving): calories **273** • fat **26g** • protein **6g** • carbs **6g** • fiber **3g**

Fruit Flower
Bouquet

EASY   option

yield: 12 servings • prep time: 20 minutes (not including time to make dip)

This cute bouquet made with only the lowest-in-sugar sweet fruits will impress your kids, and it is really quite simple to make. If a full bouquet is too much, you can cut out flower shapes and put the fruit on sticks to make the snack special. The fruit kabobs also make a great addition to a bento box (see pages 63 to 66).

1 pint blackberries

1 pint blueberries

1 pint raspberries

1 pint strawberries

1 honeydew melon

1 cantaloupe

1 batch Fruit Dip (page 371), for serving (optional; omit for dairy-free)

SPECIAL EQUIPMENT:

Flower-, star-, and/or heart-shaped cookie cutters

Small melon baller

Small vase or drinking glass

12 (12-inch) bamboo skewers

6 toothpicks, cut in half

1. Wash and pat dry the berries. Peel and slice the honeydew and cantaloupe into ½-inch-thick slices. Lay the slices flat and use the cookie cutters to cut out cute shapes, making sure to make at least 12 flowers. Use the melon baller to make ½-inch balls with the melon that is left over (for the centers of the flowers). Cut the balls in half.

2. If using a melon shell as the vase, place the shell cut side down on a serving platter. Use the sharp end of a skewer to poke holes in the shell that are spaced about ½ inch apart and angled outward slightly (to resemble a bouquet of flowers).

3. Push a half toothpick through the back of a half ball of melon, stopping before it pokes through the front, then push it into the center of a flower shape of the other color (honeydew center on cantaloupe flower and vice versa). Repeat with the remaining flowers and melon ball halves.

4. Thread the fruit onto the skewers alternating colors and sizes as you prefer, leaving 4 to 5 inches on the bottom of the skewer to go into the vase. (Note: If you have children who prefer certain fruits, let them put the fruits they like on a few skewers.) Top each skewer with a larger flower shape.

5. To make the bouquet, place the skewers in the vase or in the prepared holes in the melon shell. Serve with fruit dip, if desired. Store extras in an airtight container in the refrigerator for up to 4 days.

(per serving):
calories **99** • fat **1g** • protein **2g** • carbs **23g** • fiber **7g**

holiday fun:

At Christmastime, cut the melon into tree shapes or snowmen. For Valentine's Day, cut the melon into heart shapes.

tip:

If not using a melon shell for the vase, a vase with a small opening and a wide top works best for holding the skewers.

Sticks and Dip

MEDIUM

yield: 4 servings • prep time: 7 minutes • cook time: 20 minutes

Growing up, I often took sack lunches on field trips, and one thing my mom always packed was a store-bought package of sticks and dip—basically a stick-shaped cracker with a cheese dip. This is my take on that snack, but I think this version tastes much better! These would be great for bento boxes (see pages 63 to 66).

CHEESE DIP

2 ounces cream cheese (¼ cup)

½ cup shredded sharp cheddar cheese

2 tablespoons beef broth

STICKS

1 cup blanched almond flour

1 cup finely grated Parmesan cheese

1. Make the dip: Place the cream cheese, cheddar, and broth in a small saucepan over medium-high heat and warm until melted. (Alternatively, you can do this in the microwave.) Remove from the heat and use an immersion blender to puree until smooth. The dip will thicken up as it cools and sets. It can be made up to 3 days ahead.

2. Preheat the oven to 350°F.

3. Pulse the almond flour and Parmesan cheese in a food processor or blender. Add cold water, a bit at a time, until the mixture holds together well enough to work into a ball. Roll into ½-inch balls. Using your fingers, roll the balls back and forth until they are a stick/log shape.

4. Bake the sticks for 20 minutes, or until browned. The darker they are, the crispier they will be.

5. Store extra dip and sticks in separate airtight containers in the refrigerator for up to 4 days.

(per serving): calories **350** • fat **28g** • protein **20g** • carbs **7g** • fiber **3g**

Salmon
Jerky Fingers

MEDIUM

yield: 6 servings • prep time: 7 minutes, plus 2 hours to marinate • cook time: 1 hour

My son Micah *loves* salmon. It is one of his favorite foods! This salmon jerky is a flavorful snack that is a perfect addition to a bento box (see pages 63 to 66) or a simple breakfast on the go.

1 (1¼-pound) salmon fillet, skin and pin bones removed

Salt and pepper

MARINADE

½ cup wheat-free tamari

3 tablespoons apple cider vinegar

2 tablespoons confectioners'-style erythritol or equivalent amount of liquid or powdered sweetener (see page 77)

1 tablespoon freshly grated ginger root

1 teaspoon minced garlic, or ½ head roasted garlic (page 374)

1. Place the salmon in the freezer for 1 hour to make it easier to slice cleanly. Slice the fillet lengthwise into strips that are 4 inches long by ¼ inch thick.

2. Combine the marinade ingredients in a large shallow bowl. Submerge the strips of salmon in the marinade, cover, and place in the refrigerator to marinate for at least 2 hours or overnight.

3. Preheat the oven to 180°F. Line 2 rimmed baking sheets with parchment paper.

4. Remove the salmon strips from the marinade and season on all sides with salt and pepper. Lay the strips on the prepared baking sheet in a single layer. Bake for about 1 hour, flipping the strips over after 30 minutes, until cooked through and chewy to your liking; the longer you bake it, the chewier it gets.

5. Store extras in an airtight container in the refrigerator for up to 10 days, or freeze for up to a month.

(per serving): calories **109** • fat **3g** • protein **18g** • carbs **0.1g** • fiber **0g**

Just Like "Apples" and Dip

EASY   option

yield: 8 servings • prep time: 10 minutes

Chayote squash is technically a fruit but is much lower in carbohydrates and sugar than an apple. It has a great texture like an apple, though, and works great as a dipper for this peanut buttery dip! Mild-flavored jicama also works well. I used crunchy peanut butter, but you can use creamy if that's what your family prefers.

1 (8-ounce) package cream cheese (or Kite Hill brand cream cheese–style spread for dairy-free), softened

1 cup natural peanut butter or almond butter

¼ cup confectioners'-style erythritol or equivalent amount of liquid or powdered sweetener (see page 77)

¼ cup unsweetened almond milk

2 medium chayote squash or jicama, sliced

1. In a mixing bowl, use a hand mixer to combine the cream cheese, peanut butter, sweetener, and almond milk until smooth; taste and adjust the sweetness to your liking. Serve with the chayote slices.

2. Store extra dip and chayote in separate airtight containers in the refrigerator for up to 4 days.

(per serving):
calories **335** • fat **25g** • protein **10g** • carbs **15g** • fiber **7g**

Graham Crackers

HARD   option

yield: 24 crackers (12 servings) • prep time: 10 minutes • cook time: 20 minutes, plus 20 minutes to crisp in oven

These kid classic crackers are perfect for snacking, or you can use them to make S'mores (page 316).

2 cups blanched almond flour

⅓ cup confectioners'-style erythritol or equivalent amount of liquid or powdered sweetener (see page 77)

1 teaspoon baking powder

2 tablespoons coconut oil or unsalted butter, melted

1 large egg

2 teaspoons ground cinnamon

1½ teaspoons vanilla extract

⅛ teaspoon fine sea salt

Coconut oil spray

1. Place one oven rack in the upper third of the oven and another rack in the lower third. Preheat the oven to 325°F.

2. In a large bowl, whisk together the almond flour, sweetener, and baking powder. Stir in the melted oil. Add the egg and stir well to combine. Add the cinnamon, vanilla, and salt and stir until you have a thick dough.

3. Spray four pieces of parchment paper with coconut oil spray. Divide the dough in half and place the halves on two of the pieces of parchment. Top the dough with the other two pieces of parchment. Use a rolling pin to roll out the dough to ⅛-inch thickness. Remove the top sheet of parchment. Using a pizza cutter, cut the dough into 4 by 2-inch rectangles, then score each rectangle with the tines of a fork to make them look like graham crackers.

4. Gently slide each piece of parchment with the cracker dough onto a cookie sheet. Bake both sheets at the same time for 15 minutes. Remove the pans from the oven and score the crackers again (they will bake together otherwise), then bake for an additional 5 minutes. Turn off the oven and leave the crackers in the oven for 20 minutes to crisp. Remove from the oven and allow to cool completely before enjoying.

5. Store extras in an airtight container in the refrigerator for up to 12 days, or freeze for up to a month.

(per serving):
calories **135** • fat **12g** • protein **5g** • carbs **4g** • fiber **2g**

Swedish Fish (or Gummy Bears)

EASY

yield: about 50 gummies (10 per serving) • prep time: 5 minutes, plus 2 hours to set

My boys adore these gummies, so we make them often. I like to play around with different flavorings; our newest favorite is a touch of grape-flavored stevia. We also love to make gummies with Everly flavored drink mixes, like peach. Everly is sweetened with stevia and does not contain food dyes. If you don't have hibiscus tea, you can use 1½ tablespoons of any flavor of Everly mixed into ½ cup of water instead. This will sweeten your gummies and give them a natural color.

½ cup strong-brewed hibiscus tea, or 1½ tablespoons Everly drink mix stirred into ½ cup water

¼ cup confectioners'-style erythritol or equivalent amount of liquid or powdered sweetener (see page 77) (omit if using Everly)

3 tablespoons unflavored gelatin

1 teaspoon citric acid (optional, for sourness)

SPECIAL EQUIPMENT:

50-cavity gummy bear mold or Swedish fish mold(s)

1. Place the tea and sweetener in a small saucepan (or in a microwave-safe cup). Add the gelatin and stir until dissolved. Bring the mixture to a gentle boil over high heat while whisking, then remove from the heat. (Alternatively, microwave on high for 40 seconds, or until boiling.)

2. Add the citric acid, if using, and stir well. Pour the mixture into the gummy molds, filling them to the top, and refrigerate until set, at least 2 hours or overnight. The longer they sit, the more they will firm up.

3. Store extras in an airtight container in the refrigerator for up to 5 days.

(per serving):
calories **2** • fat **0g** • protein **0.4g** • carbs **0g** • fiber **0g**

Little
Piggy Eggs

EASY

yield: 2 servings • prep time: 10 minutes (not including time to boil eggs)

These cute eggs are perfect for bento boxes (see pages 63 to 66). This is a fun food craft to make with your kids.

4 hard-boiled eggs, peeled

1 hot dog

8 black peppercorns

Fine sea salt

SPECIAL EQUIPMENT:

Toothpicks

1. Cut a small slice off the bottom of each egg to keep it from rolling, then place the eggs on a plate.

2. Cut the hot dog into ⅛-inch-thick slices. Cut 8 triangles that are about ½ inch long for the ears. Set aside.

3. Cut a toothpick into fourths. Insert one-quarter of the toothpick into the tip of each egg, leaving a little of the toothpick exposed.

4. Push a hot dog slice onto each toothpick for the pig's nose. Place 2 peppercorns above the nose on each egg for the eyes.

5. Use a sharp knife to make 2 slits in each egg where the ears would be (a little above and outside the eyes). Push the hot dog triangles into the ear slits. Season the egg bodies with salt and serve.

6. Store extras in an airtight container in the refrigerator for up to 4 days.

(per serving):
calories **203** • fat **14g** • protein **16g** • carbs **1g** • fiber **0g**

Cookie Dough Dip

EASY option option option

yield: 8 servings • prep time: 8 minutes

During football season, I like to form this dip into a football shape and then cover it with additional chopped chocolate. (If you use store-bought chocolate, I like The Good Chocolate brand.) I decorate the top by making football laces using cream cheese! You can also make it into a heart shape for Valentine's Day or a Christmas tree shape.

1 (8-ounce) package cream cheese, softened (or Kite Hill brand cream cheese–style spread for dairy-free)

½ cup unsalted butter (or coconut oil for dairy-free), softened

⅔ cup confectioners'-style erythritol or equivalent amount of liquid or powdered sweetener (see page 77)

1 teaspoon vanilla extract

¼ teaspoon almond extract (omit for nut-free)

⅛ teaspoon fine sea salt

1 cup sugar-free chocolate chips, homemade (page 310) or store-bought, or 1 (2½-ounce) sugar-free chocolate bar, chopped

SERVING SUGGESTIONS

Chayote squash slices

Jicama slices

Strawberries

Graham Crackers (page 160)

The BEST Chocolate Chip Cookies (page 312)

1. Place the cream cheese, softened butter, sweetener, and extracts in a medium bowl. Using a hand mixer, mix on low speed until combined. Taste and adjust the sweetness to your liking. Stir in the chocolate until evenly incorporated.

2. Serve with chayote or jicama slices, strawberries, or graham crackers, or place a layer of dip between two chocolate chip cookies for the ultimate cookie sandwich! Store extras in an airtight container in the refrigerator for up to 5 days.

(per serving): calories **320** • fat **33g** • protein **2g** • carbs **2g** • fiber **0g**

No-Bake Peanut Butter Lover's Bars

EASY

yield: 9 bars (1 per serving) • prep time: 7 minutes, plus 35 minutes to chill • cook time: 2 minutes

If you're looking for a simple yet easy snack to make with your kids, this recipe is one of my testers' favorites! It would be a great first recipe to show your kids how to make healthy food.

BASE LAYER

2½ cups peanuts

¼ cup coconut oil

½ cup creamy natural peanut butter

¼ cup confectioners'-style erythritol or equivalent amount of liquid or powdered sweetener (see page 77)

1 tablespoon vanilla extract

CHOCOLATE TOPPING

¼ cup coconut oil

½ cup unsweetened cocoa powder

3 tablespoons confectioners'-style erythritol or equivalent amount of liquid or powdered sweetener (see page 77)

1 cup chopped peanuts, for topping (optional)

1. Make the base layer: Place the peanuts in a food processor and pulse until they are small pieces. Transfer the crumbled peanuts to a medium bowl. Add the coconut oil, peanut butter, sweetener, and vanilla and stir well. Taste and adjust the sweetness to your liking. Transfer to an 8-inch square baking dish and press the mixture down firmly.

2. Make the chocolate topping: In a small saucepan (or microwave-safe bowl), melt the coconut oil over low heat (or microwave it for about 20 seconds). Stir in the cocoa powder and sweetener until thickened. Pour the chocolate mixture over the base layer and sprinkle with the chopped peanuts, if using. Refrigerate for 25 to 35 minutes, until firm. Slice into bars and enjoy.

3. Store extras in an airtight container in the refrigerator for up to 10 days, or freeze for up to a month.

(per serving):
calories **359** • fat **34g** • protein **7g** • carbs **10g** • fiber **4g**

Iced
Animal Crackers

MEDIUM option

yield: 12 servings • prep time: 10 minutes, plus 15 minutes to chill dough and 10 minutes to set • cook time: 15 minutes, plus 15 minutes to crisp in oven

If you do not have animal-shaped cookie cutters, you can cut these crackers into 1-inch squares. Note that if you use allulose as the sweetener, the crackers will not be crispy like a traditional animal cracker.

2 cups blanched almond flour

2 tablespoons coconut flour

½ cup confectioners'-style erythritol or equivalent amount of liquid or powdered sweetener (see page 77)

½ cup coconut oil or unsalted butter, softened

1½ teaspoons vanilla extract

⅛ teaspoon fine sea salt

Coconut oil spray

ICING (OPTIONAL)

1 cup confectioners'-style erythritol or equivalent amount of powdered sweetener (see page 77)

¼ cup unsweetened almond milk or heavy cream

Natural pink food coloring

SPECIAL EQUIPMENT:

Small animal-shaped cookie cutters

1. Preheat the oven to 325°F. Line 2 cookie sheets with parchment paper.

2. In a food processor, pulse the almond flour, coconut flour, and sweetener until combined. Add the softened coconut oil, vanilla, and salt and pulse until a thick dough forms. Place the dough in the freezer to chill for 15 minutes for easy rolling.

3. Lightly spray a piece of parchment paper with coconut oil spray. Place the chilled dough on the parchment, top it with another sheet of parchment, and roll it out to ⅛-inch thickness. Cut into animal cracker shapes with cookie cutters. Place the shapes on the parchment-lined cookie sheets, spacing them 1 inch apart. Bake for 10 to 15 minutes, until light golden brown. Turn off the oven and leave the crackers in the oven for 15 more minutes to crisp before removing. If you are icing the crackers, allow them to cool completely in the refrigerator or freezer before icing.

4. While the crackers are cooling, make the icing, if using. Place the sweetener in a small shallow dish. Add the almond milk and stir to combine. You want an icing that isn't too thin or too thick that you can easily dip the tops of the crackers into. If needed, add a bit more milk. Transfer half of the icing to a separate shallow dish. Add a few drops of pink food coloring to one of the bowls.

5. Dip half of the animal crackers into the pink icing and the other half into the white icing. Place the dipped crackers back on the parchment paper after you dip them. Place in the refrigerator to allow the icing to set for about 10 minutes.

6. Store extras in an airtight container in the refrigerator for up to 8 days, or freeze for up to a month.

(per serving): calories **192** • fat **19g** • protein **4g** • carbs **5g** • fiber **2g**

chapter 5:
lunches that rock!

Sandwich on a Stick / 174

Antipasto on a Stick / 176

English Muffin Pizzas / 178

Chicken Protein Noodle Soup / 180

Better Than School Lunch Chicken Patties / 184

Bacon Lover's Chicken Nuggets / 186

Meat Cookies / 188

Sloppy Kai Dogs / 190

Touchdown Tacos / 192

Cheese Quesadillas / 194

Sandwich on a Stick

EASY

yield: 4 servings • prep time: 10 minutes

This is a cute idea for lunch boxes! Sharp cheddar cheese tends to crumble when placed on a skewer, so mild cheddar is a better option here.

16 slices sugar-free deli ham

16 slices sugar-free deli turkey

4 medium dill pickles

32 cherry tomatoes

16 (¾-inch) cubes cheddar cheese

16 (¾-inch) cubes farmer's cheese or mozzarella

SPECIAL EQUIPMENT:

16 (6-inch) bamboo skewers

1. Cut the ham and turkey into 1-inch strips. Cut the pickles into 1-inch segments.

2. Place a tomato on a skewer, followed by a cube of cheddar cheese, then a folded strip of ham, a pickle segment, a cube of farmer's cheese, a folded strip of turkey, and ending with another tomato. Repeat with the remaining ingredients and skewers.

3. Store extras in an airtight container in the refrigerator for up to 4 days.

(per serving):
calories **425** • fat **24g** • protein **45g** • carbs **8g** • fiber **2g**

Antipasto on a Stick

EASY

yield: 4 servings • prep time: 10 minutes

Here's another twist on the sandwich-on-a-stick theme. Why bother creating a fancy antipasto platter when you can put all the ingredients on a skewer for an easy lunch on the go?

32 grape or cherry tomatoes (yellow or red)

16 small balls fresh mozzarella cheese

16 large black olives, pitted

16 slices salami

16 large green olives, pitted

Olive oil and apple cider vinegar, for dipping (optional)

SPECIAL EQUIPMENT:

16 (6-inch) bamboo skewers

1. Place a tomato on a bamboo skewer, followed by a ball of mozzarella, then a black olive. Fold a slice of salami in half and then in half again and slide it onto the skewer, followed by a green olive, then another folded slice of salami, and ending with another tomato. Repeat with the remaining ingredients and skewers. Serve with oil and vinegar for dipping, if desired.

2. Store extras in an airtight container in the refrigerator for up to 4 days.

(per serving):
calories **328** • fat **25g** • protein **23g** • carbs **9g** • fiber **2g**

English Muffin
Pizzas

EASY   option

yield: 1 serving • prep time: 4 minutes (not including time to make muffin) • cook time: 6 minutes

When I was a little girl, my big brother Cory always made English muffin pizzas for our lunches. They were easy and delicious! This version is very similar, except it uses my healthy homemade English muffins in place of the highly processed store-bought ones.

1 Easy English Muffin (page 386)

Avocado oil spray

¼ cup sugar-free pizza sauce, homemade (page 370) or store-bought

4 slices pepperoni

2 tablespoons shredded mozzarella cheese (omit for dairy-free)

1. Preheat the oven to 400°F. Line a rimmed baking sheet with parchment paper.

2. Split the English muffin in half and spray the halves on both sides with avocado oil spray. Place on the prepared baking sheet, then toast in the oven until slightly crisp, about 3 minutes. Remove from the oven and top with the pizza sauce, pepperoni, and cheese, if using. Place back in the oven until the toppings are heated through and the cheese is melted, another 3 minutes or so.

(per serving):
calories **226** • fat **17g** • protein **15g** • carbs **6g** • fiber **2g**

Chicken Protein
Noodle Soup

MEDIUM   option

yield: 4 servings • prep time: 12 minutes • cook time: 25 minutes

Chicken noodle soup is something I always ate for lunch as a little girl; however, my soup came out of a can. The chicken pieces were tiny, and the protein wasn't nearly enough to meet a child's needs for health. This chicken protein noodle soup is so delicious, I know it will become a family favorite! Deli chicken sliced into thin strips makes a great substitute for traditional noodles—I call them protein noodles! For deli meats, I like Applegate brand.

2 (7-ounce) packages deli chicken breast

¼ cup (½ stick) unsalted butter (or coconut oil for dairy-free)

½ cup chopped celery

¼ cup chopped onions

4 boneless, skinless chicken thighs, cut into 1-inch cubes

6 cups chicken bone broth (page 392)

1 tablespoon dried parsley

1 teaspoon fine sea salt

½ teaspoon ground black pepper

½ teaspoon ground dried marjoram

1 bay leaf

1. Slice the chicken breast into long, thin strips to resemble noodles. Set aside.

2. Heat the butter in a large saucepan over medium-high heat. Add the celery and onions and sauté until soft, about 5 minutes. Add the cubed chicken thighs and sauté until slightly browned, about 5 minutes.

3. Add the broth, parsley, salt, pepper, marjoram, and bay leaf. Simmer, uncovered, until the chicken is no longer pink inside, about 15 minutes.

4. Stir in the chicken noodles. Remove from the heat, discard the bay leaf, and serve. Store extras in an airtight container in the refrigerator for up to 5 days, or freeze for up to a month.

(per serving):
calories **439** • fat **22g** • protein **52g** • carbs **7g** • fiber **1g**

variations:

To make Chinese 5-Spice Chicken Protein Noodle Soup, *add:*

2 cloves garlic, minced (when you add the onions)

3 slices fresh ginger (when you add the broth)

1 to 2 teaspoons Chinese 5-spice powder (when you add the broth)

Sliced green onions, for garnish

To make Indian-Spiced Chicken Protein Noodle Soup, *add:*

2 cloves garlic, minced (when you add the onions)

3 slices fresh ginger (when you add the broth)

1 to 3 teaspoons garam masala (when you add the broth)

Fresh cilantro leaves, for garnish

To make Thai Chicken Protein Noodle Soup, *add:*

1 cup coconut milk (in place of 1 cup of the broth)

3 slices fresh ginger (when you add the broth)

2 stalks lemongrass (when you add the broth)

1 teaspoon stevia glycerite (when you add the broth)

Fresh lime wedges, for serving

Better Than School Lunch
Chicken Patties

MEDIUM · option · option · option   yield: 6 patties (1 per serving) • prep time: 10 minutes • cook time: 10 minutes

One of my favorite school lunches was chicken patties. I loved them plain without the bun. This version is way better than any school lunch chicken patty!

PATTIES

1 pound ground chicken

2 tablespoons mayonnaise, homemade (page 365) or store-bought (omit for egg-free)

1 teaspoon dill pickle juice

1 teaspoon fine sea salt

¼ teaspoon garlic powder

¼ teaspoon onion powder

Duck fat or coconut oil, for pan-frying (optional)

COATING

1 cup pork panko or powdered Parmesan cheese (see tip, page 120)

FOR SERVING (OPTIONAL)

6 Sandwich Buns (page 384) (omit for egg-and nut-free)

Sugar-free ketchup, homemade (page 369) or store-bought

Ranch dressing, homemade (page 367 or 368) or store-bought (omit for egg-free)

Prepared yellow mustard

1. If baking the patties, preheat the oven to 400°F. Line a rimmed baking sheet with parchment paper.

2. Put the ingredients for the patties in a medium bowl and use your hands to combine well. Form the mixture into six 3½-inch patties.

3. Place the pork panko in a shallow bowl. Dredge each patty in the pork panko and use your hands to press the pork panko into a crust around the patty.

4. Place the coated patties on the prepared baking sheet, leaving space between them, and bake for 5 minutes. Flip the patties over with a spatula and bake for another 5 minutes, or until the coating is golden brown and the chicken is no longer pink inside. Alternatively, you can pan-fry the patties: Heat a few tablespoons of duck fat in a large nonstick skillet over medium-high heat. Add the patties and cook for 3 minutes, then gently flip and cook for another 3 to 4 minutes on the other side, until the patties are no longer pink inside.

5. Serve the patties in the buns, if using, and top with ketchup, ranch, and/or mustard, if desired.

6. Store extras in an airtight container in the refrigerator for up to 3 days, or freeze for up to a month. Reheat in a preheated 350°F oven for 4 minutes, or until heated through.

(per serving, with bun):
calories **402** • fat **26g** • protein **30g** • carbs **10g** • fiber **7g**

(per serving, patty only):
calories **257** • fat **15g** • protein **24g** • carbs **0.1g** • fiber **0g**

busy family tip:

If your family loves these chicken patties, I suggest making a triple batch and storing the extras uncooked in the freezer for easy meals. Place the coated patties on a rimmed baking sheet lined with parchment paper and put the baking sheet in the freezer for 2 hours. Place the frozen patties in large freezer bags and store for up to a month. Thaw in the refrigerator before baking or pan-frying as directed above.

Bacon Lover's
Chicken Nuggets

MEDIUM   option   option   yield: 4 servings • prep time: 8 minutes • cook time: 9 minutes

What's not to love about a juicy nugget wrapped in bacon? My son Micah loves these breading-free chicken nuggets, and I think that most adults will enjoy them, too!

12 thin slices bacon (pork or beef), cut in half crosswise

4 boneless, skinless chicken thighs, or 2 boneless, skinless chicken breasts, cut into 1-inch pieces

FOR GARNISH/SERVING (OPTIONAL)

Fresh flat-leaf parsley or thyme leaves

Ranch dressing, homemade (page 367 or 368) or store-bought (omit for egg-free)

Sugar-free ketchup, homemade (page 369) or store-bought

SPECIAL EQUIPMENT:

Toothpicks

1. Preheat the oven to 400°F. Line a rimmed baking sheet with parchment paper.

2. Wrap a piece of bacon around each piece of chicken and secure the ends with a toothpick.

3. Place the wrapped nuggets in a single layer on the prepared baking sheet and bake for 7 to 9 minutes, flipping them over after 4 minutes, until the bacon is slightly crispy and the chicken is cooked through. If desired, garnish with fresh parsley or thyme and serve with ranch and/or ketchup for dipping. Best served fresh.

(per serving):
calories **184** • fat **11g** • protein **22g** • carbs **0g** • fiber **0g**

Meat Cookies

EASY · option · option · option

yield: 4 servings • prep time: 5 minutes • cook time: 5 minutes

I love to make hamburgers in the oven. I started making them this way so the boys could do it themselves. I felt more comfortable having them bake the hamburgers rather than fry them.

I love my mom's meat cookies, which are really just hamburgers that we get to decorate with ketchup and mustard, but calling them meat cookies makes them extra tasty! I like to make faces with the condiments by placing pickle slices as the eyes, a mayo nose, a ketchup smile, and mustard hair. Micah and I like to eat our meat cookies without the bun.

1 pound ground beef

Fine sea salt and ground black pepper

4 slices bacon (pork or beef; optional)

4 (1-ounce) slices Muenster or Havarti cheese (omit for dairy-free)

FOR SERVING (OPTIONAL)

Baby dill pickles or sliced dill pickles

Mayonnaise, homemade (page 365) or store-bought (omit for egg-free)

Sugar-free ketchup, homemade (page 369) or store-bought

Prepared yellow mustard

Guacamole (page 376)

4 Sandwich Buns (page 384; omit for egg- and nut-free)

1. Preheat the oven to 425°F. Line a rimmed baking sheet with aluminum foil. Put a wire rack on top for the patties to sit on.

2. While the oven preheats, form the beef into 4 equal-sized patties, about ¼ inch thick. Use your thumb to press an indent in the center of each patty to prevent the burgers from being round instead of flat. Season the outsides of the patties well with salt and pepper.

3. Place the patties and bacon, if using, on the wire rack and bake for 12 to 15 minutes for medium-done burgers, or until cooked to your liking. If adding cheese, just before the burgers are cooked to your preference, remove the pan from the oven, place a slice of cheese on each burger, and allow to melt in the oven for 1 minute.

4. Decorate the meat cookies as desired with pickles, mayo, ketchup, mustard, and/or guacamole. Serve with or without buns. Store extras in an airtight container in the refrigerator for up to 4 days. To reheat, place in a greased skillet over medium heat for 2 minutes per side, or until heated through.

(per serving):
calories **382** • fat **28g** • protein **30g** • carbs **0g** • fiber **0g**

Sloppy Kai Dogs

EASY   option   option   option

yield: 4 servings • prep time: 5 minutes • cook time: 28 minutes

If you love sloppy Joes, you must try this recipe! We call them sloppy Kais because Kai loves to make a mess and rarely eats over his plate, which means his food often gets all over the table as well as all over his face. Kai is certainly my goofy boy!

2 tablespoons coconut oil or unsalted butter

¼ cup diced onions

1 clove garlic, minced

1 pound ground beef

¾ cup tomato sauce

½ cup beef bone broth

3 tablespoons confectioners'-style erythritol or equivalent amount of liquid or powdered sweetener (see page 77)

1 teaspoon prepared yellow mustard

½ teaspoon fine sea salt

⅛ teaspoon ground black pepper

4 uncured hot dogs

FOR SERVING (OPTIONAL)

4 Sandwich Buns (page 384), made into hot dog shapes (omit for egg- and nut-free)

Shredded cheddar cheese (omit for dairy-free)

1. Heat the oil in a large sauté pan over medium-high heat. Add the diced onions and cook for 2 minutes, or until softened. Add the garlic to the pan and sauté for another minute, until fragrant. Add the ground beef and cook while crumbling the meat with a wooden spoon for 5 minutes, or until barely any pink remains; drain the fat.

2. Stir in the remaining ingredients, including the hot dogs. Simmer over low heat for 10 to 20 minutes to allow the flavors to open up and the sauce to thicken.

3. If serving in buns, slice the buns in half. Place a hot dog in each bun. Ladle the ground beef mixture on top of the hot dogs. Alternatively, place a hot dog on a plate and top with the beef mixture. Top with shredded cheese, if desired.

4. Store extras in an airtight container in the refrigerator for up to 5 days, or freeze for up to a month. To reheat, place the sloppy Kai mixture in a saucepan over medium heat for 4 minutes, or until heated through.

(per serving): calories **468** • fat **34g** • protein **33g** • carbs **4g** • fiber **1g**

Touchdown
Tacos

EASY   option   option   option   yield: 4 servings • prep time: 8 minutes • cook time: 6 minutes

We are huge Packer fans, and we eat these Touchdown Tacos every football Sunday! I often make a quadruple batch of the taco meat to store for easy lunches when we are in Hawaii and want to get down to the beach fast. The boys help put fixings like guacamole, salsa, cheese, and olives in small bowls, and we all tear off leaves of lettuce, fill them with our favorite fixings, and eat them as taco wraps.

TACO MEAT

1 pound ground beef

1½ tablespoons chili powder

3 teaspoons ground cumin

2 teaspoons smoked paprika

2 teaspoons fine sea salt

½ teaspoon garlic powder

½ teaspoon onion powder

½ cup tomato sauce or salsa

1 teaspoon stevia glycerite, or a few drops of liquid stevia (optional)

FOR SERVING

1 head Boston lettuce, separated into leaves, or 8 Soft Tortillas (page 382) (use lettuce for egg- and nut-free)

½ cup salsa

½ cup guacamole (page 376)

½ cup sour cream (omit for dairy-free)

½ cup shredded cheddar cheese (omit for dairy-free)

⅓ cup chopped green onions

⅓ cup fresh cilantro leaves

¼ cup sliced black and/or green olives

1. Place the beef in a large skillet over medium heat and sprinkle on the seasonings. Brown the beef, crumbling the meat with a wooden spoon as it cooks. When the meat is no longer pink, about 6 minutes, add the tomato sauce and sweetener, if using; stir well. Use a large spoon to transfer the meat mixture to a serving dish.

2. While the beef is browning, place the lettuce or tortillas on a large plate. Place the salsa, guacamole, sour cream (if using), cheese (if using), green onions, cilantro, and olives in separate small serving dishes.

3. Assemble the tacos by filling the tortillas or lettuce leaves with a spoonful of the cooked meat and the toppings of your choice.

4. Store extra taco meat in an airtight container in the refrigerator for up to 5 days, or freeze for up to a month. To reheat, place in a skillet over medium heat for 4 minutes, or until heated through.

(per serving): calories **526** • fat **39g** • protein **32g** • carbs **11g** • fiber **4g**

Cheese Quesadillas

EASY

yield: 2 servings • prep time: 5 minutes (not including time to make tortillas) • cook time: 8 minutes

My boys love these quesadillas with my Touchdown Taco meat (page 192) added to the filling, which gives them an extra boost of protein. You could also fill them with scrambled eggs and make a breakfast quesadilla!

2 tablespoons coconut oil or unsalted butter

2 Soft Tortillas (page 382)

1 cup shredded Monterey Jack cheese

Fine sea salt

FOR SERVING/GARNISH

Guacamole (page 376)

Salsa

Sour cream

Fresh cilantro leaves

1. Heat the fat in a large skillet over medium-high heat. Place a tortilla in the skillet. Top the tortilla with half of the cheese and season with a little salt. Fold the tortilla in half over the cheese. Cook for 1 to 2 minutes per side, or until the tortilla is golden brown and the cheese is melted. Repeat with the second tortilla and remaining ½ cup of cheese, adding more fat to the skillet if needed.

2. Remove from the skillet and slice into wedges. Serve with guacamole, salsa, and/or sour cream and garnish with cilantro, if desired.

(per serving): calories **439** • fat **38g** • protein **19g** • carbs **8g** • fiber **5g**

chapter 6:
classic kid meals

Dinosaur Droppings (aka Meatballs) / **198**

Bon Vie Chicken Tenders / **200**

Protein Noodle Taco Lasagna / **202**

Fish Fingers with Easy Tartar Sauce / **204**

Baked Chicken Legs / **206**

Mama Maria's Pizza Chicken Balls / **208**

The Easiest Mac 'n' Cheese / **210**

Protein Noodle Pad Thai / **212**

Crispy Baked Ravioli / **214**

Easy Baked BBQ Chicken / **216**

Cheesy Beef and "Noodle" Casserole / **218**

Meaty Lasagna Bowls / **220**

Protein Noodle Chicken Alfredo / **222**

Pizza Party / **224**

Cheese Sticks / **227**

Breakfast for Dinner / **230**

Dinosaur Droppings
(aka Meatballs)

EASY

yield: 8 servings • prep time: 8 minutes • cook time: 20 minutes

Meatballs was one of the first foods that my boys made themselves! This recipe is quite easy: all you have to do is place the ingredients in a bowl and mix well with your hands. When they were little, Micah and Kai always loved squishing the mixture together. They called my meatballs dinosaur droppings! They still love them so much that we always make a quadruple batch and store the extras unbaked in the freezer to thaw for quick and easy meals.

1½ pounds ground beef

8 ounces ground pork (or more beef)

1 large egg

¼ cup tomato sauce

¼ cup minced yellow onions

1 tablespoon dry mustard or prepared yellow mustard

1 clove garlic, minced

2 teaspoons fine sea salt

1 teaspoon ground black pepper

FOR SERVING (OPTIONAL)

Sugar-free ketchup, homemade (page 369) or store-bought

Ranch dressing, homemade (page 367 or 368) or store-bought

1. Preheat the oven to 375°F. Line a rimmed baking sheet with parchment paper.

2. Put all the ingredients for the meatballs in a large bowl and mix with your hands until well combined. Shape into 1-inch balls and place on the prepared baking sheet. Bake the meatballs for 15 to 20 minutes, until cooked through and browned.

3. If desired, give the meatballs owl faces as directed on the opposite page. Serve with ketchup and/or ranch, if desired.

4. Store extras in an airtight container in the refrigerator for up to 4 days, or freeze for up to a month. To reheat, place in a 350°F oven for 5 minutes, or until warmed through.

busy family tip:
Use a medium-sized ice cream scoop to make uniform meatballs. If you make larger meatballs, the cooking time will increase.

(per serving):
calories **236** • fat **16g** • protein **20g** • carbs **1g** • fiber **0.2g**

variation:

Owl Meatballs. *To make these meatballs even more fun, give them owl faces! All you need are toothpicks, a few small sprigs of rosemary or dill, a mozzarella stick, black olives, cream cheese, and a bit of orange bell pepper or yellow cheese. Slice the mozzarella stick into ⅛-inch-thin rounds for eyes. Cut off the tops of the olives and use as the irises of the mozzarella eyes. Poke a toothpick cut in half through the olive and cheese to hold each eye in place. Use a tiny dot of cream cheese to cover the head of the toothpick and serve as the pupil of the eye. Cut the bell pepper or yellow cheese into small triangles for beaks. Place herb sprigs on top of the head for feathers and on the sides of the head for wings.*

Bon Vie
Chicken Tenders

MEDIUM   option

yield: 2 servings • prep time: 6 minutes, plus 2 hours to marinate •
cook time: 12 minutes

This recipe combines two childhood classics: pizza and chicken tenders! I
call them Bon Vie Chicken Tenders because *bon vie* means "the good life"
in French. I like to teach my children different languages to help them
embrace other cultures and celebrate our differences. You can skip the step of
marinating the chicken, but it adds a lot of flavor.

1 cup dill pickle juice

8 (3-inch) chicken breast
tenderloins, about 2 ounces
each

Avocado oil spray (if using an
air fryer)

1 large egg

1 cup powdered Parmesan
cheese (see tip, page 120)
(or pork panko for dairy-free)

1 teaspoon dried oregano
leaves

1 teaspoon garlic powder

1 teaspoon onion powder

½ teaspoon fine sea salt (omit
if using powdered Parmesan)

FOR SERVING (OPTIONAL)

Sugar-free pizza sauce,
homemade (page 370) or store-
bought

Sugar-free ketchup, homemade
(page 369) or store-bought

Ranch dressing, homemade
(page 367 or 368) or store-
bought

1. Place the pickle juice in a large shallow dish and add the
   chicken. Cover the bowl and place in the refrigerator to
   marinate for 2 hours or overnight.

2. If using an air fryer, spray the air fryer basket with avocado
   oil spray. If using the oven, line a rimmed baking sheet with
   parchment paper. Preheat the oven or air fryer to 400°F.

3. Crack the egg into a small shallow dish and beat lightly with
   a fork. Combine the powdered Parmesan, oregano, garlic
   powder, onion powder, and salt in a medium shallow dish.

4. Coat each chicken tenderloin on both sides with the egg, then
   coat both sides in the cheese mixture. Once coated, use your
   hands to press the coating onto the chicken. If the coating
   isn't thick, dip the chicken into the egg and then the cheese
   mixture a second time. Use your hands to press the coating
   on. Place the coated tenders in the air fryer or on the rimmed
   baking sheet.

5. Cook the tenders for 12 minutes, flipping them over after 6
   minutes, or until the tenders are no longer pink inside. Serve
   with pizza sauce, ketchup, and/or ranch, if desired.

tip:

*Using lean chicken like breast tenderloins helps the breading stay
on. Breading often slides off boneless, skinless chicken thighs.*

(per serving):
calories **594** • fat **33g** • protein **74g** • carbs **1g** • fiber **0.1g**

Protein Noodle
Taco Lasagna

MEDIUM

yield: 8 servings • prep time: 10 minutes • cook time: 45 minutes

I once adored going to Mexican restaurants for tacos and enchiladas. But when Craig lost his job and we couldn't afford to go out to eat, I started cooking our favorite restaurant meals at home. Not only was it a great way to save money, but we both lost a lot of weight eating healthier homemade versions! This recipe combines classic taco flavors with another kid favorite: lasagna. If your kids like spicy food, feel free to add an extra tablespoon of taco seasoning. If your family loves this dish, I highly suggest making four of them the next time you get all the ingredients out and storing them unbaked in the freezer for easy meals later.

2 tablespoons unsalted butter or coconut oil, divided

1 yellow onion, roughly chopped

4 cloves garlic, roughly chopped, or 1 head roasted garlic (page 374)

2 teaspoons chili powder

2 teaspoons ground cumin

1½ teaspoons fine sea salt

1½ cups chicken broth

2 (28-ounce) cans diced tomatoes or tomato puree

2 pounds ground chicken

2 tablespoons Taco Seasoning (page 388)

1 (7-ounce) package sliced deli chicken breast

3 cups shredded Monterey Jack cheese

FOR GARNISH

Sliced or diced avocado

Fresh cilantro leaves

Crumbled Cotija cheese

1. Heat 1 tablespoon of the fat in a cast-iron skillet over medium-high heat. Add the onion and sauté for 4 minutes, until softened. Reduce the heat to medium and add the garlic, chili powder, cumin, and salt. Sauté for 2 more minutes, until the garlic is light golden brown.

2. Add the broth and tomatoes and simmer over medium-high heat for 8 minutes, until aromatic. Use an immersion blender to puree the sauce, or pour the sauce into a countertop blender and blend until smooth. Set the sauce aside.

3. Place the remaining tablespoon of fat in the skillet, still over medium-high heat. Add the ground chicken and sprinkle with the taco seasoning. Cook, crumbling the meat with a wooden spoon, for about 3 minutes. Add the reserved sauce, cover, and reduce the heat to medium. Cook for 5 minutes, or until the chicken is no longer pink. Set aside.

4. Preheat the oven to 350°F.

5. Lay 5 slices of deli chicken in a 9-inch cast-iron skillet or similar-size casserole dish, overlapping them to fully cover the bottom. Layer with half of the ground chicken mixture and half of the shredded cheese. Top with the rest of the chicken slices, saucy ground chicken, and cheese. Bake for 20 minutes, until the cheese is melted and starting to brown.

(per serving):
calories **675** • fat **34g** • protein **58g** • carbs **11g** • fiber **2g**

6. Garnish with avocado, cilantro, and Cotija cheese and serve. Store extras in an airtight container in the refrigerator for up to 4 days, or freeze for up to a month. To reheat, place in a casserole dish in a 350°F oven for 5 minutes, or until heated through.

Fish Fingers with
Easy Tartar Sauce

MEDIUM   option   yield: 4 servings • prep time: 10 minutes • cook time: 25 minutes

An air fryer is basically a small high-powered convection oven, and it's great for getting a delicious crispy coating without frying. If you don't have an air fryer, you can use your oven to make these fish fingers.

1 large egg

1 cup powdered Parmesan cheese (see tip, page 120) (or pork panko for dairy-free)

¼ cup dried parsley

1 pound cod fillets, cut into sticks about ½ inch wide by 2½ inches long

Avocado or coconut oil spray

½ batch Easy Tartar Sauce (page 364), for serving

1. Preheat the oven or an air fryer to 400°F. If using the oven, line a rimmed baking sheet with parchment paper.

2. Crack the egg into a small shallow dish and beat lightly with a fork. Combine the powdered Parmesan and parsley in a medium shallow dish. Dip the fish sticks into the egg just enough to wet them, then dip them into the Parmesan mixture and coat the fish sticks well; use your hands to press the breading around each stick (dip again in both for a thicker coating). Set the coated sticks aside on a large plate. Spray the coated fish sticks with avocado oil spray.

3. If using an air fryer, place the fish sticks in the air fryer in a single layer (working in batches if needed). If using the oven, place on the prepared baking sheet. Cook for 20 to 25 minutes, flipping the fish over after 10 minutes.

4. Transfer the fish fingers to a platter and serve with the tartar sauce. Store extra fish fingers and tartar sauce in separate airtight containers in the refrigerator for up to 4 days, or freeze the fish for up to 1 month. To reheat the fish fingers, place in an air fryer or oven at 400°F for 3 minutes, or until heated through.

busy family tip:
The fish fingers freeze well; I often make a double batch and store the extras in the freezer for an easy dinner later.

(per serving):
calories **260** • fat **11g** • protein **40g** • carbs **0.2g** • fiber **0.1g**

Baked
Chicken Legs

MEDIUM option

yield: 4 servings • prep time: 8 minutes, plus 2 hours to marinate • cook time: 25 minutes

Shake 'n Bake was a mainstay in my mother's kitchen. You put the coating in a bag, add the chicken, shake it to coat, and then bake it—easy peasy! This homemade version is just as simple to prepare, but the coating packs a much bigger protein punch. You can skip the step of marinating the chicken before breading it, but the marinade adds a lot of flavor.

1 cup dill pickle juice

4 chicken legs

Avocado or coconut oil spray

1 large egg

½ cup powdered Parmesan cheese (see tip, page 120) (or pork panko for dairy-free)

¼ teaspoon ground black pepper

Chopped fresh herbs of choice, for garnish (optional)

1. Place the pickle juice in a large shallow dish and add the chicken. Cover the bowl and place in the refrigerator to marinate for 2 hours or overnight.

2. If using an air fryer, spray the air fryer basket with avocado or coconut oil spray. If using the oven, line a rimmed baking sheet with parchment paper. Preheat the oven or air fryer to 390°F.

3. Crack the egg into a small shallow dish and beat lightly with a fork. Combine the powdered Parmesan and pepper in a resealable plastic bag. Dip the chicken legs into the egg, then place them in the bag with the Parmesan mixture, seal, and shake well. Using your hands, press the cheese onto the chicken to form a nice crust. Spray the chicken with avocado or coconut oil spray.

4. Place the chicken legs on a rimmed baking sheet or in the air fryer basket. Cook for 25 minutes, or until the internal temperature of the chicken reaches 180°F. Garnish with fresh herbs, if desired, and serve.

5. Store extras in an airtight container in the refrigerator for up to 3 days. To reheat, place in a 375°F oven or air fryer for 5 minutes, or until warmed through.

(per serving):
calories **415** • fat **25g** • protein **45g** • carbs **0.2g** • fiber **0g**

Mama Maria's
Pizza Chicken Balls

MEDIUM   option

yield: 6 servings • prep time: 8 minutes • cook time: 11 minutes

Even if your kids don't like mushrooms, I encourage you to try this recipe. The mushrooms add umami and moisture to the meatballs, but you won't even notice them.

1½ pounds ground chicken

¾ cup finely chopped mushrooms

½ cup chopped fresh basil leaves

3 cloves garlic, minced, or 3 cloves roasted garlic (page 374)

1 teaspoon Italian seasoning

1 teaspoon ground dried oregano

FOR SERVING/GARNISH

1½ cups sugar-free pizza sauce, homemade (page 370) or store-bought, warmed

Shredded Parmesan cheese (optional; omit for dairy-free)

Fresh oregano leaves (optional)

1. Preheat the oven to 350°F. Line a rimmed baking sheet with parchment paper.

2. In a large bowl, use your hands to mix together the ground chicken, mushrooms, and basil. Add the garlic, Italian seasoning, and oregano and use your hands to combine well.

3. Shape the mixture into balls about 1½ inches in diameter and place on the prepared baking sheet. Bake the meatballs for 11 minutes, or until the internal temperature reaches 160°F.

4. Pour the pizza sauce onto a serving platter and place the cooked meatballs on top. Garnish with shredded Parmesan and oregano, if desired.

5. To reheat, place the meatballs on a rimmed baking sheet in a 350°F oven for 4 minutes, or until heated through.

(per serving):
calories **423** • fat **18g** • protein **39g** • carbs **4g** • fiber **1g**

The Easiest
Mac 'n' Cheese

EASY   option

yield: 6 servings • prep time: 8 minutes • cook time: 15 minutes

This recipe is extra easy because instead of having to make a cheese sauce on the stovetop, you mix the ingredients together in a bowl and add to the cauliflower. The cheese mixture melts perfectly when baked, and you can freeze it! I like to use flavorful cheeses so my boys' palates get used to different tastes; however, you can use a mild cheddar in place of the sharp cheddar.

I love making this mac 'n' cheese in individual ramekins because it cuts down on the baking time so lunch or dinner can be ready in minutes. I also like to store extra ramekins in the freezer. All I have to do is thaw them and then place them in the oven for easy meals when life gets busy!

2 cups frozen chopped cauliflower, thawed

¼ cup shredded farmer's cheese, mozzarella, or Gruyère

¼ cup shredded sharp cheddar cheese

2 ounces cream cheese (¼ cup), softened

2 tablespoons finely diced onions

3 tablespoons beef broth

¼ teaspoon fine sea salt

TOPPING

¼ cup pork panko or blanched almond flour

¼ cup (½ stick) unsalted butter, melted, plus more for greasing the ramekins

4 slices bacon (pork or beef), finely diced

Chopped fresh flat-leaf parsley, thyme, or chives, for garnish (optional)

1. Preheat the oven to 375°F.

2. Place the cauliflower on a paper towel and pat dry. Cut any large pieces of cauliflower into ½-inch pieces.

3. In a medium bowl, stir together the cheeses and onions. Slowly stir in the broth until well combined. Add the salt and stir to combine. Add the cauliflower and gently mix the cauliflower into the cheese mixture.

4. Grease six 4-ounce ramekins with butter. Divide the cauliflower mixture evenly among the ramekins, filling each about three-quarters full.

5. Make the topping: In a small bowl, stir together the pork panko, melted butter, and bacon until well combined. Divide the topping evenly among the ramekins.

6. Bake for 11 to 15 minutes, until the topping is browned and the bacon is crispy. Garnish with fresh herbs, if desired, and serve.

7. Store extras in the ramekins covered with foil in the refrigerator for up to 4 days, or freeze for up to a month. To reheat, place in a 375°F oven for 6 minutes, or until the cauliflower is heated through and the topping is crispy.

(per serving):
calories **198** • fat **17g** • protein **8g** • carbs **2g** • fiber **1g**

Protein Noodle
Pad Thai

MEDIUM

yield: 4 servings • prep time: 12 minutes • cook time: 8 minutes

Traditionally, pad thai has a kick to it. My boys like it mild, but if you want it to have some heat, feel free to add 1 teaspoon of hot sauce, such as Frank's RedHot, to the sauce in Step 1. Or the adults can drizzle their bowls with hot sauce at the end if they want. I like to serve this dish with chopsticks to make it extra festive! But most of the time, we all need to resort to forks to eat it.

 This protein pad thai is delicious, and it's easier to make than most pad thai recipes because you don't have to boil the noodles. It also makes yummy leftovers!

½ cup chicken broth

½ cup confectioners'-style erythritol or equivalent amount of liquid or powdered sweetener (see page 77)

¼ cup lime juice

3 tablespoons creamy natural peanut butter or almond butter

2 tablespoons fish sauce

1 tablespoon coconut oil

1 pound ground chicken

2 cloves garlic, minced, or ½ head roasted garlic (page 374)

1½ teaspoons grated fresh ginger

2 (7-ounce) packages sliced deli chicken breast

4 large eggs, lightly beaten

½ teaspoon fine sea salt

FOR GARNISH

¼ cup chopped fresh chives or scallions

Handful of peanuts

Fresh cilantro leaves

1. In a small bowl, whisk together the broth, sweetener, lime juice, peanut butter, and fish sauce. Set aside.

2. Heat the oil in a large skillet or wok over medium-high heat. Add the ground chicken, garlic, and ginger and sauté until the chicken is no longer pink, about 5 minutes.

3. Meanwhile, prepare the protein noodles: Slice the deli chicken into thin noodle-like strips. Gently heat them in a large skillet over low heat or in the microwave for 1 minute. Transfer the noodles to a large serving bowl.

4. Once the ground chicken is cooked through, pour in the peanut sauce and stir well to coat. If you prefer a thicker sauce, cook the mixture over medium heat for 5 to 10 minutes, until thickened to your liking; otherwise, remove the pan from the heat immediately. Scoop the ground chicken mixture on top of the protein noodles in the serving bowl.

5. Place the eggs in the skillet and scramble over medium heat until set, about 2 minutes. Season the eggs with the salt. Top the chicken mixture in the serving bowl with the eggs. Garnish with the chives, peanuts, and cilantro.

6. Store extras in an airtight container in the refrigerator for up to 4 days. To reheat, place the mixture in a saucepan over medium heat for 4 minutes, or until heated through.

(per serving):
calories **665** • fat **31g** • protein **65g** • carbs **8g** • fiber **1g**

Crispy
Baked Ravioli

HARD option   yield: 6 servings • prep time: 15 minutes • cook time: 12 minutes

In this recipe, deli turkey takes the place of traditional ravioli dough and is stuffed with a cheesy filling. To make the ravioli dairy-free, you could use Kite Hill brand cream cheese–style spread in place of the shredded cheese and cream cheese, or you could fill them with cooked ground sausage.

1 cup shredded Swiss cheese

6 ounces cream cheese (¾ cup), softened

8 ounces thinly sliced deli turkey (12 very large slices)

2 large eggs

1 cup pork panko or blanched almond flour

Avocado oil spray

FOR GARNISH/SERVING (OPTIONAL)

Fresh parsley leaves

Ranch dressing, homemade (page 367 or 368) or store-bought

Sugar-free pizza sauce, homemade (page 370) or store-bought, warmed

1. Preheat the oven to 400°F. Line a rimmed baking sheet with parchment paper.

2. In a small bowl, stir together the shredded Swiss and cream cheese until well combined.

3. Assemble the ravioli: Lay a slice of turkey on a sheet of parchment paper. Spoon about 2 heaping tablespoons of the cheese filling into the center of the turkey. Fold one end of the turkey over the filling, making sure the turkey completely covers the filling and meets the turkey on the other side; otherwise, the filling will leak out. Fold the ends around the filling to make a square, making sure that the filling is covered well. Using your fingers, press down around the filling to even out the ravioli into a square shape. Repeat with the rest of the turkey and filling; you should have 12 ravioli.

4. Crack the eggs into a shallow bowl and beat well with a fork. Place the pork panko in another shallow bowl.

5. Gently dip each ravioli into the egg mixture, then dredge it in the pork panko. Use your hands to press the pork panko into the ravioli, coating it well. Spray the ravioli with avocado oil spray and place on the prepared baking sheet. Make sure to leave space between the ravioli.

6. Bake the ravioli for 12 minutes, or until crispy, gently flipping them over after 6 minutes. Allow to cool for a few minutes before serving so the hot cheese does not burn your mouth. If desired, garnish with fresh parsley and serve with ranch or pizza sauce on the side for dipping.

7. Store extras in an airtight container in the refrigerator for up to 4 days. To reheat, place in a 400°F oven for 3 minutes, or until heated through.

(per serving):
calories **346** • fat **25g** • protein **28g** • carbs **1g** • fiber **0g**

Easy Baked BBQ Chicken

EASY

yield: 2 servings • prep time: 5 minutes • cook time: 35 minutes

I grew up eating BBQ chicken about once a week. During the cold Wisconsin winters when the grill would be covered in snow, we had to make it indoors! To make this simple recipe even easier, feel free to use garlic paste from a jar if you don't want to smash a clove to a paste. If you use chicken thighs rather than legs, the baking time will be closer to 45 to 50 minutes.

¾ cup tomato sauce

⅓ cup confectioners'-style erythritol or equivalent amount of liquid or powdered sweetener (see page 77)

1 tablespoon apple cider vinegar

1 clove garlic, smashed to a paste, or ½ head roasted garlic (page 374)

1 teaspoon onion salt or fine sea salt

1 teaspoon liquid smoke

1 pound bone-in, skin-on chicken legs or thighs

1. Preheat the oven to 400°F.

2. Place the tomato sauce, sweetener, vinegar, garlic, onion salt, and liquid smoke in a small bowl. Stir well, then pour half of the sauce into another bowl and set aside for serving.

3. Place the chicken in an 8-inch square baking dish and baste with the other half of the sauce. Cover with foil and bake for 25 minutes. Uncover and bake for another 10 minutes, or until the chicken is no longer pink inside.

4. Serve the chicken with the reserved sauce. Store extras in an airtight container in the refrigerator for up to 4 days, or freeze for up to a month. To reheat, place the chicken in a 375°F oven for 10 minutes, or until warmed through.

(per serving):
calories **333** • fat **17g** • protein **41g** • carbs **5g** • fiber **1g**

Cheesy Beef and "Noodle" Casserole

EASY option

yield: 4 servings • prep time: 5 minutes • cook time: 29 minutes

Hamburger Helper was a staple in my mother's pantry. We ate it quite often. In this much healthier version, I use eggplant instead of noodles! Eggplant works great in this recipe because it is like a sponge and soaks up the delicious flavor of the sauce. A helpful tip from one of my recipe testers: make sure to peel the eggplant before you cut it.

2 tablespoons coconut oil, lard, or tallow

1 small onion, diced

1 small eggplant

1½ teaspoons fine sea salt or garlic salt, divided

1 pound ground beef

2 cups tomato sauce

2 teaspoons prepared yellow mustard

1 cup shredded cheddar cheese (omit for dairy-free)

Fresh parsley, for garnish

1. Place the oil in a Dutch oven or other large pot over medium-high heat. Add the onion and sauté for 4 minutes, or until the onion is starting to soften.

2. Meanwhile, peel the eggplant and cut it into ½-inch cubes. Add the eggplant to the pot. Season with ½ teaspoon of the salt. Cook over medium heat, stirring occasionally, for 5 minutes, or until the eggplant is starting to soften.

3. Add the ground beef to the pot and season with the rest of the salt. Cook, crumbling the meat with a wooden spoon, for 5 minutes, or until it is almost cooked through. Drain off any excess fat, if desired.

4. Add the tomato sauce and mustard to the pot. Cook over medium-low heat, stirring occasionally, for 20 minutes, or until the eggplant is very tender.

5. Top with the cheese, if using, and garnish with fresh parsley. Store extras in an airtight container in the refrigerator for up to 5 days. To reheat, place into a pot over medium heat, stirring occasionally, for 3 minutes, or until heated through.

(per serving): calories **475** • fat **35g** • protein **30g** • carbs **12g** • fiber **3g**

Meaty Lasagna Bowls

MEDIUM

yield: 8 servings • prep time: 10 minutes • cook time: 13 minutes

These lasagna bowls are great for quick and easy meals. Just assemble the ingredients in the bowls, cover, and store unbaked in the refrigerator; then, when you're ready to eat, just pop a bowl in the microwave or toaster oven!

2 tablespoons unsalted butter or coconut oil

¼ cup chopped onions

2 cloves garlic, minced, or ½ head roasted garlic (page 374)

1 pound ground beef

1 pound ground Italian sausage (or more beef)

4 cups marinara sauce, homemade (page 372) or store-bought

1 (8-ounce) package sliced deli chicken breast

1 pound ricotta or cottage cheese

12 ounces mozzarella cheese, sliced

¾ cup grated Parmesan cheese

1. Preheat the oven to 375°F.

2. Melt the butter in a large pot over medium-high heat. Add the onions and garlic and sauté for 3 minutes, or until the onions are soft. Add the ground beef and sausage and cook, crumbling the meats with a wooden spoon, until they are well browned, about 5 minutes. Stir in the marinara sauce and remove from the heat.

3. To assemble, divide the saucy meaty mixture evenly among 8 oven-safe serving bowls. Arrange a slice of chicken over the meat sauce in each bowl. Dollop the ricotta over the chicken. Top with a sprinkle of mozzarella and Parmesan. Repeat the layers, using the rest of the meat sauce, chicken slices, ricotta, mozzarella, and Parmesan.

4. Place the bowls in the oven and bake for 3 to 5 minutes, or until the cheese is melted (or heat individual bowls in the microwave for 1 minute). Store extras covered in the refrigerator for up to 4 days, or freeze for up to a month.

(per serving): calories **622** • fat **42g** • protein **50g** • carbs **9g** • fiber **1g**

Protein Noodle
Chicken Alfredo

MEDIUM

yield: 8 servings • prep time: 6 minutes • cook time: 17 minutes

This chicken Alfredo recipe is so good, you are going to want to make a full batch to have plenty of leftovers! However, you can easily cut the recipe in half if you prefer. Instead of using regular noodles, I use deli chicken cut into noodle-like strips—"protein noodles"!

I like to use roasted garlic instead of raw garlic because it is a more mild and sweeter flavor that appeals to the palates of children.

ALFREDO SAUCE

1 cup unsalted butter

1 head roasted garlic (page 374), or 2 cloves garlic, minced

1 (8-ounce) package cream cheese

1 cup grated Parmesan cheese, plus more for garnish

⅔ cup chicken or beef broth

NOODLES

4 (7-ounce) packages sliced deli chicken breast

1. Make the sauce: Place the butter and garlic in a saucepan and cook over medium-high heat for 2 minutes, stirring constantly so the garlic doesn't burn, until the garlic is light golden brown. Stir in the cream cheese, Parmesan, and broth. Simmer uncovered for at least 15 minutes; the flavors will open up if you simmer it longer. If the sauce separates, add a few tablespoons of broth and whisk well.

2. While the sauce simmers, slice the chicken into fettuccine-shaped noodles.

3. Once the sauce is finished, stir the chicken noodles into the sauce, sprinkle with Parmesan, and enjoy!

4. Store extras in an airtight container in the refrigerator for up to 4 days. To reheat, place the noodles and sauce in a small saucepan over medium heat for 3 minutes, or until heated through.

(per serving):
calories **522** • fat **39g** • protein **42g** • carbs **2g** • fiber **0g**

Pizza Party

 HARD option   yield: one 12-inch pizza (8 servings) • prep time: 10 minutes • cook time: 15 minutes

I grew up in Medford, Wisconsin, which is the birthplace of frozen pizza: Tombstone brand! We always had pizzas in the freezer for easy meals. Now I keep "healthified" pizzas in my freezer. I recommend par-baking the crust, putting the toppings on, and then freezing the pizza.

I present three options below, but feel free to top this crust with your favorite sauce and toppings. You could use pesto instead of pizza sauce, for example. I like making personal-sized pizzas so that everyone gets to make their favorite. You can make the pizzas any shape you want, too. Try a heart shape for Valentine's Day!

I call this a party, but in reality, it's a great way to get the family to spend time together and work as a team to prep meals for the month!

Store extra pizza in an airtight container in the refrigerator for up to 4 days, or freeze for up to a month. To reheat, place slices on a rimmed baking sheet or pizza stone in a 375°F oven for 5 minutes, or until heated through.

Pizza Crust

1 ¾ cups shredded mozzarella cheese

2 tablespoons cream cheese

¾ cup pork panko or blanched almond flour

1 large egg

⅛ teaspoon fine sea salt

Avocado or olive oil, for brushing (optional)

1. If you have a pizza stone, place it in the oven. Preheat the oven to 425°F.

2. To make the crust, place the mozzarella and cream cheese in a heat-safe bowl and microwave for 1 to 2 minutes, until the cheese is entirely melted. Stir well.

3. Add the pork panko, egg, and salt and combine well using a hand mixer.

4. Put the dough on a greased piece of parchment paper and form it into a circle about 12 inches in diameter. Brush with avocado or olive oil for an extra crispy crust, if desired.

5. If using a pizza stone, slide the parchment with the crust onto the hot pizza stone in the oven. Otherwise, place the crust on a rimmed baking sheet. Par-bake for 5 minutes, or until the crust starts to get a little golden.

6. Remove from the oven, top as desired, and finish baking (see the variations that follow for details).

(per serving):
calories **247** • fat **19g** • protein **22g** • carbs **0.2g** • fiber **0g**

Pepperoni Pizza

1 cup sugar-free pizza sauce, homemade (page 370) or store-bought

1 par-baked pizza crust (above)

1 cup shredded mozzarella cheese

14 slices pepperoni

Spread the sauce all over the par-baked crust and top with the cheese and pepperoni. Bake at 425°F until the cheese is melted, about 10 minutes. Remove from the oven and serve.

(per serving):
calories **320** • fat **24g** • protein **27g** • carbs **2g** • fiber **1g**

Bacon Cheeseburger Pizza

TOPPINGS

8 ounces ground beef

1 teaspoon fine sea salt

1 cup shredded cheddar cheese

3 slices bacon (pork or beef), diced

A few yellow onion slices

A few dill pickle slices (optional)

SAUCE

¾ cup sugar-free ketchup, homemade (page 369) or store-bought, or tomato sauce

2 tablespoons prepared yellow mustard

1 teaspoon stevia glycerite, or a few drops of liquid stevia

1 par-baked pizza crust (page 225)

1. Place the ground beef in a cast-iron skillet and season with the salt. Cook over medium-high heat, crumbling the meat with a wooden spoon, for about 5 minutes, until no pink remains. Remove from the heat.

2. Make the sauce: Place all the ingredients in a small bowl and stir well to combine.

3. Spread the sauce all over the par-baked crust and top with the cooked ground beef, cheese, bacon, and onion slices.

4. Bake at 425°F until the cheese is melted, about 10 minutes. Remove from the oven, top with the pickles, if desired, and serve.

(per serving): calories **447** • fat **33g** • protein **36g** • carbs **2g** • fiber **1g**

Meat Lover's Pizza

4 slices bacon (pork or beef), diced

1 (4-ounce) Italian sausage link, sliced, or 4 ounces ground Italian sausage or ground beef

1 cup sugar-free pizza sauce, homemade (page 370) or store-bought

1 par-baked pizza crust (page 225)

1 cup shredded mozzarella cheese, divided

14 slices pepperoni

14 small slices Canadian bacon

1. Cook the bacon in a cast-iron skillet over medium-high heat until slightly crisp, about 5 minutes, then crumble with a wooden spoon. Transfer the bacon to a paper towel–lined plate and set aside.

2. Cook the sausage in the same skillet over medium-high heat, crumbling it with the wooden spoon if using ground meat, until browned on both sides or cooked through, about 4 minutes. Transfer to the plate with the bacon, keeping the meats separate.

3. Spread the sauce over the par-baked crust and top with half of the cheese, the sausage, pepperoni, and Canadian bacon. Top with the rest of the cheese, then the crumbled bacon.

4. Bake at 425°F until the cheese is melted, about 10 minutes. Remove from the oven and serve.

chapter 6: **classic kid meals**

(per serving): calories **415** • fat **32g** • protein **32g** • carbs **1g** • fiber **0.4g**

Cheese
Sticks

MEDIUM option option

yield: 4 servings • prep time: 5 minutes (not including time to make crust) • cook time: 8 minutes

What's a pizza party without a side of cheesy breadsticks? When I was a girl, I would go roller-skating at the Skateway. My friends and I would eat cheese sticks for lunch in between skating. I think these healthy sticks taste way better, but they still bring me back to my roller-skating days!

1 par-baked pizza crust (page 225)

1 cup shredded mozzarella cheese

½ cup shredded Parmesan cheese

Fresh parsley leaves, for garnish

1 cup sugar-free pizza sauce, homemade (page 370) or store-bought, or marinara sauce, homemade (page 372) or store-bought, for serving

1. Preheat the oven to 425°F.

2. Place the par-baked pizza crust on a pizza stone or rimmed baking sheet and top with the mozzarella and Parmesan. Bake for 5 to 8 minutes, until the cheese is melted. Slice the crust in half lengthwise, then cut crosswise into 1½-inch strips. Garnish with parsley and serve with pizza sauce for dipping.

(per serving):
calories 246 • fat 17g • protein 22g • carbs 2g • fiber 0.3g

Breakfast for Dinner

MEDIUM · option · option

yield: 4 servings • prep time: 10 minutes (not including time to make pancake batter or jam) • cook time: 15 minutes

Breakfast for dinner—we call it brinner!—is a meal my whole family looks forward to, and I love it because it's cheap and easy to make. Allow each family member to arrange the components as they like. Micah likes to make a pancake slider by topping a pancake with slices of bacon, a layer of scrambled eggs, and a smear of strawberry jam, followed by another pancake. Kai, who despises bacon, prefers to keep his pancakes separate from his sausage and eggs.

PANCAKE SLIDERS

4 slices bacon (pork or beef; omit for vegetarian)

4 sugar-free breakfast sausage links (omit for vegetarian)

1½ teaspoons coconut oil, or more if needed, for the skillet

1 batch Blender Pancake batter (page 102)

8 large eggs

1 tablespoon unsalted butter (or coconut oil for dairy-free)

Fine sea salt and ground black pepper

Sugar-Free Strawberry Jam (page 378), for serving (omit for vegetarian)

SUGGESTED ACCOMPANIMENTS

Cinnamon Rolls (page 116) or Cinnamon Roll Chaffles (page 340)

2 cups plain low-carb yogurt (omit for dairy-free)

1 cup blueberries

1 cup strawberries

1. Bake the bacon and sausages, if using, according to the instructions on page 90.

2. While the meats bake, cook the pancakes: Heat the oil in a large skillet over medium heat. Once hot, pour half of the batter into the skillet, making four 3-inch pancakes. Cook until golden brown, about 2 minutes, then flip and cook until browned on the other side, another 1 to 2 minutes. Remove from the pan and repeat with the remaining batter, adding more oil to the skillet if needed.

3. Crack the eggs into a blender and puree until fluffy (or place in a large bowl and use an immersion blender to puree). Heat a large nonstick skillet over medium heat. Add the butter and swirl to coat the pan. Once melted, pour in the eggs and gently scramble until set and creamy, about 4 minutes. Remove from the heat and season with salt and pepper.

4. Place the meats and pancakes on separate serving plates. Put the scrambled eggs and jam in separate serving bowls. Place your desired accompaniments, such as cinnamon rolls or chaffles, yogurt, and berries, in separate bowls and serve.

5. Store extra components in separate airtight containers in the refrigerator for up to 4 days. To reheat the bacon, sausages, pancakes, and eggs, place in a greased skillet over medium heat for 3 minutes, or until heated through.

(per serving):
calories **641** • fat **38g** • protein **63g** • carbs **7g** • fiber **2g**

chapter 7:
instant pot & slow cooker recipes

Chicken Sloppy Joes / **234**

Pizza Dog Casserole / **236**

Cheeseburger Lettuce Wraps / **238**

Spaghetti Bolognese / **240**

Epic Cheesy Beef Nachos / **242**

Shredded BBQ Chicken / **244**

Chicken Enchiladas / **246**

Sweet 'n' Sour Chicken Wings / **248**

Egg Roll in a Bowl / **250**

Chicken
Sloppy Joes

EASY   option   option

yield: 4 servings • prep time: 5 minutes (not including time to make paffles/ chaffles/buns, if using) • cook time: 12 minutes (Instant Pot) or 3 to 6 hours (slow cooker)

I grew up on sloppy Joes. It is still one of my favorite dinners; I just make it a little differently now. I cut the sugar out of the sauce and serve the meat wrapped in lettuce leaves or on chaffles instead of sandwich buns. My whole family enjoys this recipe!

1 tablespoon unsalted butter (or coconut oil for dairy-free)

2 tablespoons chopped onions

1 clove garlic, minced

1 pound ground chicken or beef

1 cup tomato sauce

½ cup beef broth

¼ cup tomato paste

3 tablespoons confectioners'-style erythritol or equivalent amount of liquid or powdered sweetener (see page 77) (optional)

1½ teaspoons coconut or apple cider vinegar

½ teaspoon prepared yellow mustard

½ teaspoon fine sea salt

⅛ teaspoon ground black pepper

FOR SERVING (OPTIONAL)

Butter lettuce leaves

Basic Savory Paffles or Chaffles (page 334) or Sandwich Buns (page 384) (optional; omit for egg-free)

Baby dill pickles

Halved cherry tomatoes

1. Make the chicken sloppy Joe mixture using either of the following methods:

   INSTANT POT METHOD: Coat the bottom of a 6-quart Instant Pot with the butter. Add the onions and garlic and press Sauté. Cook for 2 minutes, or until the onions are soft. Add the ground chicken and cook while crumbling the meat for 5 minutes, or until the chicken is almost cooked through. Press Cancel to stop the Sauté. Drain the excess grease. Stir in the remaining ingredients. Seal the lid, press Pressure Cook or Manual, and set the timer for 5 minutes. Once finished, let the pressure release naturally. Remove the lid and stir well before serving.

   SLOW COOKER METHOD: Place the onions, garlic, and ground chicken in a 6-quart slow cooker. Stir in the remaining ingredients. Cover and cook on high for 3 hours or on low for 6 hours, until the chicken is cooked through. About 1 hour into cooking, stir to crumble the meat. Stir well again before serving.

2. To serve, wrap the meat mixture in lettuce leaves, or serve it on paffles, chaffles, or buns, if desired. Top with pickles and tomatoes.

3. Store extras in an airtight container in the refrigerator for up to a week, or freeze for up to a month. To reheat, place in a saucepan over medium heat, stirring occasionally, for 5 minutes, or until heated through.

(per serving): calories **288** • fat **8g** • protein **39g** • carbs **10g** • fiber **3g**

Pizza Dog Casserole

yield: 8 servings • prep time: 10 minutes • cook time: 10 minutes (Instant Pot) or 40 minutes (stovetop/oven)

My boys love pizza and they love hot dogs! I married the two and made the most delicious casserole that they gobble up fast. If you don't have an Instant Pot, you can bake this casserole in the oven.

1 tablespoon unsalted butter (or coconut oil for dairy-free)

½ cup diced onions

2 cloves garlic, minced

1 pound ground beef

1 teaspoon fine sea salt

3 cups sugar-free pizza sauce, homemade (page 370) or store-bought

8 uncured hot dogs, sliced in half lengthwise and then in half crosswise

1 cup shredded mozzarella or Parmesan cheese (omit for dairy-free)

Fresh basil leaves, for garnish (optional)

INSTANT POT METHOD:

1. Place the butter in a 6-quart Instant Pot and press Sauté. Once melted, add the onions and garlic and cook for 3 minutes, or until the onions are soft. Add the ground beef and salt and cook while crumbling the beef with a wooden spoon until the meat is almost cooked through, about 5 minutes. Press Cancel to stop the Sauté. Drain the excess fat if needed. Stir in the pizza sauce and hot dogs.

2. Seal the lid, press Pressure Cook or Manual, and set the timer for 5 minutes. Once finished, let the pressure release naturally. Remove the lid and stir well. Top with the cheese and garnish with basil, if using, and serve.

STOVETOP/OVEN METHOD:

1. Preheat the oven to 375°F.

2. Melt the butter in a large cast-iron skillet or other oven-safe skillet over medium heat. Add the onions and garlic and cook for 3 minutes, or until the onions are soft. Add the ground beef and salt and cook while crumbling the beef with a wooden spoon until the meat is no longer pink, about 5 minutes. Drain the excess fat if needed. Stir in the pizza sauce and simmer, uncovered, for 20 minutes.

3. Lay the hot dog slices on top of the mixture in the skillet. Cover everything with the shredded cheese, if using. Transfer the skillet to the oven and bake for 15 minutes, or until the cheese is bubbly and melted. Garnish with basil, if desired, and serve.

Store extras in an airtight container in the refrigerator for up to 3 days. Reheat in a baking dish in a 350°F oven for a few minutes, until warmed through.

(per serving): calories **338** • fat **25g** • protein **22g** • carbs **6g** • fiber **2g**

Cheeseburger
Lettuce Wraps

EASY   option

yield: 4 servings • prep time: 9 minutes • cook time: 3 minutes (Instant Pot) or 2 hours (slow cooker)

If you love McDonald's Big Macs, you are going to love this recipe! My kids have never had a Big Mac, but they do love this recipe. This recipe is so amazing, you will never miss the bun. The sauce can be made ahead and stored in the refrigerator for up to two weeks. Using fish sauce adds umami, but you can opt for regular salt if you don't have fish sauce on hand.

SPECIAL SAUCE

½ cup mayonnaise, homemade (page 365) or store-bought

¼ cup chopped dill pickles

3 tablespoons tomato sauce

2 tablespoons confectioners'-style erythritol or equivalent amount of liquid or powdered sweetener (see page 77)

⅛ teaspoon fish sauce or fine sea salt

FILLING

2 teaspoons unsalted butter (or coconut oil for dairy-free)

2 tablespoons diced onions

1 clove garlic, smashed to a paste or minced

1 pound ground beef

1 teaspoon fine sea salt

¼ teaspoon ground black pepper

FOR GARNISH/SERVING

1 cup shredded cheddar cheese (omit for dairy-free)

Toasted sesame seeds

Dill pickle slices

Boston leaf lettuce

1. Make the sauce: Place the ingredients in a pint-sized jar, seal the lid, and shake well to combine. Set aside.

2. Make the filling using either of the following methods:

   INSTANT POT METHOD: Place the butter in a 6-quart Instant Pot and press Sauté. Once melted, add the onions and sauté for 2 minutes, or until soft. Add the garlic and sauté for another minute, until fragrant. Add the ground beef, salt, and pepper and stir well to break up the beef. Seal the lid, press Pressure Cook or Manual, and set the timer for 1 minute. Once finished, press Quick Release. Drain any excess grease.

   SLOW COOKER METHOD: Place the butter, onions, garlic, ground beef, salt, and pepper in a 6-quart slow cooker and stir well to break up the beef. Cover and cook on low for 2 hours, or until the beef is cooked through. Drain any excess grease.

3. To serve, top the ground beef mixture with the cheese, if using. Garnish with toasted sesame seeds and pickles. Serve wrapped in lettuce leaves and drizzled with the sauce.

4. Store extra filling and sauce in separate airtight containers in the refrigerator for up to 4 days. To reheat the filling, place in a lightly greased skillet over medium heat for 3 minutes, or until heated through.

(per serving):
calories **468** • fat **38g** • protein **28g** • carbs **1g** • fiber **0g**

busy family tip:

If you don't have ground beef thawed, you can make this recipe with frozen meat. Start by sautéing the onions and garlic in the butter in the Instant Pot, then remove from the pot and set aside. Rinse the pot with hot water and dry the outside well. Insert the trivet and pour in 1 cup of cold water. Place the frozen beef on the trivet and seal the lid. Cook on high pressure for 35 minutes, then press Quick Release. In the meantime, prep the sauce and garnishes; you'll likely have time to set the table and wash your prep dishes, too. When the beef is cooked through (it should read at least 160°F on a meat thermometer), put it in a bowl and break it up, add the onion mixture, and top with the cheese, if using. Ta-da!

Spaghetti Bolognese

EASY   option

yield: 8 servings • prep time: 15 minutes • cook time: 19 minutes (Instant Pot) or 4 to 8 hours (slow cooker)

I have the great opportunity to teach nutrition in Italy with MilleVie Travel Agency every year. One year we visited the most beautiful farm overlooking the Amalfi Coast. They made the most delicious spaghetti Bolognese and served it over zoodles for us. I will never forget that meal! This recipe is in memory of my travels to Italy.

4 ounces bacon (pork or beef), diced

½ cup chopped onions

1 head roasted garlic (page 374), or 1 clove garlic, minced

1 teaspoon fine sea salt

½ teaspoon ground black pepper

¼ cup fresh flat-leaf parsley

3 tablespoons chopped fresh oregano

3 tablespoons chopped fresh thyme

2 bay leaves

1 pound ground beef

8 ounces ground Italian sausage

2 cups marinara sauce, homemade (page 372) or store-bought

4 cups crushed tomatoes with juices

¼ cup beef broth

½ teaspoon stevia glycerite (optional)

¼ cup heavy cream (omit for dairy-free)

2 tablespoons unsalted butter (omit for dairy-free)

2 medium zucchini, or 2 (7-ounce) packages deli turkey breast, sliced into thin "noodles," for serving

1 cup grated Parmesan cheese, for serving (omit for dairy-free)

1. Make the Bolognese sauce using either of the following methods:

   INSTANT POT METHOD: Place the diced bacon in a 6-quart Instant Pot and press Sauté. Cook, crumbling occasionally with a wooden spoon, for 4 minutes, or until the bacon is starting to crisp and the fat is rendered. Add the onions and cook for another 4 minutes, stirring frequently, until soft. Add the garlic, salt, pepper, and herbs. Cook for 30 seconds, stirring. Add the beef and Italian sausage and stir well to combine. Add the marinara sauce, tomatoes, broth, and stevia, if using. Seal the lid, press Pressure Cook or Manual, and set the timer for 10 minutes. Once finished, allow the pressure to release naturally.

   SLOW COOKER METHOD: Place the diced bacon in a large skillet over medium-high heat. Cook, crumbling occasionally with a wooden spoon, for 4 minutes, or until the bacon is starting to crisp and the fat is rendered. Add the onions and cook for another 4 minutes, stirring frequently, until soft. Add the garlic, salt, pepper, and herbs. Cook for 30 seconds, stirring. Transfer the mixture to a 6-quart slow cooker, add the beef and Italian sausage, and stir well to combine. Add the marinara sauce, tomatoes, broth, and stevia, if using. Cover and cook on low for 8 hours or on high for 4 hours, or until the meat is cooked through.

(per serving): calories **465** • fat **35g** • protein **26g** • carbs **11g** • fiber **2g**

2. To serve, stir in the cream and butter, if using. Adjust the seasoning to taste and remove the bay leaves. Serve over the noodles and top with the Parmesan cheese, if desired.

3. Store extra Bolognese sauce in an airtight container in the refrigerator for up to 4 days, or freeze for up to a month. To reheat, place in a large skillet over medium heat for 5 minutes, or until heated through.

Epic Cheesy Beef Nachos

EASY

yield: 4 servings • prep time: 10 minutes • cook time: 21 minutes (Instant Pot) or 1 to 3 hours (slow cooker)

This epic nacho recipe is better than the nachos of my childhood—the homemade cheese sauce will knock your socks off! You can also use this cheese sauce on Touchdown Tacos (page 192) or as a dip with vegetables.

SEASONED BEEF

2 teaspoons unsalted butter (for Instant Pot method)

¼ cup diced onions

1 pound ground beef

1½ teaspoons chili powder

½ teaspoon garlic powder

½ teaspoon onion powder

1 teaspoon paprika

1 teaspoon ground cumin

1 teaspoon fine sea salt

¼ cup beef broth

2 tablespoons tomato sauce

NACHO CHEESE SAUCE

1 tablespoon unsalted butter

½ cup beef broth

1 cup shredded Monterey Jack or sharp cheddar cheese

4 ounces cream cheese (½ cup)

1 teaspoon fine sea salt

⅛ teaspoon cayenne pepper (optional)

FOR SERVING

4 cups shredded lettuce

1 (1.5-ounce) bag Chicken Breast Carnivore Crisps or plain pork rinds

¼ cup sliced black olives

1. Make the seasoned beef using either of the following methods:

   INSTANT POT METHOD: Place the butter in a 6-quart Instant Pot and press Sauté. Once melted, add the onions and cook for 3 minutes, or until soft. Add the beef. Sprinkle on the seasonings, then pour in the broth and tomato sauce. Seal the lid, press Pressure Cook or Manual, and set the timer for 18 minutes. Once finished, press Quick Release. Transfer the beef mixture to a serving bowl.

   SLOW COOKER METHOD: Place the onions and beef in a 6-quart slow cooker. Sprinkle on the seasonings, then pour in the broth and tomato sauce. Cover and cook on low for 3 hours or on high for 1 hour. Stir well to break up the beef. Transfer the mixture to a serving bowl.

2. While the beef is cooking, make the cheese sauce: Melt the butter in a medium saucepan over medium heat. Add the rest of the ingredients and stir well until melted, about 3 minutes. Use an immersion blender to puree the sauce until smooth.

3. To serve, place the shredded lettuce on a serving platter. Top with the chicken crisps, cooked beef, cheese sauce, and olives.

4. Store extra beef mixture and cheese sauce in separate airtight containers in the refrigerator for up to 4 days. To reheat the beef, place in a lightly greased skillet over medium heat for 3 minutes, or until heated through. To reheat the sauce, place in a saucepan over medium heat for 3 minutes, or until heated through.

(per serving):
calories **591** • fat **46g** • protein **37g** • carbs **5g** • fiber **2g**

Shredded
BBQ Chicken

EASY

yield: 6 servings • prep time: 5 minutes • cook time: 20 minutes (Instant Pot) or 4 hours (slow cooker)

Before I started eating keto, I always loved a shredded BBQ chicken sandwich from Famous Dave's restaurant. Now I like to make it at home! Using frozen chicken breasts means that you don't have to plan ahead and have the chicken thawed. Smoked salt gives it an extra smoky flavor, but you can use regular salt if you prefer. This chicken is so delicious left over, I suggest making extra for easy meals on busy evenings.

Coconut oil, for greasing

6 (6-ounce) frozen boneless, skinless chicken breasts

½ cup diced onions

2 cups tomato sauce

¼ cup confectioners'-style erythritol or equivalent amount of liquid or powdered sweetener (see page 77)

1 tablespoon apple cider vinegar

1 teaspoon liquid smoke

1 teaspoon smoked salt or fine sea salt

Boston leaf lettuce or Sandwich Buns (page 384), for serving (optional)

1. Make the BBQ chicken using either of the following methods:

   INSTANT POT METHOD: Grease a 6-quart Instant Pot with coconut oil. Place the chicken, onions, tomato sauce, sweetener, vinegar, liquid smoke, and smoked salt in the prepared pot. Seal the lid, press Pressure Cook or Manual, and set the timer for 20 minutes. Once finished, press Quick Release. Open the lid and shred the chicken with two forks.

   SLOW COOKER METHOD: Grease a 6-quart slow cooker with coconut oil. Place the chicken, onions, tomato sauce, sweetener, vinegar, liquid smoke, and smoked salt in the prepared slow cooker. Cook on low for 4 hours, or until the chicken is fork-tender. Shred the meat with two forks.

2. Serve the chicken wrapped in lettuce leaves or on buns, if desired.

3. Store extras in an airtight container in the refrigerator for up to 5 days, or freeze for up to a month. To reheat, place in an oven-safe dish in a 350°F oven for 5 minutes, or until heated through.

(per serving): calories **197** • fat **4g** • protein **36g** • carbs **6g** • fiber **1g**

Chicken
Enchiladas

EASY   option

yield: 4 servings • prep time: 6 minutes • cook time: 20 minutes (Instant Pot) or 4½ to 8½ hours (slow cooker)

I'm all about fast and easy cooking when it comes to weeknight meals. I know that many of you are pressed for time and want simple recipes—but especially when feeding kids, you need recipes that are also very tasty! If your family loves Mexican food, you must try these simple enchiladas. You can prep the sauce up to 3 days ahead and the filling up to 2 days ahead. If you really like this dish, make a triple batch and store two batches in the freezer for easy meals later.

ENCHILADA SAUCE

1 cup salsa

2 tablespoons tomato sauce

¾ cup beef or chicken broth

2 tablespoons chili powder

¼ teaspoon ground cumin

¼ teaspoon garlic powder

FILLING

2 (6-ounce) boneless, skinless chicken breasts

½ cup chicken broth

¼ cup diced onions

1 (4½-ounce) can diced green chilies, drained

TORTILLAS

12 thin slices deli chicken breast

OPTIONAL TOPPINGS

Shredded Monterey Jack or sharp cheddar cheese (omit for dairy-free)

Sour cream (omit for dairy-free)

Chopped fresh cilantro leaves

1. Make the sauce: Place all the sauce ingredients in a blender and blend until smooth. Set aside.

2. Make the filling using either of the following methods:

INSTANT POT METHOD:

Place all the filling ingredients in a 6-quart Instant Pot. Seal the lid, press the Pressure Cook or Manual button, and set the timer for 20 minutes. Once finished, allow the pressure to release naturally. Shred the chicken with two forks and remove it to a bowl; wipe the pot clean.

Pour the sauce into the Instant Pot. Lay a slice of deli chicken on a clean work surface; this will serve as your tortilla. Place a few tablespoons of the shredded chicken filling in the center of the slice of chicken. Roll up like an enchilada. Set the enchilada on top of the sauce in the Instant Pot. Repeat with the remaining filling and "tortillas." Top with cheese, if using. Seal the lid, press Pressure Cook or Manual, and set the timer for 2 minutes. Once finished, allow the pressure to release naturally.

SLOW COOKER METHOD:

Place all the filling ingredients in a 6-quart slow cooker. Cook on low for 6 to 8 hours or on high for 4 hours, or until the chicken is fork-tender. Shred the chicken with two forks and remove it to a bowl; wipe the slow cooker clean.

Pour the sauce into the slow cooker. Lay a slice of deli chicken on a clean work surface; this will serve as your tortilla. Place a few tablespoons of the shredded chicken filling in the

(per serving): calories **257** • fat **8g** • protein **36g** • carbs **9g** • fiber **2g**

busy family tip:

For those of you who do not want to have to cook anything, here's an even faster way to make the filling for this dish. Pick up an organic rotisserie chicken at the grocery store and shred the meat with two forks. Then open a can of diced green chilies and combine well with the shredded chicken. This will be your filling. But seriously, making shredded chicken in an Instant Pot or slow cooker is very easy!

center of the slice of chicken. Roll up like an enchilada. Set the enchilada on top of the sauce in the slow cooker. Repeat with the remaining filling and "tortillas." Top with cheese, if using. Cover and cook on high for 30 minutes, or until the enchiladas are heated through and the cheese is melted.

3. To serve, use a large serving spoon to dish out the enchiladas and top with sour cream and/or cilantro, if desired.

4. Store extras in an airtight container in the refrigerator for up to 5 days, or freeze for up to a month. To reheat, place in a casserole dish in a 350°F oven for 6 minutes, or until the cheese is melted and the enchiladas are heated through.

Sweet 'n' Sour Chicken Wings

EASY

yield: 8 servings • prep time: 10 minutes • cook time: 23 minutes (Instant Pot) or 3 to 4 hours (slow cooker)

My boys love chicken wings! We also love sweet 'n' sour chicken! Why not marry the two to make delicious kid-friendly chicken wings? (If you're a fan of wings, also check out Kai's Chicken Wings on page 132.) For this recipe, you'll need your oven as well as an Instant Pot or slow cooker.

SAUCE

½ cup chicken broth

⅓ cup confectioners'-style erythritol or equivalent amount of liquid or powdered sweetener (see page 77)

¼ cup tomato sauce

2 tablespoons wheat-free tamari

1 tablespoon lime juice

1 teaspoon grated fresh ginger

2 cloves garlic, smashed to a paste, or 1 head roasted garlic (page 374)

2 pounds chicken wings or drumettes

½ teaspoon fine sea salt

Sliced green onions or sesame seeds, for garnish

1. Make the sauce: Place all the ingredients in a large skillet and whisk to combine. Simmer over medium heat until reduced and thickened, about 10 minutes.

2. Meanwhile, prepare the chicken: Pat the wings dry and season with the salt. Cook the wings using either of the following methods:

   INSTANT POT METHOD: Set a trivet inside a 6-quart Instant Pot and pour in ½ cup of water. Set the wings on the trivet. Seal the lid, press Pressure Cook or Manual, and set the timer for 5 minutes. Once finished, let the pressure release naturally.

   SLOW COOKER METHOD: Place the seasoned wings in a 6-quart slow cooker. Cover and cook on low for 3 to 4 hours, until the juices run clear when the thickest part of the chicken is cut to the bone (or the internal temperature reaches 165°F).

3. Place an oven rack one notch above the center position and preheat the oven to broil. Line a rimmed baking sheet with parchment paper.

4. Brush the cooked chicken wings with the sauce. Place the wings on the lined baking sheet and broil for 6 to 8 minutes, until they are crispy on the edges. Garnish with green onions or sesame seeds and serve.

5. Store extras in an airtight container in the refrigerator for up to 5 days, or freeze for up to a month. To reheat, place in a 400°F oven for 5 minutes, or until heated through.

(per serving): calories **335** • fat **22g** • protein **31g** • carbs **1g** • fiber **0.1g**

Egg Roll in a Bowl

EASY

yield: 4 servings • prep time: 10 minutes • cook time: 6 minutes (Instant Pot) or 1 to 2 hours (slow cooker)

This simple and delicious meal tastes like the inside of an egg roll! Many of my recipe testers loved this recipe so much, they would make it often and bring it to work with them for an easy portable meal! You can use green or purple cabbage in this recipe, or a mix of both.

1 pound ground pork or chicken

1 tablespoon untoasted, cold-pressed sesame oil

1 tablespoon finely grated fresh ginger

2 teaspoons minced garlic

1 tablespoon wheat-free tamari

1 teaspoon fish sauce (optional, for umami)

6 cups finely shredded cabbage

2 tablespoons confectioners'-style erythritol or equivalent amount of liquid or powdered sweetener (see page 77)

¼ cup chopped green onions, for garnish

1. Make the egg roll mixture using either of the following methods:

   INSTANT POT METHOD: Place the ground pork, sesame oil, ginger, garlic, tamari, and fish sauce in a 6-quart Instant Pot. Press Sauté and cook, crumbling the meat with a wooden spoon, until it is almost cooked through, about 5 minutes. Stir in the cabbage. Seal the lid, press Manual, and set the timer for 1 minute. Once finished, press Quick Release. Stir in the sweetener.

   SLOW COOKER METHOD: Place the ground pork, sesame oil, garlic, ginger, tamari, and fish sauce in a large skillet over medium-high heat. Cook, crumbling the meat with a wooden spoon, until it is almost cooked through, about 5 minutes. Place the cabbage in a 6-quart slow cooker. Top with the pork mixture. Cover and cook on low for 2 hours or on high for 1 hour, or until the cabbage is very soft. Stir in the sweetener.

2. To serve, divide the egg roll mixture among 4 bowls or plates and garnish with the green onions.

3. Store extras in an airtight container in the refrigerator for up to 5 days, or freeze for up to a month. To reheat, place in a skillet over medium heat, stirring occasionally, for 5 minutes, or until heated through.

(per serving): calories **364** • fat **27g** • protein **32g** • carbs **9g** • fiber **3g**

chapter 8:
holiday fun

Fluffy Bunny Scrambled Eggs / 254

Valentine's Day Breakfast / 256

Christmas Tomato Soup with Grilled Cheese Stars and Trees / 258

Zombie Spaghetti and Eyeballs / 260

Christmas Tree Pizza / 262

Heart-Shaped Eggs / 264

Valentine Deviled Eggs / 266

Holiday Tree Cheese Ball / 268

Halloween Spooky Skeleton with BBQ Riblets / 270

Taco Meatball Holiday Tree / 272

Spooky Breadstick Fingers / 274

Easy Red, White, and Blueberry Sundaes / 276

Strawberry Cheesecake Santas / 278

Holiday Jigglers / 280

Bombdiggity Pops / 282

Shamrock Shake Gummies / 284

Pumpkin Pie Gummies / 286

Valentine's Day Muffin Pan Ice Cream Cakes / 288

Fluffy Bunny
Scrambled Eggs

EASY

yield: 4 servings • prep time: 5 minutes • cook time: 17 minutes

No matter what the holiday is, I like to make simple foods such as scrambled eggs fit the holiday theme. On Easter, I always make these Fluffy Bunny Scrambled Eggs. I like to whip my eggs in a blender before scrambling them to make them extra light and fluffy! You can skip that step and just beat the eggs with a fork if you prefer.

4 slices bacon (pork or beef), cut in half lengthwise

8 large eggs

1 tablespoon unsalted butter

Fine sea salt

2 tablespoons cream cheese, softened

8 small blueberries

4 raspberries

1 string cheese stick

1. Bake the bacon (see page 90) and set aside.

2. While the bacon cooks, make the scrambled eggs. Crack the eggs into a blender and puree until fluffy (or place in a large bowl and use an immersion blender to puree until fluffy). Heat a large nonstick skillet over medium heat. Add the butter and swirl to coat the pan. Once melted, pour in the eggs. Cook, gently scrambling the eggs, until they are set and creamy, about 4 minutes. Season with salt. Remove from the heat and divide evenly among 4 plates.

3. Cut the cream cheese into 8 equal-sized pieces and roll each piece into a 1-inch ball, then flatten it slightly.

4. Shape the eggs into 3-inch circles for the bunny faces. Place 2 half-slices of cooked bacon on top of each circle for ears. In the middle of each face, place 2 discs of cream cheese for eyes, then place the blueberries in the center of the cream cheese discs for pupils. Center a raspberry under the eyes for the nose. Pull the string cheese into thin strips and cut into 3-inch-long whiskers. Place 3 whiskers on each side of the raspberry nose. Best served fresh.

(per serving):
calories **256** • fat **20g** • protein **17g** • carbs **2g** • fiber **0.3g**

Valentine's Day
Breakfast

EASY

yield: 2 servings • prep time: 5 minutes (not including time to make chaffle sandwiches) • cook time: 19 minutes

For this cute breakfast, you will need a heart-shaped cookie cutter. If you do not have one, you can use a sharp knife to cut the over-easy eggs into heart shapes. For the photo, I also made chaffles using a heart-shaped mini waffle maker, which cost less than $10, but if you don't have one of those, either, you can cut the chaffles into heart shapes with the knife.

4 slices bacon (pork or beef)

6 strawberries

1 teaspoon unsalted butter

4 large eggs

Fine sea salt

2 Strawberry Shortcake Chaffle Sandwiches (page 350)

SPECIAL EQUIPMENT:

Heart-shaped cookie cutter

Mini waffle maker

1. Preheat the oven to 400°F. Line a rimmed baking sheet with parchment paper.

2. Place a slice of bacon on the prepared baking sheet and form into a heart shape. Repeat with the remaining slices. Place another baking sheet on top of the bacon hearts to keep the bacon from curling up. Bake for 15 minutes, or until cooked to your liking.

3. Meanwhile, use a sharp knife to cut around the top of a strawberry as if you were carving a jack-o-lantern. Cut the strawberry in half lengthwise. Cut the top of each strawberry half to make a V-shape to form a heart-shaped strawberry. Repeat with the remaining strawberries.

4. To make the eggs, melt the butter in a large nonstick skillet over medium heat. Crack the eggs into the skillet without breaking the yolks. Sprinkle with salt. Cook until the whites are just set and the yolks are soft, about 4 minutes. Remove the eggs from the skillet and place on a cutting board. Use a heart-shaped cookie cutter to cut the eggs into hearts.

5. Place 2 eggs on each plate with a chaffle sandwich, 2 bacon hearts, and 6 heart-shaped strawberries. Best served fresh.

(per serving):
calories **671** • fat **54g** • protein **40g** • carbs **7g** • fiber **1g**

Christmas Tomato Soup
with Grilled Cheese Stars and Trees

MEDIUM   option

yield: 8 servings • prep time: 15 minutes • cook time: 15 minutes

My baby brother Vince's favorite childhood lunch was a grilled cheese sandwich made with Wonder Bread served with Campbell's tomato soup. We both adored it. I love this play on our favorite childhood lunch because it tastes just as amazing and is sugar-free!

Halloumi is a firm and slightly rubbery cheese that is on the salty side. I love cutting it into cute shapes. This cheese is extra special because you can grill or fry it. When heated, Halloumi gets creamy, and the saltiness declines into a robust savory morsel. It serves as the perfect "grilled cheese sandwich" without bread! If you can't find Halloumi, you can use cheddar cheese, but do not heat it. Cut the cheddar into star or tree shapes with a cookie cutter and serve with the hot soup.

SOUP

1 tablespoon unsalted butter or coconut oil

¼ cup finely chopped onions

1 teaspoon minced garlic, or ½ head roasted garlic (page 374)

1 cup chicken broth (or vegetable broth for vegetarian), divided

1 (14½-ounce) can diced tomatoes, or 1 large tomato, diced, with juices

1½ cups tomato sauce

½ teaspoon stevia glycerite, or more to taste

1½ teaspoons fine sea salt

2 ounces cheddar cheese slices, cut into star shapes, for garnish

AVOCADO CREAM

2 medium ripe avocados, peeled, halved, and pitted

1 cup sour cream or plain low-carb yogurt

1 clove raw or roasted garlic (page 374)

¼ teaspoon fine sea salt

GRILLED CHEESE

8 ounces Halloumi cheese, cut into ¼-inch-thick slices and then into star and tree shapes (see note above)

1 tablespoon melted unsalted butter

1. Make the soup: Heat the butter in a large saucepan over medium heat. Add the onions and garlic and cook, stirring often, until soft, about 4 minutes. Whisk in the broth, tomatoes with juices, tomato sauce, stevia, and ½ teaspoon of the salt. Simmer for 5 minutes, stirring occasionally, to allow the flavors to meld; do not allow the soup to come to a boil. Remove the pan from the heat and puree the soup with an immersion blender until smooth. Taste and adjust the salt and/or sweetness to your liking. Return the pan to low heat and cover to keep warm while you prepare the other components.

2. Make the avocado cream: Place the avocados, sour cream, garlic, and salt in a blender or food processor and puree until smooth. Taste and adjust the seasoning to your liking. Transfer the mixture to a resealable plastic bag. Set aside.

(per serving):
calories **287** • fat **24g** • protein **10g** • carbs **10g** • fiber **4g**

3. Make the grilled cheese: Preheat a medium skillet, grill pan, or panini maker to medium-high heat. Brush both sides of the cheese shapes with the butter. Place in the hot pan and cook for about 3 minutes per side, until golden brown (and with grill marks if using a grill pan or panini maker).

4. To serve, place 1 cup of soup in a bowl. Cut a ¼-inch hole in a corner of the plastic bag with the avocado cream. Pipe a Christmas tree shape on top of the soup. (Tip: If, like me, you are not the best artist, use a large Christmas tree–shaped cookie cutter to outline the avocado cream.) Top each tree with a cheddar cheese star. Serve the soup with the grilled cheese.

5. Store extra soup and grilled cheese in separate airtight containers in the refrigerator for up to 4 days. To reheat the soup, place it in a pot over medium heat for 3 minutes, or until heated through. Reheat the grilled cheese on the panini maker or grill pan.

Zombie Spaghetti and Eyeballs

MEDIUM   option

yield: 4 servings (3 meatballs per serving) • prep time: 8 minutes • cook time: 35 minutes

Even if you don't like mushrooms, do not leave them out of this recipe! Sure, the meatballs will still turn out if you do not add the mushrooms; however, mushrooms add umami, which is the special flavor that makes food extra delicious. They also add moisture. Check out this mushroom testimonial:

"I have a new favorite. According to Maria, adding diced mushrooms to your meatballs makes them extra delicious since they have 'umami.' Umami is the Japanese word for savory. Using certain foods with umami greatly enhances flavor. All I can tell you is it really does make them taste so much better! You do not taste the mushrooms, but the flavor of the meatballs, in my opinion, goes up dramatically!!!" —Christy

1 pound ground beef

1 cup finely chopped mushrooms (about 8 ounces)

1½ cups marinara sauce, homemade (page 372) or store-bought, divided

½ cup grated Parmesan cheese (omit for dairy-free)

¼ cup chopped onions

1 clove garlic, minced, or ½ head roasted garlic (page 374)

1 large egg

1 tablespoon Italian seasoning

½ teaspoon fine sea salt

⅛ teaspoon ground black pepper

8 sliced black olives

1 (1-ounce) mozzarella cheese stick, cut into ¼-inch rounds (or 1 hard-boiled egg white for dairy-free)

2 medium zucchini, spiral-sliced into thin noodles, or 12 ounces thinly sliced deli turkey breast, cut into thin noodles

Sliced fresh oregano or basil leaves, for garnish

SPECIAL EQUIPMENT:

Drinking straw

1. Preheat the oven to 375°F.

2. Make the meatballs: In a large bowl, use your hands to combine the ground beef, mushrooms, ½ cup of the marinara sauce, the Parmesan cheese, onions, garlic, egg, Italian seasoning, salt, and pepper. The mixture should be very moist but still able to hold its shape when rolled into balls. Form the mixture into 2¼-inch meatballs. Arrange the meatballs in a single layer on a rimmed baking sheet. Bake for 35 minutes, turning occasionally, until evenly browned.

3. While the meatballs are in the oven, make the eyeballs: Use a straw to cut small round pupils from the black olives and to poke a hole in the center of each string cheese round. Insert the olive pupil into the string cheese hole.

4. Remove the meatballs from the oven and let cool a little. Meanwhile, prepare the zucchini noodles, if using, by placing them in a colander over a sink. Sprinkle with 2 teaspoons

(per serving):
calories **409** • fat **27g** • protein **30g** • carbs **9g** • fiber **2g**

busy family tip:

To save time, I often use Rao's marinara sauce when making this recipe. Use a medium cookie scoop to make uniform meatballs. If you make larger meatballs, the baking time will increase.

of salt. Let stand for at least 5 minutes and allow the excess moisture to drain. Press gently to remove more moisture.

5. Warm the remaining marinara sauce in a small saucepan over medium heat.

6. Once the meatballs have cooled slightly, divide the zoodles among 4 plates. Top with the warmed marinara sauce and the meatballs. Place 2 eyeballs on top of each meatball. Garnish with fresh oregano.

7. Store extra meatballs in an airtight container in the refrigerator for up to 4 days, or freeze for up to 2 months. To reheat, place in a preheated 350°F oven for 3 minutes, or until heated through.

Christmas Tree
Pizza

MEDIUM · option · option

yield: 1 pizza (8 servings) • prep time: 10 minutes • cook time: 15 minutes

I had the great opportunity to speak in Russia in November 2019 about the ketogenic diet and epilepsy. After my speech, I made my healthy pizza for a small group of VIPs. I made the pizza into a Christmas tree shape, and the group loved how fun and delicious the pizza was!

CRUST

1¾ cups shredded mozzarella cheese

2 tablespoons cream cheese

¾ cup pork panko or blanched almond flour

1 large egg

⅛ teaspoon fine sea salt

Avocado or olive oil, for brushing (optional)

TOPPINGS

1 cup sugar-free pizza sauce, homemade (page 370) or store-bought

1 cup shredded mozzarella cheese

Sliced cherry tomatoes

Thinly sliced red bell pepper

1 slice Canadian bacon, cut into a large star shape (use a slice of cheese for vegetarian)

Fresh basil leaves, for garnish (optional)

1. If you have a pizza stone, place it in the oven. Preheat the oven to 425°F. Grease a piece of parchment paper.

2. To make the dough for the crust, place the mozzarella and cream cheese in a heat-safe bowl and microwave for 1 to 2 minutes, until the cheese is entirely melted. Stir well. Add the pork panko, egg, and salt and combine well using a hand mixer.

3. Put the dough on the greased parchment paper and form it into a Christmas tree shape (or a heart shape for Valentine's Day). Brush with avocado or olive oil for an extra crispy crust.

4. If using a pizza stone, slide the crust on the parchment onto the hot pizza stone in the oven. Otherwise, place the crust on a rimmed baking sheet. Par-bake the crust for 5 minutes, or until it starts to get a little golden.

5. Remove the par-baked crust from the oven and top with the sauce and cheese. Place the tomato slices around the tree to look like ornaments. Lay the bell pepper slices along the tree to look like garland. Top the pizza tree with the Canadian bacon star.

6. Bake the topped pizza for 8 minutes, or until the cheese starts to brown. Garnish with basil leaves, if desired.

7. Store extras in an airtight container in the refrigerator for up to 5 days, or freeze for up to a month.

(per serving): calories **243** • fat **17g** • protein **22g** • carbs **1g** • fiber **0.3g**

Heart-Shaped Eggs

EASY

yield: 4 servings • prep time: 10 minutes • cook time: 11 minutes

Trying to make Valentine's Day special without sugar? How about some cute healthy eggs? My sister-in-law showed me this trick for making heart-shaped eggs. All you have to do is hard-boil some eggs, peel them, and, while they are still very warm, place each one in a V-shaped piece of cardboard with a chopstick over the top and secure with a rubber band. Allow to cool in the fridge and ta-da! So cute! Use these heart-shaped eggs to make Valentine Deviled Eggs (page 266).

4 large eggs

SPECIAL EQUIPMENT:

4 (2½-inch) squares of clean cardboard

4 chopsticks

4 rubber bands

1. Place the eggs in a medium saucepan and cover with cold water. Bring to a boil, then immediately cover the pan and remove it from the heat. Allow the eggs to cook in the hot water for 11 minutes. After 11 minutes, drain the water and rinse the eggs with very cold water for a minute or two to stop the cooking process. Peel the boiled eggs.

2. Bend each piece of cardboard to make a "V" shape. Place one peeled egg in the "V" of each cardboard. Place a chopstick on the egg that sticks out from the cardboard. Loop the rubber band around the cardboard to secure the chopstick onto the egg so it presses into the egg to make a heart shape.

3. Set the eggs in the fridge to chill for 30 minutes. Remove the eggs from the cardboard and use to make Valentine Deviled Eggs (page 266) or cut into ¼-inch-thick heart-shaped slices.

(per serving):
calories **74** • fat **5g** • protein **6g** • carbs **0.4g** • fiber **0g**

Valentine
Deviled Eggs

MEDIUM

yield: 6 servings (4 egg halves per serving) • prep time: 30 minutes
(not including time to cook eggs)

Watermelon radishes are a striking and lovely vegetable. They can be hard
to find, however. I buy them at the local farmers market during the summer
months here in Wisconsin. If you can't find them, you can omit them from the
garnish.

1 cup sliced red onions

1 cup apple cider vinegar

12 Heart-Shaped Eggs
(page 264)

½ cup mayonnaise, homemade
(page 365) or store-bought

2 teaspoons prepared yellow
mustard

½ teaspoon fine sea salt

FOR GARNISH

Fresh dill sprigs

Watermelon radishes, thinly
sliced and then cut into small
heart shapes

1. Place the red onions and vinegar in a blender and puree until
    smooth. Place the heart-shaped boiled eggs in the vinegar
    mixture. The red onion will dye the outsides of the eggs pink.
    Allow to sit for 20 minutes, or until the pink color is to your
    liking.

2. Remove the eggs from the vinegar mixture and pat dry. Cut
    the eggs in half lengthwise.

3. Remove the egg yolks and place them in a bowl. Mash the
    yolks with a fork until they have the texture of very fine
    crumbles. Add the mayonnaise, mustard, and salt and mix
    until evenly combined.

4. Pipe the yolk mixture into the egg white halves. Garnish with
    fresh dill sprigs and watermelon radish hearts.

5. Store extras in an airtight container in the refrigerator for up
    to 3 days.

(per serving):
calories **292** • fat **25g** • protein **13g** • carbs **3g** • fiber **0.4g**

Holiday Tree
Cheese Ball

EASY

yield: 8 servings • prep time: 5 minutes, plus 1 hour to chill • cook time: 15 minutes

Funny story: to cut the bell pepper stars for this holiday-themed cheese ball, I used the star-shaped pieces from the popular family game Perfection. Sometimes parents need to get creative!

CHEESE BALL

1 (8-ounce) package cream cheese, softened

½ cup thick salsa

1 cup shredded pepper jack or sharp cheddar cheese

COATING

1 red bell pepper

1 thin slice cheddar cheese

⅓ cup chopped fresh cilantro

SERVING SUGGESTIONS

Sliced red and green bell peppers

Celery sticks

Cucumber slices

Parmesan crostini

1. Make the cheese ball: Place the cream cheese, salsa, and shredded cheese in a large bowl and stir until smooth and well combined. Form into a ball, wrap in parchment paper, and place in the refrigerator for 1 hour to set.

2. Meanwhile, use a tiny star-shaped cookie cutter and cut about 30 stars out of the red bell pepper. First, cut the pepper into ½-inch slices. Then lay the slices flat and cut out the stars. Cut a star out of the slice of cheese for the top of the tree. Alternatively, you can use a sharp knife to cut the pepper and cheese into diamond shapes.

3. Place the chilled cheese ball on a serving tray and form it into a tree shape. Press the chopped cilantro all over the tree, then decorate with the bell pepper stars and top with the cheddar cheese star. Serve with red and green bell pepper slices or other dippers of choice. Store extras in an airtight container in the refrigerator for up to 5 days.

(per serving):
calories **155** • fat **13g** • protein **5g** • carbs **2g** • fiber **0g**

Halloween Spooky Skeleton with BBQ Riblets

MEDIUM

yield: 4 servings • prep time: 10 minutes • cook time: 50 minutes or about 3 hours, depending on method

My son Kai's birthday is in October, and his favorite holiday is Halloween. Often, when we think of Halloween, our minds automatically go to candy and chocolate. My family celebrates Halloween without the sugar, and so can yours! We go a little crazy with decorations and fun, healthy Halloween food. I hope that when my boys grow up, they remember the Halloween treats that I made for them!

1 rack baby back ribs

1 cup tomato sauce

2 tablespoons apple cider vinegar

½ teaspoon fine sea salt

2 tablespoons confectioners'-style erythritol or equivalent amount of liquid or powdered sweetener (see page 77)

1 pork or beef rope sausage spiral, about 12 ounces

½ red bell pepper, stem, seeds, and ribs removed

1 (3-ounce) package prosciutto

1 (3-ounce) package salami

3 pimento-stuffed olives

SPECIAL EQUIPMENT:
1 plastic skeleton head

1. Place the ribs in a 6-quart Instant Pot or slow cooker. Add the tomato sauce, vinegar, sweetener, and salt. Stir to coat the ribs. If using an Instant Pot, seal the lid, press Pressure Cook or Manual, and set the timer for 25 minutes. Once finished, let the pressure release naturally for 10 minutes, then turn the valve to venting for a quick release. If using a slow cooker, cover and cook on high for 2 to 3 hours, until the ribs are fork-tender.

2. Remove the ribs from the pot or slow cooker. Slice into individual riblets and set aside.

3. Preheat the oven to 475°F.

4. Place the bell pepper cut side down on a rimmed baking sheet lined with parchment paper. Place in the oven to roast for 15 minutes, or until charred and soft.

5. Meanwhile, bring a pot of water to a boil. Add the sausage and boil for 8 minutes, or until cooked through. Remove the sausage from the water.

6. Finish the sausage by placing it on the rimmed baking sheet with the bell pepper and roasting in the oven to crisp the skin for 2 minutes on each side.

7. Place the riblets on a large serving platter in a manner resembling a skeleton body. Place the charred bell pepper in the center of the ribs to represent the heart. Place the cooked sausage below the heart to replicate the intestines.

8. Wrap the prosciutto around the skeleton face. Wrap the salami around the brain area. Set the head at the top of the body and place the olives in the eye sockets and nose. Serve warm!

(per serving):
calories **654** • fat **49g** • protein **50g** • carbs **4g** • fiber **1g**

Taco Meatball
Holiday Tree

MEDIUM **option**   yield: 4 servings • prep time: 5 minutes • cook time: 15 minutes

If your family loves these taco meatballs like mine does—whether you present them as a festive holiday tree or serve them as is—make a triple batch and store the unbaked meatballs in the freezer. All you have to do in anticipation of a busy night is thaw the frozen meatballs in the refrigerator, place on a rimmed baking sheet, and bake.

TACO MEATBALLS

2 pounds ground beef

1 cup salsa

1 large egg

2 tablespoons Taco Seasoning (page 388)

1 teaspoon fine sea salt

FOR GARNISH/SERVING

10 Boston leaf or Bibb lettuce leaves

2 cups salsa

1 thin slice cheddar cheese (omit for dairy-free)

Shredded cheddar cheese (omit for dairy-free)

Guacamole (page 376) (optional)

Fresh cilantro leaves

1. Preheat the oven to 375°F.

2. Make the meatballs: Place the ground beef, salsa, egg, taco seasoning, and salt in a large bowl. Use your hands to combine the ingredients well, then shape the mixture into 1-inch meatballs and place on a rimmed baking sheet. Bake the meatballs for 15 to 20 minutes, until cooked through and browned.

3. Meanwhile, arrange the lettuce leaves in a tree shape on a large white serving platter, placing 4 leaves at the bottom of the tray, followed by 3 leaves, then 2, then 1 at the top. Place the salsa in a small bowl for dipping at the bottom of the lettuce tree for the tree stand.

4. Use a star-shaped cookie cutter to cut a star out of the slice of cheese and place the star at the top of the lettuce tree.

5. Once the meatballs are done, place 1 or 2 meatballs in each lettuce cup, then garnish with shredded cheese, guacamole, and/or fresh cilantro.

6. Store extra meatballs in an airtight container in the refrigerator for up to 4 days, or freeze for up to a month.

(per serving):
calories **573** • fat **38g** • protein **46g** • carbs **8g** • fiber **0.5g**

Spooky
Breadstick Fingers

MEDIUM   option

yield: 4 servings • prep time: 10 minutes (not including time to make dough) • cook time: 30 minutes

I made my easy bun recipe into spooky fingers for Halloween, and my boys loved dipping them into pizza sauce to look like blood—extra creepy!

1 batch Sandwich Buns dough (page 384)

12 whole almonds

1¼ cups sugar-free pizza sauce, homemade (page 370) or store-bought

1. Preheat the oven to 325°F. Line a rimmed baking sheet with parchment paper.

2. Make the breadstick fingers: Divide the dough into 12 equal-sized pieces. Roll each piece into a 5-inch-long, ½-inch-wide finger (they will puff up in the oven). Place the fingers about 2 inches apart on the prepared baking sheet. Use a sharp knife to make 2 slits near the center of each finger for knuckles that are about ¼ inch deep. Place an almond on one end of each finger with the pointy end of the almond facing out. Press the almond into the dough to secure it.

3. Bake the fingers for 15 to 20 minutes, or until cooked through. Remove from the oven and allow to cool for a few minutes; the almonds will be extra hot on the inside.

4. While the breadstick fingers are cooling, warm the pizza sauce in a small saucepan over medium heat, about 3 minutes.

5. Serve the breadsticks with the warmed pizza sauce. Store extra breadsticks in an airtight container in the refrigerator for up to 4 days, or freeze for up to a month. To reheat, place in a 325°F oven for 4 minutes, or until heated through, or serve cold.

(per serving):
calories **124** • fat **9g** • protein **8g** • carbs **5g** • fiber **2g**

Easy Red, White, and Blueberry Sundaes

EASY option

yield: 4 servings • prep time: 10 minutes • cook time: 30 minutes

I love using my whipped cream dispenser for recipes like this one. If you have a dispenser, just fill it with heavy cream up to the fill line. Add the sweetener and seal following the manufacturer's directions. Shake and use between the strawberry and blueberry layers.

6 large strawberries, sliced ¼ inch thick

1 cup heavy cream (or coconut cream for dairy-free)

2 tablespoons confectioners'-style erythritol or equivalent amount of liquid or powdered sweetener (see page 77)

1 cup blueberries

1. If not using a whipped cream dispenser, chill a large metal bowl for about 30 minutes.

2. Divide the sliced strawberries evenly among 4 sundae glasses.

3. If not using a whipped cream dispenser, place the heavy cream in the chilled bowl and use a hand mixer to whip until soft peaks form. Add the sweetener and whip until medium peaks form.

4. Divide the whipped cream evenly between the sundae glasses. Top with the blueberries and decorate each sundae with a paper flag, if desired.

5. Store extras covered in the refrigerator for up to 4 days.

(per serving):
calories **230** • fat **23g** • protein **2g** • carbs **9g** • fiber **1g**

Strawberry Cheesecake Santas

EASY option option

yield: 24 Santas (2 per serving) • prep time: 15 minutes

These sugar-free cheesecake Santas are really delicious! They are a little tedious for me because I'm not the best artist; however, these Santas are a fun Christmas food craft to make with your kids. As the boys and I gathered in the kitchen making these Santas, we talked about life, and we had a lot of laughs!

24 large strawberries

1 (8-ounce) package cream cheese (or Kite Hill brand cream cheese–style spread for dairy-free), softened

¼ cup confectioners'-style erythritol, or a few drops of stevia glycerite

1 teaspoon vanilla extract

CHOCOLATE EYES AND BUTTONS

1 tablespoon coconut oil or unsalted butter, softened

1½ teaspoons unsweetened cocoa powder

1½ teaspoons confectioners'-style erythritol, or a few drops of stevia glycerite

1. Using a sharp knife, slice the stems off the strawberries. Cut as evenly as possible because the stem end of the strawberry will serve as the base of the Santa. Set aside.

2. Cut off the top third of each strawberry, which will be the Santa hat. Set the tops aside.

3. In a medium bowl, stir together the warmed cream cheese, sweetener, and vanilla until well combined. Taste and adjust the sweetness to your liking. Transfer the cream cheese mixture to a resealable plastic bag and cut a ½-inch hole in one corner of the bag.

4. Place the stem end of the sliced strawberry facedown as the base. Top the strawberry with the cream cheese mixture, then the strawberry hats. Repeat with the remaining strawberries and cream cheese mixture, reserving some of the cream cheese mixture for decoration.

5. Snip a ⅛-inch hole in the opposite corner of the plastic bag. Use this end to make Santa's scarf by going around the lower part of his face, dot 2 dots on the base for jacket buttons, and squirt a dollop on the top of his hat. Repeat with the remaining Santas.

6. Place the softened coconut oil, cocoa powder, and sweetener in a small bowl. Stir well. Transfer the chocolate mixture to a resealable plastic bag. Cut a tiny hole in one corner of the bag. Carefully pipe 2 eyes on each cream cheese face and 2 dots on top of the cream cheese jacket buttons.

7. Store extras in an airtight container in the refrigerator for up to 3 days.

(per serving):
calories **174** • fat **14g** • protein **3g** • carbs **5g** • fiber **1g**

Holiday
Jigglers

EASY

yield: 8 servings • prep time: 5 minutes, plus 3 hours to chill

I had the great opportunity to speak at the Low Carb Denver conference one year. One of the doctors who presented talked about how easy the keto diet can be and said that if you need a low-carb dessert, you can just make a package of sugar-free Jell-O. I couldn't believe my ears! A medical doctor was recommending a store-bought "food" filled with artificial dye, aspartame, and other chemicals? This fun recipe is super easy, yet so much healthier.

1 tablespoon plus 1 teaspoon unflavored gelatin

1 cup cold water

1 cup boiling water

3 tea bags (blueberry, chai, peach, lemon, pomegranate, or other flavor of choice)

2 tablespoons confectioners'-style erythritol, or a few drops of stevia glycerite

1 teaspoon blueberry, pineapple, lemon, or strawberry extract (optional)

1 teaspoon citric acid, or more for a more intense sour taste

SPECIAL EQUIPMENT (OPTIONAL):

Silicone gummy mold

1. Have on hand a silicone gummy mold, or line an 8-inch square baking dish with parchment paper and set aside.

2. Soak the gelatin in the cold water for a few minutes to soften it.

3. Meanwhile, drop the tea bags into the boiling water and let steep for 3 to 5 minutes. Remove the tea bags, squeeze out the water, and add the gelatin mixture to the hot tea. Add the remaining ingredients and stir until thoroughly blended.

4. Pour the mixture into the gummy mold or prepared baking dish. Refrigerate until set, about 3 hours. If you used a baking dish, cut the gummy into the desired shapes using cookie cutters or a knife and enjoy.

(per serving):
calories **4** • fat **0g** • protein **1g** • carbs **0g** • fiber **0g**

Bombdiggity Pops

EASY   option

yield: 8 pops (1 per serving) • prep time: 10 minutes, plus 3 hours 40 minutes to chill

These ice pops—a riff on the classic red, white, and blue Bomb Pop—are a great way to sneak in healthy protein from the yogurt! I use Two Good brand yogurt, which is the lowest in carbs and sugar. Sweetening the pops with allulose keeps them soft.

1 cup fresh or frozen strawberries or raspberries

¾ cup powdered allulose, divided

Fine sea salt

2 cups plain low-carb yogurt (or coconut cream for dairy-free)

1 cup fresh or frozen blueberries

SPECIAL EQUIPMENT:

8 star-shaped ice pop molds

1. Place the strawberries, ¼ cup of the sweetener, and a tiny pinch of salt in a blender. Puree until smooth. Taste and adjust the sweetness to your liking. Transfer the mixture to the ice pop molds. Place in the freezer to set for 20 minutes. Rinse the blender clean.

2. Place the yogurt in a medium bowl and add ¼ cup of the sweetener and a pinch of salt. Stir well to combine. Taste and adjust the sweetness to your liking.

3. Once the strawberry layer is chilled, divide the yogurt evenly among the molds. Place in the freezer to set for another 20 minutes.

4. Place the blueberries, the remaining ¼ cup of sweetener, and a tiny pinch of salt in the blender. Puree until smooth. Taste and adjust the sweetness to your liking. Once the yogurt layer is chilled, divide the blueberry mixture evenly among the molds. Place in the freezer to set for another 3 hours, or until frozen.

5. Store extras in the freezer for up to 1 month.

(per serving):
calories 37 • fat 1g • protein 3g • carbs 5g • fiber 1g

tips:

Leave ¼ inch of space at the top of the ice pop molds to allow for expansion. If the pops expand too much, they become difficult to remove from the molds and can make a mess in your freezer.

Feel free to layer the colors as you like. For example, you could do a thin layer of red, a thin layer of white, a thin layer of red, a thin layer of white, and a thicker layer of blue. Mix it up as you prefer!

If you do not have ice pop molds, you can use paper cups and insert wood craft sticks after you fill the cups with the strawberry mixture.

Shamrock Shake
Gummies

EASY   option   option

yield: 4 servings • prep time: 4 minutes, plus 3 hours to set • cook time: 1 minute

If you don't have a gummy mold, you can pour the mixture into a parchment-lined baking dish and cut it into 1-inch squares.

1⅓ cups unsweetened almond milk (or heavy cream for nut-free)

3 tablespoons confectioners'-style erythritol or equivalent amount of liquid or powdered sweetener (see page 77)

2 tablespoons unflavored gelatin

1 medium ripe avocado, halved, peeled, and pitted

½ teaspoon mint extract

½ teaspoon vanilla extract

⅛ teaspoon fine sea salt

¼ cup vanilla-flavored collagen peptides (optional)

SPECIAL EQUIPMENT:

4-leaf clover gummy mold

1. Place the almond milk and sweetener in a small saucepan. Whisk in the gelatin and allow to soften for a minute. Heat over medium-high heat until the mixture is simmering and the gelatin has dissolved, 1 to 2 minutes. Remove from the heat.

2. Add the avocado, extracts, and salt to the pan. Use an immersion blender to puree until smooth (or transfer the gummy mixture to a countertop blender to puree). Taste and adjust the sweetness to your liking.

3. Set the gummy mold on a rimmed baking sheet. Gently pour the mixture into the gummy mold. Place the sheet in the fridge for 3 hours or overnight to set, then remove the gummies from the mold and enjoy. Store extras in an airtight container in the refrigerator for up to 5 days.

(per serving):
calories **139** • fat **8g** • protein **13g** • carbs **5g** • fiber **4g**

Pumpkin Pie
Gummies

EASY   option   option

yield: 4 servings • prep time: 4 minutes, plus 2 hours to set •
cook time: 1 minute

I always loved a gummy bear, gummy worm, or any type of gummy candy, so I thought to put a twist on a sugar-free gummy and make a pumpkin pie gummy recipe! These cute pumpkins are perfect for Halloween or Thanksgiving.

¼ cup unsweetened almond milk (or heavy cream for nut-free)

2 tablespoons unflavored gelatin

¼ cup pumpkin puree

2 tablespoons confectioners'-style erythritol or equivalent amount of liquid or powdered sweetener (see page 77)

½ teaspoon pumpkin pie spice

½ teaspoon vanilla extract

SPECIAL EQUIPMENT:

Small pumpkin-shaped cookie cutter

1. Line an 8-inch square baking dish with parchment paper. Set aside.

2. Place the almond milk in a small saucepan (or a microwave-safe cup). Add the gelatin and whisk until dissolved. Bring to a boil over high heat while whisking, about 2 minutes, then remove from the heat (or microwave on high for 40 seconds, or until boiling). Whisk in the pumpkin puree, sweetener, pumpkin pie spice, and vanilla. Taste and adjust the sweetness to your liking.

3. Pour the mixture into the prepared baking dish. Place in the refrigerator until set, about 2 hours or overnight. The longer it sits, the more it will firm up. Use a pumpkin-shaped cookie cutter to cut out shapes or use a knife to cut into 1-inch squares.

4. Store extras in an airtight container in the refrigerator for up to 5 days.

(per serving):
calories **23** • fat **0.2g** • protein **3g** • carbs **1g** • fiber **0.4g**

Valentine's Day Muffin Pan
Ice Cream Cakes

EASY

yield: 24 cakes (1 per serving) • prep time: 10 minutes, plus 15 minutes for ice cream to soften and 1 hour to chill (not including time to make ice cream, donuts, or chocolate hearts)

In the process of creating a cookbook, there are times when recipes just don't turn out right. Testing recipes is a difficult job, and I feel so disappointed when they do not work. One of these difficult recipes was my Easy Blender Chocolate Donuts. They tasted good, but the first ten batches kept crumbling. One of my recipe testers, Leisa, who always sees the bright side of things, used the crumbled donuts to make little ice cream cakes with the donuts as the crust! I had to include her delicious idea in this book.

1 batch No-Churn Strawberries and Cream Ice Cream (page 318)

1 batch Easy Blender Donuts (page 104)

FOR GARNISH

Whipped cream

24 strawberries

1 batch Sugar-Free Chocolate (page 310), made in heart-shaped molds that are about 1½ inches in diameter

1. Take the ice cream out of the freezer to soften for 15 to 25 minutes. Line a standard-sized 24-well muffin pan with cupcake liners or plastic wrap.

2. Crumble the donuts and place 2 tablespoons of the crumbs in each muffin well. Press down to form the crusts for the cakes.

3. Scoop ⅔ cup of ice cream on top of each crust. Run a butter knife under warm water and smooth the tops with the warm knife. Place the muffin pan in the freezer to set for about 1 hour.

4. To serve, remove the set cakes from the freezer and dollop with a tablespoon of whipped cream. Arrange a strawberry and a chocolate heart on top of the whipped cream. Store extras in an airtight container in the freezer for up to a month.

(per serving):
calories **212** • fat **19g** • protein **4g** • carbs **7g** • fiber **3g**

chapter 9:

desserts

No-Bake Strawberry Panna Cotta / 292

Just Like Oreos Sandwich Cookies / 294

Protein Hot Chocolate / 296

Raspberries and Cream Ice Pops / 298

Extreme Chocolate Blender Birthday Cake / 300

Baseball Blender Cupcakes / 302

Chocolate Hazelnut Whoopie Pies / 304

Kai's Puppy Chow / 306

Crispy Candy / 308

Sugar-Free Chocolate Bars or Chips / 310

The BEST Chocolate Chip Cookies / 312

Marshmallows / 314

S'mores / 316

No-Churn Ice Cream Five Ways / 317

Dairy-Free No-Churn Ice Cream / 322

Raspberry Sorbet / 324

Truffles Five Ways / 326

No-Bake Strawberry
Panna Cotta

EASY option   option

yield: 6 servings • prep time: 8 minutes, plus 5 hours to chill • cook time: 2 minutes

Panna cotta is a lovely custard-like dessert, and it is one of my favorite no-bake treats. The name may sound fancy, but it's similar to a custard, only it's prepared without eggs. I made it in heart-shaped dishes to make Valentine's Day extra special.

When making panna cotta or anything else with gelatin, remember that gelatin can get rubbery if it sits too long. If you are making this dessert to consume in a day or two rather than right away, I suggest using ¼ teaspoon less gelatin.

1 cup unsweetened almond milk (or unsweetened hemp milk for nut-free)

2 teaspoons unflavored gelatin

1 pound strawberries, plus extra for garnish if desired

1 cup heavy cream (or coconut milk for dairy-free)

½ cup confectioners'-style erythritol or equivalent amount of liquid or powdered sweetener (see page 77)

1 teaspoon strawberry or vanilla extract

⅛ teaspoon fine sea salt

1. Place the milk in a medium saucepan; slowly whisk in the gelatin. Let stand until the gelatin softens, about 10 minutes.

2. Meanwhile, place the strawberries in a blender or food processor and puree until smooth. Press the puree through a fine-mesh sieve and discard the seeds.

3. To the saucepan with the gelatin mixture, add the strawberry puree, heavy cream, sweetener, extract, and salt. Whisk over medium heat just until the gelatin dissolves, about 2 minutes. Remove the pan from the heat. Divide the panna cotta among cute dessert dishes or ramekins. Cover and chill until set, at least 5 hours or overnight.

4. Serve garnished with sliced strawberries, if desired. Store extras covered in the refrigerator for up to 4 days. Do not freeze.

(per serving):
calories **163** • fat **15g** • protein **2g** • carbs **7g** • fiber **1g**

Just Like Oreos
Sandwich Cookies

HARD   option

yield: 24 cookies (1 per serving) • prep time: 12 minutes, plus time to chill • cook time: 20 minutes, plus 15 minutes to crisp in oven

This recipe is based on the classic Oreo cookie. Oreos come in various flavors throughout the year, and I love doing the same for my boys! In the fall, I add pumpkin pie spice to the filling. In the winter, I add nutmeg or peppermint extract. I serve these cookies with a glass of unsweetened almond milk for dipping—just like I had when I was a little girl!

COOKIES

2 cups blanched almond flour

¼ cup plus 2 tablespoons unsweetened cocoa powder

⅓ cup confectioners'-style erythritol or equivalent amount of powdered sweetener (see page 77)

1 teaspoon baking powder

⅛ teaspoon fine sea salt

3 tablespoons unsalted butter (or coconut oil for dairy-free), melted

1 large egg

1 teaspoon vanilla extract

FILLING

6 tablespoons (¾ stick) unsalted butter (or coconut oil for dairy-free), softened

2 ounces cream cheese (¼ cup) (or Kite Hill brand cream cheese–style spread for dairy-free), softened

2 tablespoons heavy cream (or unsweetened coconut or almond milk for dairy-free), room temperature

⅓ cup confectioners'-style erythritol or equivalent amount of liquid or powdered sweetener (see page 77)

⅛ teaspoon fine sea salt

½ teaspoon flavored extract of choice, or a dash of nutmeg or pumpkin pie spice (optional)

1. Preheat the oven to 300°F. Line a cookie sheet with parchment paper.

2. Make the cookies: In a large bowl, whisk together the almond flour, cocoa powder, sweetener, baking powder, and salt. Add the melted butter, egg, and vanilla and stir well to combine into a thick dough.

3. Roll out the dough on a large piece of parchment until it is ¼ inch thick. Use a round cookie cutter that is 1½ inches in diameter to cut out the cookie shapes. Place the cookies on the prepared cookie sheet.

4. Bake for 18 to 20 minutes, until the edges are lightly browned. Turn off the oven and leave the cookies in the oven for 15 more minutes to crisp up. Remove and allow to cool completely.

5. While the cookies are cooling, make the filling: Put the butter, cream cheese, and heavy cream in a medium bowl and use a hand mixer to mix well. Stir in the sweetener, salt, and extract or spice, if using. Taste and adjust the sweetness to your liking.

6. Once the cookies are cool, pipe or spread a tablespoon of the filling on a cookie. Top the filling with another cookie to make a sandwich. Repeat with the remaining cookies and filling.

7. Store extras in an airtight container in the refrigerator for up to 5 days.

(per serving):
calories **117** • fat **11g** • protein **3g** • carbs **3g** • fiber **1g**

Protein
Hot Chocolate

MEDIUM   option   option

yield: 1 serving • prep time: 3 minutes • cook time: 1 minute

What's not to love about rich, creamy hot chocolate? Honestly, I feel good about having this option for my boys. It packs healthy protein from the eggs and collagen, and it is sugar-free and delicious! I would let my boys drink this for breakfast.

1½ cups unsweetened almond milk or heavy cream

2 large eggs

¼ cup chocolate- or vanilla-flavored collagen peptides

3 tablespoons unsweetened cocoa powder, or more for a richer chocolate flavor

½ teaspoon vanilla extract

A few drops of chocolate-flavored liquid stevia

Pinch of fine sea salt

Marshmallows (page 314), for garnish (optional)

1. Heat the almond milk in a small saucepan over high heat until simmering.

2. Meanwhile, puree the eggs, collagen, cocoa powder, vanilla, stevia, and salt in a blender. With the blender running on low speed, pour in the hot milk. Taste and adjust the sweetness to your liking.

3. Pour the hot chocolate into a mug and garnish with marshmallows, if desired.

(per serving):
calories **289** • fat **14g** • protein **32g** • carbs **4g** • fiber **3g**

Raspberries and Cream Ice Pops

EASY option option

yield: 8 ice pops (1 per serving) • prep time: 4 minutes, plus 2 hours to set

In the summer, I am all about easy recipes. Ice pops are something that even my boys can make, and they are so tasty on a hot day! I *always* have sugar-free ice pops stocked in my freezer, and this recipe is Micah's favorite. He avoids dairy, so I make it with coconut cream.

½ cup heavy cream (or coconut cream for dairy-free)

½ cup unsweetened almond milk (or more heavy cream or coconut cream for nut-free)

½ cup raspberries

¼ cup powdered allulose or equivalent amount of liquid sweetener (see page 77)

2 teaspoons strawberry extract

Pinch of fine sea salt

SPECIAL EQUIPMENT:

8 ice pop molds

Place all the ingredients in a blender and puree until smooth. Taste and adjust the sweetness to your liking. Pour the mixture into 8 ice pop molds. Place in the freezer to set for at least 2 hours before serving.

(per serving):
calories **56** • fat **6g** • protein **0.5g** • carbs **1g** • fiber **1g**

Extreme Chocolate
Blender Birthday Cake

MEDIUM   option

yield: one 9-inch layer cake (14 servings) • prep time: 15 minutes • cook time: 35 minutes

Kai *loves* superheroes! He generally thrives in chaos, but when it comes to his superheroes, he is very organized. He lays them out in a neat row on his pillow when he leaves for the day. He also made a chart of the superheroes' birthdays. When we had a party for Ant-Man, I made him a Little Debbie Birthday Cake (find the recipe on KetoMaria.com). For Captain America's birthday, I didn't have a lot of time to prepare. I needed something easy, so I decided to throw all the ingredients into my blender and see if it worked. It did! This blender cake is easy *and* delicious! I had many testers test this recipe, and they all were very impressed. One tester mentioned that the cake was extremely moist, but that's exactly what I was aiming for—an ooey-gooey cake.

CAKE

1½ cups confectioners'-style erythritol or equivalent amount of powdered sweetener (see page 77)

1 cup unsweetened vanilla-flavored almond milk or heavy cream

½ cup unsalted butter (or coconut oil for dairy-free), softened

2 large eggs

2 teaspoons vanilla extract

2 cups blanched almond flour or peanut flour

¾ cup unsweetened cocoa powder

¼ cup coconut flour

1½ teaspoons baking powder

1½ teaspoons baking soda

1 teaspoon fine sea salt

1 cup hot water

FROSTING

¾ cup (1½ sticks) unsalted butter (or coconut oil for dairy-free), softened

6 ounces cream cheese (¾ cup) (or Kite Hill brand cream cheese–style spread for dairy-free), softened

2 cups confectioners'-style erythritol or equivalent amount of powdered sweetener (see page 77)

1½ cups unsweetened cocoa powder

¾ cup unsweetened vanilla-flavored almond milk or heavy cream

1 teaspoon vanilla extract

1. Preheat the oven to 350°F. Grease two 9-inch cake pans.

2. Make the cakes: Put the sweetener, almond milk, butter, eggs, and vanilla in a blender and pulse until well blended and smooth. Add the almond flour, cocoa powder, coconut flour, baking powder, baking soda, and salt. Pour the hot water over the top; it will start to bubble as it hits the baking powder and soda. Pulse until smooth, scraping down the sides of the blender once or twice. Pour the batter evenly into the prepared pans.

3. Bake for 30 to 35 minutes, until a toothpick inserted in the center of a cake comes out clean. Let cool for 10 minutes before removing to a wire rack to cool completely.

(per serving): calories **357** • fat **32g** • protein **8g** • carbs **10g** • fiber **5g**

4. While the cakes are cooling, make the frosting: Place the butter and cream cheese in a medium bowl and use a hand mixer to blend until light and fluffy. Add the sweetener and cocoa powder and mix to combine. Add the almond milk and vanilla and beat to a spreadable consistency. Taste and adjust the sweetness to your liking.

5. Cut the cooled cakes in half horizontally, making 4 thin layers. Using an offset spatula or a butter knife, cover the top of each layer with frosting, then stack them on a cake plate and frost the outside of the cake. Slice and serve.

6. Store extras in an airtight container in the refrigerator for up to 5 days.

Baseball
Blender Cupcakes

MEDIUM option

yield: 20 cupcakes (1 per serving) • prep time: 15 minutes • cook time: 25 minutes

When I was really little, my mom made cupcakes that looked like baseballs. She always adds little details like that for us. I think it makes her food taste better! I not only taste the love she puts into our food, I see it, too.

CUPCAKES

1½ cups confectioners'-style erythritol or equivalent amount of powdered sweetener (see page 77)

1 cup unsweetened almond or cashew milk or heavy cream

½ cup (1 stick) unsalted butter, melted (or coconut oil for dairy-free)

2 large eggs

1 teaspoon vanilla extract

2 cups blanched almond flour

¾ cup unsweetened cocoa powder

¼ cup coconut flour

2 teaspoons baking powder

1 teaspoon baking soda

½ teaspoon fine sea salt

1 cup very hot water

FILLING AND FROSTING

2 (8-ounce) packages cream cheese (or Kite Hill brand cream cheese–style spread for dairy-free), softened

½ cup confectioners'-style erythritol or equivalent amount of liquid or powdered sweetener (see page 77)

2 tablespoons unsweetened almond milk or heavy cream

DECORATION

½ cup melted sugar-free chocolate, homemade (page 310) or store-bought

1. Preheat the oven to 350°F and grease 20 wells of a standard-sized muffin pan well with butter or avocado or coconut oil spray. (Bake the muffins in 2 batches if your pan has only 12 wells.)

2. Make the cupcakes: Put the sweetener, milk, butter, eggs, and vanilla in a blender and pulse until well blended and smooth. Add the almond flour, cocoa powder, coconut flour, baking powder, baking soda, and salt. Pour the hot water over the top; it will start to bubble as it hits the baking powder and soda. Pulse until smooth, scraping down the sides of the blender once or twice.

3. Pour the batter into the prepared muffin pan, filling the wells two-thirds full. Bake for 20 to 25 minutes, until a toothpick inserted in the center of a cupcake comes out clean. Remove from the oven and allow to cool in the pan for about 10 minutes before turning out onto a wire rack to cool completely.

4. While the cupcakes are cooling, make the filling: Place the cream cheese and sweetener in a medium bowl. Using a hand mixer, mix until smooth. Slowly beat in the almond milk to thin the filling. Transfer the filling to a piping bag.

5. When the cupcakes are cool, poke a hole in the bottom of each cupcake and pipe in the filling. Spread a thin layer of the filling over the tops of the cupcakes. Set the cupcakes upright on a serving platter.

(per serving):
calories **351** • fat **32g** • protein **8g** • carbs **9g** • fiber **4g**

6. To make the baseball design, place the melted chocolate in a piping bag or a small resealable plastic bag. Cut a very small hole in one corner of the plastic bag. Pipe two half-circles angling outward on the top of each cupcake, moving from one end to the other. Make very short laces through the half-circles to resemble a baseball.

7. Store extras in an airtight container in the refrigerator for up to 4 days, or freeze for up to 1 month. Allow to thaw to room temperature before serving.

Chocolate Hazelnut
Whoopie Pies

MEDIUM option

yield: 6 whoopie pies (1 per serving) • prep time: 10 minutes (not including time to make chocolate hazelnut spread) • cook time: 14 minutes

If you love Nutella, you must try these decadent whoopie pies! *Note:* If you don't have a batch of my Sugar-Free Chocolate Hazelnut Spread handy, you can use almond butter or natural peanut butter instead.

CAKES

1¼ cups blanched almond flour, or ½ cup coconut flour

¼ cup unsweetened cocoa powder

½ teaspoon baking soda

¼ teaspoon fine sea salt

¼ cup (½ stick) unsalted butter (or coconut oil for dairy-free), softened

⅓ cup confectioners'-style erythritol or equivalent amount of liquid or powdered sweetener (see page 77)

3 large eggs (or 6 eggs plus ¼ cup unsweetened almond milk if using coconut flour)

1 teaspoon hazelnut or vanilla extract

FILLING

½ cup unsalted butter, softened (or coconut oil for dairy-free)

¾ cup Sugar-Free Chocolate Hazelnut Spread (page 380)

¾ cup confectioners'-style erythritol or equivalent amount of liquid or powdered sweetener (see page 77)

1 tablespoon heavy cream (or unsweetened almond milk for dairy-free)

1 teaspoon hazelnut or vanilla extract

CHOCOLATE DRIZZLE

¼ cup heavy cream (or coconut cream for dairy-free)

2 tablespoons confectioners'-style erythritol or equivalent amount of liquid or powdered sweetener (see page 77)

½ ounce unsweetened chocolate, finely chopped

½ teaspoon hazelnut or vanilla extract

SPECIAL EQUIPMENT:

12-well whoopie pie pan or muffin top pan

1. Preheat the oven to 325°F. Grease a 12-well whoopie pie pan or muffin top pan.

2. Make the cakes: In a mixing bowl, whisk together the flour, cocoa powder, baking soda, and salt. In a separate bowl, beat the butter, sweetener, eggs, and extract with a hand mixer until smooth. Stir the wet ingredients into the dry ingredients until fully incorporated. Spoon the batter into the prepared pan, filling each well about two-thirds full. Bake for 12 minutes, or until a toothpick inserted in the center of a cake comes out clean. Allow to cool completely in the pan.

3. While the cakes are cooling, make the filling: Using the hand mixer, cream the butter, chocolate hazelnut spread, and sweetener in a medium bowl. Beat in the heavy cream to thin it out a little, then add the extract and mix to combine. Set the filling aside.

4. Make the drizzle: Bring the heavy cream to a simmer in a small saucepan over medium-high heat. Once it reaches a simmer, remove the pan from the heat and stir in the sweetener and chopped chocolate until the chocolate is melted, then stir in the extract. Taste and add more sweetener, if desired.

(per serving): calories **824** • fat **75g** • protein **22g** • carbs **21g** • fiber **13g**

5. To assemble, place one cake flat side up on a plate. Top with 2 tablespoons of the filling, then another cake. Repeat with the rest of the cakes and filling. Drizzle the chocolate over the whoopie pies.

6. Store extras in an airtight container in the refrigerator for up to 4 days.

Kai's
Puppy Chow

EASY   option   yield: 4 servings • prep time: 4 minutes

When I was a kid, my sister taught me how to make puppy chow, a crispy snack made with cereal, peanut butter, and chocolate. (It's also known as muddy buddies.) It was so good and really easy to make. I was pondering how to make a grain-free, sugar-free puppy chow, and my Pork Rind Cereal recipe on KetoMaria.com has been a big hit, so I thought I would try to make a pork rind puppy chow! Personally, I don't care for plain pork rinds—I find the flavor of most brands unappealing. However, the combination of peanut butter, butterscotch, and chocolate makes this sugar-free treat irresistible! You could also omit the peanut butter and coconut oil and use 1 cup of my Sugar-Free Chocolate Hazelnut Spread (page 380) to coat the pork rinds.

2 cups plain pork rinds

½ cup natural peanut butter or almond butter

½ cup unsalted butter (or butter-flavored coconut oil for dairy-free), melted

¼ cup granular erythritol sweetener or equivalent amount of liquid or powdered sweetener (see page 77), or ¼ teaspoon butterscotch toffee–flavored stevia

1 teaspoon butterscotch extract

1½ tablespoons unsweetened cocoa powder

Confectioners'-style erythritol, for dusting (optional)

1. Break the pork rinds into 1-inch pieces. Divide the pieces between 2 medium bowls.

2. Place the peanut butter and melted butter in a third medium bowl and stir well to combine. Stir in the sweetener and extract. Taste and adjust the sweetness to your liking. Drizzle half of the peanut butter mixture over one bowl of pork rinds and toss to coat.

3. Add the cocoa powder to the remaining half of the peanut butter mixture and stir well. Drizzle the chocolate–peanut butter mixture over the other bowl of pork rinds and toss to coat. Dust both bowls with confectioners'-style sweetener, if desired, and combine the flavors if you like.

4. Place in the refrigerator to cool for 15 minutes before serving. Store extras in an airtight container in the refrigerator for up to 5 days.

(per serving):
calories **492** • fat **45g** • protein **15g** • carbs **7g** • fiber **2g**

Crispy
Candy

EASY   option

yield: 4 servings • prep time: 4 minutes • cook time: 12 minutes

This candy is perfect as a crispy treat, as a topping for no-churn ice cream (pages 317 to 323), or to use in my Candy Bar Truffles recipe (page 329). If you use allulose instead of erythritol, it will be more chewy, like toffee. The recipe calls for butterscotch extract, but you can use any flavor you like—try strawberry, banana, lemon, or peppermint!

1 cup confectioners'-style erythritol or equivalent amount of powdered sweetener (see page 77)

3 tablespoons coconut oil or unsalted butter

2 teaspoons butterscotch extract

1. Preheat the oven to 350°F. Line the bottom of a 6-inch pie plate with parchment paper.

2. In a medium bowl, combine the sweetener, coconut oil, and extract with a fork until small crumbs form. Place the mixture in the lined pie plate and spread into a thin layer.

3. Bake for 10 to 12 minutes, until the mixture is completely melted and the sweetener has dissolved. Remove from the oven and allow to cool on the counter. Once cool to the touch, set in the refrigerator to cool completely. The candy will harden as it cools. Break into pieces and enjoy!

4. Store extras in an airtight container in the refrigerator for up to 1 month.

(per serving):
calories **88** • fat **11g** • protein **0g** • carbs **0g** • fiber **0g**

Sugar-Free Chocolate
Bars or Chips

EASY   option

yield: 1 large chocolate bar or 2 cups chocolate chips (4 servings) •
prep time: 10 minutes • cook time: 3 minutes

You can eat this chocolate plain, use the bars to make S'mores (page 316), or use the chips in The BEST Chocolate Chip Cookies (page 312), Cookie Dough Dip (page 166), or Chocolate Chip Cookie Dough Truffles (page 331). You can also use it to make chocolate bowls for no-churn ice cream (pages 317 to 323); see the variation below.

¼ cup heavy cream (or coconut cream for dairy-free)

4 tablespoons (½ stick) unsalted butter (or coconut oil for dairy-free)

5 ounces unsweetened chocolate, finely chopped

⅓ cup confectioners'-style erythritol or equivalent amount of liquid or powdered sweetener (see page 77)

2 teaspoons vanilla extract

⅛ teaspoon fine sea salt

SPECIAL EQUIPMENT:

Chocolate bar or chip molds

1. Place the heavy cream and butter in a small saucepan over medium-high heat. Once the mixture reaches a simmer, remove the pan from the heat, add the chopped chocolate and sweetener, and stir well until the chocolate is melted. Add the vanilla and salt and stir until smooth and thick.

2. If making a bar, pour the mixture into a chocolate bar mold. Or, to make chips, line a cookie sheet with parchment paper. Transfer the chocolate mixture to a piping bag or a large resealable plastic bag. Cut a small hole in one corner of the plastic bag. Pipe ¼-teaspoon chocolate chip shapes onto the parchment. Place in the refrigerator to set.

3. Store in an airtight container in the refrigerator for up to 6 days.

variation:

Chocolate Ice Cream Bowls. *Blow up small balloons so they are about 3 inches in diameter (or whatever size you want to make the bowls). Hold a balloon at the knotted end and dip the other end halfway into the melted chocolate, then place on a parchment-lined baking sheet. Repeat with the remaining balloons and chocolate. Place the baking sheet in the refrigerator for 10 to 20 minutes, until the chocolate has hardened. To remove the chocolate from the balloons, hold the balloon just below the knot and gently poke a small hole in it. Slowly release the air by opening your fingers a tiny bit. Fill the chocolate bowl with ice cream.*

(per serving):
calories **347** • fat **30g** • protein **5g** • carbs **10g** • fiber **5g**

The BEST Chocolate Chip Cookies

MEDIUM option

yield: 24 cookies (1 per serving) • prep time: 7 minutes • cook time: 20 minutes

Make sure the oven is fully preheated for this recipe; otherwise, the cookies will melt and end up flat and crispy. Allulose gives them a chewy texture. Also, almond flour is a sensitive nut that burns easily, so make sure your oven isn't running too hot. For baking almond flour cookies, 325°F is the proper temperature.

1 cup coconut oil or unsalted butter, softened

1½ cups allulose

1 large egg

1½ cups blanched almond flour

½ cup coconut flour

1 teaspoon baking powder

½ teaspoon fine sea salt

2 cups sugar-free chocolate chips, homemade (page 310) or store-bought, or 1 (2½-ounce) sugar-free milk chocolate bar, chopped

1. Place one oven rack in the upper third of the oven and one in the lower third. Preheat the oven to 325°F.

2. In a medium bowl, use a hand mixer to cream the coconut oil, allulose, and egg until very fluffy. In a separate bowl, whisk together the almond flour, coconut flour, baking powder, and salt. Slowly add the dry ingredients to the wet and mix until smooth. Stir in the chocolate chips.

3. Roll 2 tablespoons of the dough into a ball in your hands (for a uniform shape), place on a cookie sheet, then press down until the cookie is about ¾ inch thick. Repeat with the remaining dough, using two cookie sheets and spacing the cookies about 2 inches apart. You should get 24 cookies.

4. Bake both sheets of cookies for 17 to 20 minutes, until golden around the edges. Let cool completely on the cookie sheet before removing and enjoying. Store extras in an airtight container in the refrigerator for up to 6 days, or freeze for up to a month.

tips:

If I don't have homemade chocolate chips on hand, I like to use The Good Chocolate brand chocolate bars for this recipe.

You can use these cookies to make ice cream sandwiches with No-Churn Vanilla Bean Ice Cream (page 317) for an extra special treat.

(per serving):
calories **154** • fat **14g** • protein **3g** • carbs **5g** • fiber **2g**

Marshmallows

MEDIUM option

yield: 4 servings • prep time: 15 minutes, plus 5 hours to set •
cook time: 5 minutes

These marshmallows taste great in Protein Hot Chocolate (page 296), S'mores
(page 316), and Rocky Road Ice Cream (page 319).

Coconut oil, for greasing the
baking dish

1 cup cold water, divided

2 tablespoons unflavored
gelatin

¾ cup confectioners'-style
erythritol or equivalent
amount of powdered
sweetener (see page 77)

½ cup liquid allulose

2 teaspoons vanilla extract

⅛ teaspoon almond extract
(omit for nut-free)

SPECIAL EQUIPMENT:

Candy thermometer

1. Lightly grease an 8-inch square baking dish with coconut oil.
   Place ½ cup of the water in a stand mixer (or in a large bowl
   if using a hand mixer) and whisk in the gelatin. Let sit for
   2 minutes to allow the gelatin to soften.

2. Heat the sweeteners and remaining ½ cup of water in a small
   saucepan over high heat, whisking continuously, until the
   mixture reaches 235°F to 240°F (soft ball stage), 3 to 5 minutes.
   Remove the pan from the heat and stir in the extracts.

3. With the mixer on low speed, slowly add the hot syrup to the
   gelatin mixture. After all the syrup has been added, increase
   the speed to high and mix for about 5 minutes, until the
   marshmallow mixture has medium peaks (it will look like
   whipped egg whites).

4. Working quickly to prevent the marshmallow mixture from
   setting up in the bowl, pour it into the prepared baking dish.
   Allow the marshmallow to set at room temperature, about
   5 hours, then cut to the desired size. By the next day, the cut
   marshmallows will have dried out enough to resemble store-
   bought marshmallows.

5. Store extras in an airtight container for up to a week.

tips:

*If you prefer thinner marshmallows, use a larger baking dish, or
put the marshmallow mixture in a piping bag and pipe it onto a
parchment-lined cookie sheet to make shapes.*

*If the marshmallow mixture hardens as you are working, return it
to the mixing bowl and set the bowl over a pot of simmering water
to melt the marshmallow again, then rewhip.*

(per serving):
calories **19** • fat **0g** • protein **3g** • carbs **0.3g** • fiber **0g**

variation:

Coated Marshmallows. *Dip the top of a marshmallow in melted chocolate (page 310) and then dip into crushed graham crackers (page 160). Store the coated marshmallows in an airtight container in the refrigerator for up to 6 days.*

S'mores

EASY   option

yield: 12 s'mores (2 per serving) • prep time: 8 minutes (not including time to make graham crackers or marshmallows)

1 batch Graham Crackers (page 160)

1 (2½-ounce) sugar-free chocolate bar, homemade (page 310) or store-bought, broken into 2-inch squares

1 batch Marshmallows (page 314)

1. Place a graham cracker on a plate. Top with a square of chocolate followed by a marshmallow. Top with another graham cracker. Repeat with the remaining ingredients.

2. If desired, gently heat the s'mores in a 300°F oven for 1 minute, or until the marshmallows are starting to soften. Enjoy immediately.

(per serving):
calories **408** • fat **36g** • protein **11g** • carbs **12g** • fiber **6g**

No-Churn
Ice Cream Five Ways

No-churn ice cream is so easy to make, and you can change up the flavor in so many ways. I've given you several options here. It's important to use allulose as the sweetener because it keeps the ice cream soft. If the ice cream is too hard when you take it out of the freezer, allow it to sit out at room temperature for about 8 minutes before serving.

 One of my favorite cooking gadgets is my mom's immersion blender. It is really fun and works great for making no-churn ice cream!

No-Churn Vanilla Bean Ice Cream

EASY   option

yield: 1 quart (8 servings) • prep time: 5 minutes, plus 2 hours to chill

1½ cups heavy cream

⅔ cup powdered allulose

½ cup unsweetened almond milk (or more heavy cream for nut-free)

Seeds scraped from 1 vanilla bean, or 2 teaspoons vanilla extract

¼ teaspoon fine sea salt

1. Pour the heavy cream into a blender, or put it in a large bowl and use an immersion blender, and blend until stiff peaks form. (Alternatively, you can whip the cream in a chilled bowl with a chilled hand mixer.) Transfer to a large bowl, if needed.

2. Place the allulose, almond milk, vanilla bean seeds, and salt in another bowl and stir well. Gently fold the vanilla mixture into the whipped cream. Taste and adjust the sweetness to your liking. Place in the freezer to chill for at least 2 hours.

3. Store in an airtight container in the freezer for up to a month.

tip:
Use this vanilla ice cream to make ice cream sandwiches with The BEST Chocolate Chip Cookies (page 312).

(per serving):
calories **159** • fat **17g** • protein **1g** • carbs **3g** • fiber **0g**

No-Churn Strawberries and Cream Ice Cream

EASY   option

yield: 1 quart (8 servings) • prep time: 5 minutes, plus 2 hours to chill

1 cup heavy cream

2 cups strawberries, stems removed

⅔ cup powdered allulose

½ cup unsweetened almond milk (or more heavy cream for nut-free)

¼ teaspoon fine sea salt

1. Pour the heavy cream into a blender, or put it in a large bowl and use an immersion blender, and blend until stiff peaks form. (Alternatively, you can whip the cream in a chilled bowl with a chilled hand mixer.) Transfer to a large bowl, if needed.

2. Place the strawberries, allulose, almond milk, and salt in the blender and puree until smooth. Gently fold the strawberry mixture into the whipped cream. Taste and adjust the sweetness to your liking. Place in the freezer to chill for at least 2 hours.

3. Store in an airtight container in the freezer for up to a month.

(per serving):
calories **118** • fat **11g** • protein **1g** • carbs **5g** • fiber **1g**

No-Churn Blue Moon Ice Cream

EASY   option

yield: 1 quart (8 servings) • prep time: 5 minutes, plus 2 hours to chill

1½ cups heavy cream

⅔ cup powdered allulose

½ cup unsweetened almond milk (or more heavy cream for nut-free)

½ teaspoon lemon extract

½ teaspoon raspberry extract

½ teaspoon vanilla extract

¼ teaspoon almond extract

¼ teaspoon fine sea salt

A few drops of natural blue food coloring (optional)

1. Pour the cream into a blender, or put it in a large bowl and use an immersion blender, and blend until stiff peaks form. (Alternatively, you can whip the cream in a chilled bowl with a chilled hand mixer.) Transfer to a large bowl, if needed.

2. Place the allulose, almond milk, extracts, salt, and food coloring, if using, in another bowl and stir well. Gently fold the almond milk mixture into the whipped cream. Taste and adjust the sweetness to your liking. Place in the freezer to chill for at least 2 hours.

3. Store in an airtight container in the freezer for up to a month.

(per serving):
calories **160** • fat **17g** • protein **1g** • carbs **3g** • fiber **0g**

No-Churn Chocolate Ice Cream

EASY   option

yield: 1 quart (8 servings) • prep time: 5 minutes, plus 2 hours to chill

⅔ cup powdered allulose

½ cup unsweetened almond milk (or more heavy cream for nut-free)

¼ teaspoon fine sea salt

2 ounces unsweetened baking chocolate, finely chopped

2 teaspoons vanilla or almond extract

1½ cups heavy cream

1. Bring the allulose, almond milk, and salt to a simmer in a small saucepan over medium-high heat. Once simmering, remove the pan from the heat and add the chopped chocolate. Stir until the chocolate is melted and the mixture is smooth. Stir in the extract. Set in the refrigerator to chill for 30 minutes.

2. Pour the heavy cream into a blender, or put it in a large bowl and use an immersion blender, and blend until stiff peaks form. (Alternatively, you can whip the cream in a chilled bowl with a chilled hand mixer.) Transfer to a large bowl, if needed.

3. Gently fold the chilled chocolate mixture into the whipped cream. Taste and adjust the sweetness to your liking. Place in the freezer to chill for at least 2 hours.

4. Store in an airtight container in the freezer for up to a month.

variation:

Rocky Road Ice Cream. *To the chocolate ice cream mixture, add 1 cup of Marshmallows (page 314) cut into ¼-inch pieces, 1 (2½-ounce) sugar-free chocolate bar (page 310) cut into ¼-inch pieces, and 1 cup of sliced almonds.*

(per serving):
calories **209** • fat **21g** • protein **2g** • carbs **5g** • fiber **1g**

Dairy-Free
No-Churn Ice Cream

EASY   option

yield: 1 quart (8 servings) • prep time: 10 minutes, plus time to chill coconut cream and bowl and chill almond milk mixture

The flavor of this ice cream reminds me of a Wendy's Frosty—especially if you use almond extract. Adding gelatin helps keep this dairy-free ice cream soft. It only needs to sit out for a couple of minutes before it becomes soft enough to eat. Also, the immersion blender is key! Using a hand mixer to whip coconut cream tends to make a mess. Besides, kids love using immersion blenders!

2 (13.5-ounce) cans coconut cream

1 cup unsweetened almond milk (or hemp milk for nut-free)

1½ teaspoons unflavored gelatin

½ cup powdered allulose

3 tablespoons unsweetened cocoa powder

1 teaspoon almond or vanilla extract

¼ teaspoon fine sea salt

SPECIAL EQUIPMENT:

Immersion blender

1. Chill the coconut cream and a large mixing bowl in the refrigerator for at least 30 minutes or overnight.

2. Place the almond milk in a small saucepan (or a microwave-safe bowl) and sprinkle in the gelatin. Whisk until there are no lumps. Heat over medium-high heat just until simmering (or heat it in the microwave). Whisk well, transfer to a bowl, if needed, and set in the refrigerator to cool.

3. Once the almond milk mixture is cool, place the chilled coconut cream in the chilled bowl and use an immersion blender to whip until fluffy. Slowly add the milk mixture, allulose, cocoa powder, extract, and salt. Taste and adjust the sweetness to your liking.

4. This ice cream often gets a bit hard in the freezer, so I recommend that you divide it into individual portions before storing; one serving will thaw faster for a delicious treat.

(per serving):
calories **197** • fat **19g** • protein **1g** • carbs **0.1g** • fiber **0.1g**

Raspberry
Sorbet

EASY   option

yield: 2 cups (4 servings) • prep time: 7 minutes, plus time to chill milk mixture • cook time: 2 minutes

I made this sorbet for my boys when they were toddlers. They absolutely loved the taste, and I love that it is naturally dairy-free! If you prefer, you can use water in place of the almond or coconut milk, but I find that using milk gives the sorbet a better texture. If you use canned coconut milk, the sorbet has a tropical raspberry flavor! Using allulose keeps the sorbet soft, and adding gelatin and salt keeps it from hardening as much in the freezer.

⅓ cup unsweetened almond milk (or unsweetened coconut milk for nut-free)

1½ teaspoons unflavored gelatin

⅓ cup powdered allulose or equivalent amount of liquid sweetener (see page 77)

2½ cups frozen raspberries or strawberries

1 tablespoon lemon juice

½ teaspoon fine sea salt

1. Place the almond milk in a small saucepan (or a microwave-safe bowl) and sprinkle in the gelatin. Whisk until there are no lumps. Heat over medium-high heat just until simmering (or heat it in the microwave). Whisk well, transfer to a bowl, if needed, and set in the refrigerator to cool.

2. Once the almond milk mixture is cool, place all the ingredients in a high-powered blender or food processor and puree until very smooth and fluffy, about 4 minutes. Taste and adjust the sweetness to your liking. Enjoy right away or store in an airtight container in the freezer for up to 1 month.

note:

If the sorbet is too hard straight out of the freezer, allow it to sit at room temperature for about 8 minutes before serving.

(per serving):
calories **57** • fat **1g** • protein **3g** • carbs **11g** • fiber **5g**

Truffles
Five Ways

When I was writing this book, my best friend from grade school, Marla, messaged me and asked me to include some easy truffle recipes for her girls. This message warmed my heart so much! After over a decade apart, I still love Marla dearly, so I had to create a few recipes for her family.

Brownie Truffles

EASY   option

yield: 12 truffles (1 per serving) • prep time: 10 minutes, plus 2½ hours to chill

FILLING

1 cup almond butter

½ cup unsalted butter (or coconut oil for dairy-free)

⅓ cup confectioners'-style erythritol or equivalent amount of liquid or powdered sweetener (see page 77)

¼ cup unsweetened cocoa powder

1 teaspoon vanilla extract

⅛ teaspoon fine sea salt

COATING

½ cup heavy cream (or coconut cream for dairy-free)

1 ounce unsweetened chocolate, finely chopped

¼ cup confectioners'-style erythritol or equivalent amount of liquid or powdered sweetener (see page 77)

1 teaspoon vanilla extract

1. Make the filling: Place the almond butter and melted butter in a medium bowl and stir well to combine. Add the sweetener, cocoa powder, vanilla, and salt and mix well. Taste and adjust the sweetness to your liking. Use a small cookie scoop to make 12 small balls. Place on a parchment-lined baking sheet. Put the baking sheet in the freezer for 20 to 30 minutes while you make the coating.

2. Make the coating: Bring the heavy cream to a simmer in a small saucepan over medium-high heat. Once it reaches a simmer, remove the pan from the heat, add the chopped chocolate and sweetener, and stir well until the chocolate is melted. Add the vanilla and stir until smooth and thick.

3. One at a time, dip the frozen truffles into the melted chocolate mixture. Use a fork to remove from the chocolate and place on the parchment-lined baking sheet. Drizzle extra chocolate over the coated truffles for decoration, if desired.

4. Place in the refrigerator for 2 hours, or until set. Store extras in an airtight container in the fridge for up to 6 days.

tip:

To make these truffles extra chocolatey, reduce the amount of erythritol in the filling to ¼ cup and add 5 drops of chocolate-flavored liquid stevia.

(per serving):
calories **255** • fat **25g** • protein **6g** • carbs **6g** • fiber **3g**

Strawberry Cheesecake Truffles

EASY   option

yield: 16 truffles (1 per serving) • prep time: 10 minutes, plus 2½ hours to chill (not including time to make graham crackers)

FILLING

1 (8-ounce) package cream cheese (or Kite Hill brand cream cheese–style spread for dairy-free), softened

1 cup crushed Graham Crackers (page 160)

¼ cup confectioners'-style erythritol or equivalent amount of liquid or powdered sweetener (see page 77)

⅛ teaspoon fine sea salt

¼ teaspoon strawberry or vanilla extract (optional)

¼ cup plus 2 tablespoons finely chopped strawberries

COATING

½ cup unsalted butter (or coconut cream for dairy-free)

1 ounce cocoa butter, finely chopped

¼ cup confectioners'-style erythritol or equivalent amount of liquid or powdered sweetener (see page 77)

¼ teaspoon strawberry or vanilla extract

1 drop natural pink food coloring (optional)

1. Make the filling: Place the cream cheese, crushed graham crackers, sweetener, salt, and extract, if using, in a medium bowl and stir well to combine. Gently stir in the strawberries. Taste and adjust the sweetness to your liking.

2. Use a small cookie scoop to make 16 small balls. Place the balls on a parchment-lined baking sheet. Put the baking sheet in the freezer for 20 to 30 minutes while you make the coating.

3. Make the coating: Melt the butter in a small saucepan over medium-high heat. Once it reaches a simmer, remove the pan from the heat, add the chopped cocoa butter and sweetener, and stir well until the cocoa butter is melted. Add the extract and stir until smooth and thick. Taste and adjust the sweetness to your liking.

4. One at a time, dip the frozen truffles into the melted white chocolate mixture. Use a fork to remove from the coating and place on the parchment-lined baking sheet. If desired, add a drop of pink food coloring to the rest of the white chocolate and drizzle over the coated truffles for decoration. Place in the refrigerator for 2 hours, or until set.

5. Store extras in an airtight container in the fridge for up to 6 days.

tip:

For Valentine's Day, you can design a heart shape on the top of each truffle with the pink drizzle.

(per serving):
calories **223** • fat **21g** • protein **5g** • carbs **4g** • fiber **2g**

Candy Bar Truffles

EASY   option

yield: 12 truffles (1 per serving) • prep time: 10 minutes, plus 2½ hours to chill (not including time to make candy)

FILLING

1 cup natural peanut butter or almond butter

½ cup unsalted butter (or coconut oil for dairy-free), melted

1 batch Crispy Candy (page 308), plus more for garnish

⅓ cup confectioners'-style erythritol or equivalent amount of liquid or powdered sweetener (see page 77)

1 teaspoon butterscotch or vanilla extract

⅛ teaspoon fine sea salt

COATING

½ cup heavy cream (or coconut cream for dairy-free)

1 ounce unsweetened chocolate, finely chopped

¼ cup confectioners'-style erythritol or equivalent amount of liquid or powdered sweetener (see page 77)

1 teaspoon vanilla extract

1. Make the filling: Place the peanut butter and melted butter in a medium bowl and stir well to combine. Crush the candy and reserve 3 tablespoons for garnish. Add the rest of the crushed candy, the sweetener, extract, and salt to the bowl with the peanut butter mixture. Taste and adjust the sweetness to your liking.

2. Use a small cookie scoop to make 12 small balls. Place the balls on a parchment-lined baking sheet. Put the baking sheet in the freezer for 20 to 30 minutes while you make the coating.

3. Make the coating: Bring the heavy cream to a simmer in a small saucepan over medium-high heat. Once it reaches a simmer, remove the pan from the heat, add the chopped chocolate and sweetener, and stir well until the chocolate is melted. Add the vanilla and stir until smooth and thick.

4. Dip the frozen truffles into the melted chocolate mixture. Use a fork to remove from the chocolate and place on the parchment-lined baking sheet. Sprinkle the reserved crushed candy over the truffles while the coating is still wet. Place in the refrigerator for 2 hours, or until set.

5. Store extras in an airtight container in the fridge for up to 6 days.

note:
These truffles were inspired by Butterfinger candy bars.

(per serving):
calories **283** • fat **27g** • protein **5g** • carbs **5g** • fiber **2g**

Red Velvet Truffles

EASY   option

yield: 16 truffles (1 per serving) • prep time: 10 minutes, plus 2½ hours to chill (not including time to make graham crackers)

FILLING

1 (8-ounce) package cream cheese (or Kite Hill brand cream cheese–style spread for dairy-free), softened

1 cup crushed Graham Crackers (page 160)

¼ cup confectioners'-style erythritol or equivalent amount of liquid or powdered sweetener (see page 77)

1 tablespoon plus 1 teaspoon unsweetened cocoa powder

¼ teaspoon vanilla extract

⅛ teaspoon fine sea salt

A few drops of natural red food coloring

COATING

½ cup unsalted butter (or coconut cream for dairy-free)

1 ounce cocoa butter, finely chopped

¼ cup confectioners'-style erythritol

¼ teaspoon strawberry or vanilla extract

1 drop natural red food coloring (optional)

1. Make the filling: Place the cream cheese, crushed graham crackers, sweetener, cocoa powder, vanilla, salt, and food coloring in a medium bowl and stir well to combine. Taste and adjust the sweetness to your liking. Use a small cookie scoop to make 16 small balls. Place on a parchment-lined baking sheet. Put the baking sheet in the freezer for 20 to 30 minutes while you make the coating.

2. Make the coating: Melt the butter in a small saucepan over medium-high heat. Once the butter starts to sizzle, remove the pan from the heat, add the chopped cocoa butter and sweetener, and stir well until the cocoa butter is melted. Add the extract and stir until smooth and thick. Taste and adjust the sweetness to your liking.

3. One at a time, dip the frozen truffles into the melted white chocolate. Use a fork to remove from the coating and place on the parchment-lined baking sheet. If desired, add a drop of red food coloring to the rest of the white chocolate and drizzle over the coated truffles for decoration. Place in the refrigerator for 2 hours, or until set.

4. Store extras in an airtight container in the fridge for up to 6 days.

tip:
For Valentine's Day, you can design a heart shape on the top of each truffle with the pink drizzle.

(per serving):
calories **160** • fat **16g** • protein **3g** • carbs **2g** • fiber **1g**

Chocolate Chip Cookie Dough Truffles

EASY   option

yield: 12 truffles (1 per serving) • prep time: 10 minutes, plus 2½ hours to chill

FILLING

1 cup almond butter

½ cup unsalted butter (or coconut oil for dairy-free), softened

⅓ cup confectioners'-style erythritol or equivalent amount of liquid or powdered sweetener (see page 77)

1 cup sugar-free chocolate chips, homemade (page 310) or store-bought, or 1 (2½-ounce) sugar-free chocolate bar, chopped

1 teaspoon vanilla extract

⅛ teaspoon fine sea salt

COATING

½ cup heavy cream (or coconut cream for dairy-free)

1 ounce unsweetened chocolate, finely chopped

¼ cup confectioners'-style erythritol or equivalent amount of liquid or powdered sweetener (see page 77)

1 teaspoon vanilla extract

1. Make the filling: Place the almond butter and softened butter in a medium bowl and stir well to combine. Add the sweetener, chocolate, vanilla, and salt. Taste and adjust the sweetness to your liking.

2. Use a small cookie scoop to make 12 small balls. Place on a parchment paper–lined baking sheet. Put the baking sheet in the freezer for 20 to 30 minutes while you make the coating.

3. Make the coating: Bring the heavy cream to a simmer in a small saucepan over medium-high heat. Once it reaches a simmer, remove the pan from the heat, add the chopped chocolate and sweetener, and stir well until the chocolate is melted. Add the vanilla and stir until smooth and thick.

4. One at a time, dip the frozen truffles into the melted chocolate mixture. Use a fork to remove from the chocolate and place on the parchment-lined baking sheet. Place in the refrigerator for 2 hours, or until set.

5. Store extras in an airtight container in the fridge for up to 6 days.

tip:

If I don't have homemade chocolate chips on hand, I like to use The Good Chocolate brand chocolate bars for this recipe.

(per serving): calories **247** • fat **25g** • protein **3g** • carbs **3g** • fiber **1g**

chapter 10:
chaffles & waffles

Basic Savory Chaffles or Paffles / 334

Easy Blender Waffles / 336

Chaffle Breakfast Sammie / 338

Cinnamon Roll Chaffles / 340

Blueberry Muffin Chaffles / 342

Chocolate Hazelnut Waffles / 344

Drive-Thru Chaffle Burger / 346

Crispy Taco Chaffles / 348

Strawberry Shortcake Chaffle Sandwiches / 350

"Apple" Pie Waffles / 352

Glazed Pumpkin Mini Waffles / 354

Waffle Cone Mini Waffles / 356

Bacon Cheeseburger Waffle / 358

Chocolate Waffle Sandwich / 360

Basic Savory Chaffles or Paffles

EASY   option

yield: 2 chaffles (1 serving) • prep time: 5 minutes • cook time: 6 minutes

A chaffle is a mini waffle made of cheese and egg. It is simple to prepare; most kids can make one on their own! I have also included a dairy-free option made with pork panko (crushed pork rinds) because my son Micah avoids dairy. We call these "paffles"! Chaffles and paffles work great for sandwiches—just add your favorite fixings and wrap in parchment. You can make extra chaffles or paffles to store in the freezer; they will keep for up to a month.

½ cup shredded cheddar cheese or pork panko

1 large egg

Avocado or coconut oil spray

1. Preheat a mini waffle maker.

2. Place the cheese and egg in a small bowl and use a fork to combine well.

3. Grease the waffle maker with avocado or coconut oil spray. Place half of the cheese mixture in the waffle maker and press the lid down. Cook for 2 to 3 minutes, until golden brown and cooked through. Use a fork to gently remove the chaffle or paffle from the waffle maker or gently flip the waffle maker to release the waffle onto a plate. Repeat with the remaining batter.

variations:

Pizza Chaffles or Paffles. *Add 1 teaspoon of Italian seasoning to the batter. Place the chaffles or paffles side by side on a plate and top with pizza sauce and your favorite pizza toppings.*

Chaffle or Paffle Sub Sandwich. *Add ½ teaspoon of smoked paprika to the batter. Place 2 slices of turkey or ham on a chaffle or paffle and top with 2 lettuce leaves and a tomato slice. Smear 1 tablespoon of mayonnaise or mustard on the other chaffle or paffle and place on top of the sandwich.*

(per serving–chaffles):
calories 294 • fat 23g • protein 20g • carbs 0.4g • fiber 0g

(per serving–paffles):
calories 354 • fat 23g • protein 38g • carbs 0.4g • fiber 0g

Easy Blender Waffles

EASY   option

yield: 4 waffles (2 per serving) • prep time: 2 minutes • cook time: 8 minutes

Waffles are great to have in the freezer; your kids can pop them into the toaster oven themselves for easy meals. You can use a regular-size waffle maker or a mini waffle maker to make them.

½ cup blanched almond flour

2 tablespoons confectioners'-style erythritol or equivalent amount of liquid or powdered sweetener (see page 77)

1 teaspoon baking powder

½ teaspoon fine sea salt

2 ounces cream cheese (¼ cup), softened (or Kite Hill brand cream cheese–style spread or 1 hard-boiled egg for dairy-free)

2 large eggs

2 tablespoons unsalted butter (or coconut oil for dairy-free), melted

1 teaspoon vanilla or almond extract

Avocado or coconut oil spray

SERVING SUGGESTIONS

Butter (omit for dairy-free)

Blueberries, raspberries, and/or sliced strawberries

Whipped cream (omit for dairy-free)

1. Preheat a waffle maker to high heat.

2. Place the almond flour, sweetener, baking powder, and salt in a blender. Pulse 3 times to combine. Add the softened cream cheese, eggs, butter, and extract and pulse until smooth.

3. Grease the waffle maker with avocado or coconut oil spray. Place one-quarter of the batter in the center (or one-eighth if using a mini waffle maker) and press the lid down. Cook for 3 to 4 minutes, until golden brown and crisp. Remove from the waffle maker. Repeat with the remaining batter, making a total of 4 waffles (or 8 mini waffles).

4. Serve the waffles topped with butter, berries, and/or whipped cream, if desired.

5. Store extras in an airtight container in the refrigerator for up to 4 days, or freeze for up to a month. To reheat, place the waffles in a toaster oven or 350°F oven for 2 minutes, or until heated through and crispy.

(per serving):
calories **465** • fat **41g** • protein **15g** • carbs **9g** • fiber **3g**

Chaffle
Breakfast Sammie

EASY option

yield: 1 serving • prep time: 5 minutes (not including time to make chaffles) • cook time: 4 minutes

My boys love this egg sandwich for breakfast on the go. It is a twist on a popular fast-food breakfast sandwich, but we think this version tastes way better. One of my recipe testers commented: *"My hubby says this recipe is better than any McMuffin he's eaten! I love them because they are quick, simple, and yummy!"* If you use ground pork to make a patty, grease will come out the sides of the waffle maker. Be prepared and have a rimmed baking sheet under the waffle maker to catch any drips.

1 large egg

⅛ teaspoon fine sea salt

2½ ounces ground pork, or 1 ounce thinly sliced deli ham or turkey

2 Basic Savory Chaffles or Paffles (page 334)

1 slice cheddar cheese (omit for dairy-free)

1. Preheat a mini waffle maker. If using ground pork, place the maker on a rimmed baking sheet to catch any grease.

2. Crack the egg into a small bowl and sprinkle with salt. Scramble with a fork and place in the waffle maker. Cook for 1 to 2 minutes, until set. Gently flip the waffle maker on its side and remove the egg using a fork; set aside.

3. If using ground pork, form the pork into a hockey puck shape. Season the outside with the salt. Place in the waffle maker and press the lid down. Cook for 1½ to 2 minutes, until cooked to your liking. Remove from the waffle maker.

4. Place one chaffle on a plate, then layer with the pork patty or sliced ham, cheese (if using), and egg. Top with the other chaffle. Best served fresh.

(per serving):
calories **634** • fat **49g** • protein **50g** • carbs **1g** • fiber **0g**

Cinnamon Roll
Chaffles

EASY

yield: 2 chaffles (1 per serving) • prep time: 5 minutes • cook time: 6 minutes

I loved cinnamon rolls when I was a little girl. These cinnamon roll chaffles are super delicious but much easier than making homemade cinnamon rolls!

CHAFFLES

½ cup shredded mozzarella cheese

¼ cup almond butter

2 tablespoons confectioners'-style erythritol or equivalent amount of liquid or powdered sweetener (see page 77)

1 large egg

¼ teaspoon vanilla extract

2 teaspoons ground cinnamon, plus more for garnish if desired

Avocado or coconut oil spray

FROSTING

1 tablespoon unsalted butter, softened

1 tablespoon cream cheese, softened

1 tablespoon confectioners'-style erythritol

1 tablespoon unsweetened almond milk or heavy cream

¼ teaspoon vanilla extract

1. Preheat a mini waffle maker.

2. Place the cheese, almond butter, sweetener, egg, and vanilla in a small bowl and use a fork to combine well. Swirl in the cinnamon so there are streaks of cinnamon.

3. Grease the waffle maker with avocado or coconut oil spray. Place half of the batter in the waffle maker and press the lid down. Cook for 2 to 3 minutes, until golden brown and cooked through. Use a fork to gently remove the chaffle from the waffle maker or gently flip the waffle maker to release the chaffle onto a plate. Repeat with the remaining batter.

4. Meanwhile, make the frosting: Place the butter, cream cheese, and sweetener in a small bowl and use a fork to stir well. Add the almond milk and extract and stir well. Taste and adjust the sweetness to your liking.

5. Drizzle the chaffles with the frosting and sprinkle with additional cinnamon, if desired. Best served fresh.

(per serving):
calories **376** • fat **32g** • protein **18g** • carbs **8g** • fiber **4g**

Blueberry Muffin
Chaffles

EASY

yield: 2 chaffles (1 serving) • prep time: 5 minutes • cook time: 6 minutes

My son Kai loves making my blueberry muffin chaffles. They are really easy to make and taste amazing. He often makes extra chaffle batter and stores it in the fridge. All he has to do is turn the chaffle maker on, and he has an easy snack ready in minutes!

½ cup shredded mozzarella cheese

2 tablespoons blanched almond flour

1 tablespoon confectioners'-style erythritol or equivalent amount of liquid or powdered sweetener (see page 77)

½ teaspoon ground cinnamon

1 large egg

2 tablespoons small blueberries

Avocado or coconut oil spray

SERVING SUGGESTIONS

Cream cheese

Butter

1. Preheat a mini waffle maker.

2. Place the cheese, almond flour, sweetener, cinnamon, and egg in a small bowl and use a fork to combine well. Gently stir in the blueberries.

3. Grease the waffle maker with avocado or coconut oil spray. Place half of the batter in the waffle maker and press the lid down. Cook for 2 to 3 minutes, until golden brown and cooked through. Use a fork to gently remove the chaffle from the waffle maker or gently flip the waffle maker to release the chaffle onto a plate. Repeat with the remaining batter.

4. Place the chaffles on a plate and top with cream cheese or butter, if desired. Best served fresh.

(per serving):
calories **296** • fat **22g** • protein **22g** • carbs **7g** • fiber **2g**

Chocolate Hazelnut
Waffles

EASY   option

yield: 2 mini waffles (1 serving) • prep time: 5 minutes • cook time: 6 minutes

Are you a fan of Nutella? Then you will love these waffles! *Note:* If you don't have hazelnut flour, you can grind toasted hazelnuts into a fine powder in a food processor or blender.

3 tablespoons hazelnut flour

2 tablespoons unsweetened cocoa powder

2 tablespoons confectioners'-style erythritol or equivalent amount of liquid or powdered sweetener (see page 77)

Pinch of fine sea salt

2 large eggs

Avocado or coconut oil spray

SERVING SUGGESTIONS

¼ batch Cream Cheese Glaze (page 354)

Sugar-Free Chocolate Hazelnut Spread (page 380)

Butter (omit for dairy-free)

Raspberries, for garnish

1. Preheat a mini waffle maker.

2. Place the hazelnut flour, cocoa powder, sweetener, salt, and eggs in a small bowl and use a fork to combine well.

3. Grease the waffle maker with avocado or coconut oil spray. Place half of the batter in the waffle maker and press the lid down. Cook for 2 to 3 minutes, until golden brown and cooked through. Use a fork to gently remove the waffle from the waffle maker or gently flip the waffle maker to release the waffle onto a plate. Repeat with the remaining batter.

4. Place the waffles on a plate. Drizzle with the glaze or top with chocolate hazelnut spread or butter, if desired. Garnish with fresh berries. Best served fresh.

(per serving): calories **323** • fat **24g** • protein **18g** • carbs **9g** • fiber **5g**

Drive-Thru Chaffle Burger

EASY   option

yield: 1 to 2 servings • prep time: 5 minutes (not including time to make chaffles) • cook time: 4 minutes

This chaffle burger is like a healthy Big Mac! The special sauce on this burger tastes just like McDonald's sauce. Don't be afraid to add the fish sauce. Fish sauce adds umami, which gives food an extra special flavor.

When making the burger patties for this sandwich, grease will come out of the sides of the waffle maker. It's okay; just be prepared. I place my waffle maker on a rimmed baking sheet to catch the grease.

⅓ pound ground beef

¼ teaspoon fine sea salt

2 Basic Savory Chaffles or Paffles (page 334)

1 slice cheddar cheese (omit for dairy-free)

4 dill pickle slices

2 leaves iceberg lettuce, shredded

¼ cup diced yellow onions

1 teaspoon toasted sesame seeds, for garnish (optional)

SPECIAL SAUCE
(makes about 1 cup)

½ cup mayonnaise, store-bought

¼ cup chopped dill pickles

3 tablespoons tomato sauce or sugar-free ketchup, homemade (page 369) or store-bought

1 teaspoon stevia glycerite, or a few drops of liquid stevia or monk fruit extract

⅛ teaspoon fine sea salt

⅛ teaspoon fish sauce (optional)

1. Preheat a mini waffle maker. Place the waffle maker on a rimmed baking sheet to catch any grease.

2. Divide the beef into 2 equal portions and form each into a patty. Season the outsides with the salt.

3. Place one patty in the waffle maker and press the lid down. Cook for 1½ to 2 minutes, until cooked to your liking. Remove from the waffle maker and repeat with the second beef patty.

4. Make the sauce: Place all the ingredients in a small bowl and stir well to combine. Taste and adjust the sweetness to your liking.

5. Place one chaffle on a plate, top with the beef patties, cheese, pickle slices, shredded lettuce, and onions, and drizzle with 2 tablespoons of the sauce. (You will have leftover sauce; it will keep in the fridge for up to a week.) Garnish with sesame seeds, if desired, and top with the other chaffle.

note:

If this double burger is too large for your little ones, feel free to slice it in half for sharing.

(chaffle sandwich with 2 tablespoons sauce): calories **1041** • fat **81g** • protein **68g** • carbs **7g** • fiber **1g**

Crispy Taco Chaffles

EASY   option

yield: 4 tacos (2 per serving) • prep time: 5 minutes (not including time to make taco meat or guacamole) • cook time: 12 minutes

One thing that my mom always has in the fridge is extra taco meat. We like to eat that all the time. It tastes great added to scrambled eggs, wrapped in lettuce leaves, served as nachos with pork rinds, or in crispy taco chaffles!

CHAFFLE TACO SHELLS

1 cup shredded cheddar cheese (or pork panko for dairy-free)

2 large eggs

Avocado or coconut oil spray

FILLINGS

½ cup Touchdown Taco meat (page 192), warmed

4 tablespoons shredded Monterey Jack cheese (omit for dairy-free)

4 tablespoons shredded lettuce

4 tablespoons guacamole (page 376)

4 tablespoons diced tomatoes or salsa

Fresh cilantro leaves, for garnish (optional)

1. Preheat a mini waffle maker. Place the waffle maker on a rimmed baking sheet to catch any grease.

2. Place the cheese and eggs in a small bowl and use a fork to combine well.

3. Grease the waffle maker with avocado or coconut oil spray. Place one-quarter of the cheese mixture in the waffle maker and press the lid down. Cook for 2 to 3 minutes, until golden brown and cooked through. Remove the chaffle from the waffle maker and place around a small ladle or wooden spoon handle so it forms a taco shell shape as it cools. Repeat with the remaining batter.

4. Fill each taco shell with 2 tablespoons of taco meat and 1 tablespoon each of the shredded cheese, lettuce, guacamole, and diced tomatoes. Garnish with cilantro, if desired. Best served fresh.

(per serving):
calories **691** • fat **54g** • protein **46g** • carbs **4g** • fiber **2g**

Strawberry Shortcake
Chaffle Sandwiches

EASY   option

yield: 2 sandwiches (1 per serving) • prep time: 5 minutes • cook time: 12 minutes

To make these Strawberry Shortcake Chaffles extra special for Valentine's Day, make them in a heart-shaped waffle maker!

CHAFFLES

1 cup shredded mozzarella cheese

2 large eggs

2 tablespoons confectioners'-style erythritol, or a few drops of stevia glycerite

¼ teaspoon strawberry, vanilla, or almond extract

Avocado or coconut oil spray

CHEESECAKE FILLING

2 ounces cream cheese (¼ cup), softened

1 large strawberry

2 tablespoons confectioners'-style erythritol, or a few drops of stevia glycerite

TOPPING (OPTIONAL)

¼ cup heavy cream

1 tablespoon confectioners'-style erythritol, or a few drops of stevia glycerite

Sliced strawberries

1. Preheat a mini waffle maker.

2. Place the mozzarella, eggs, sweetener, and extract in a small bowl and use a fork to combine well.

3. Grease the waffle maker with avocado or coconut oil spray. Place one-quarter of the cheese mixture in the waffle maker and press the lid down. Cook for 2 to 3 minutes, until golden brown and cooked through. Use a fork to gently remove the chaffle from the waffle maker or gently flip the waffle maker to release the chaffle onto a plate. Repeat with the remaining batter.

4. Meanwhile, make the filling: Place all the ingredients for the filling in a food processor and puree until smooth. Taste and adjust the sweetness to your liking.

5. Make the topping: Place the heavy cream and sweetener in a whipped cream dispenser.

6. Place one chaffle on a plate, top with half of the cheesecake filling, and top with another chaffle. Top the chaffle with a few sliced strawberries and some whipped cream, or place the toppings on the plate next to the chaffle sandwich, as pictured. Repeat with the remaining ingredients. Best served fresh.

(per serving):
calories **503** • fat **43g** • protein **23g** • carbs **3g** • fiber **0.2g**

"Apple" Pie
Waffles

EASY   option

yield: 4 waffles (1 per serving) • prep time: 2 minutes (not including time to make waffle batter) • cook time: 8 minutes

Mild-flavored zucchini makes a great low-sugar substitute for apples! We love this "apple" topping so much that I make a double batch to keep in the fridge for an easy waffle topping. It also tastes great over pork chops, inside of protein crêpes (page 88), or over No-Churn Vanilla Bean Ice Cream (page 317).

"APPLE" PIE TOPPING

1 small zucchini

¼ cup unsalted butter or coconut oil

3 tablespoons allulose (brown sugar–style preferred) or equivalent amount of powdered sweetener (see page 77)

1 tablespoon lemon juice

2 teaspoons vanilla extract

1 teaspoon ground cinnamon

1 batch Easy Blender Waffle batter (page 336)

1. Make the "apple" pie topping: Peel the zucchini, cut it lengthwise into quarters, and remove the seeds. Cut the zucchini into ¼-inch cubes.

2. If using butter, place the butter in a medium saucepan over medium-high heat and whisk often until brown flecks appear. Keep whisking until the butter is a deep brown color. Otherwise, heat the coconut oil in a medium saucepan over medium heat. Add the zucchini and the remaining ingredients and sauté for 8 minutes, or until softened to your liking. The longer you cook it, the softer it will be.

3. While the "apple" topping cooks, make the waffles as directed on page 336.

4. Serve the waffles topped with a few tablespoons of the "apple" topping.

5. Store extra topping and waffles in separate airtight containers in the refrigerator for up to 4 days, or freeze for up to a month. To reheat the topping, place it in a small saucepan over medium heat for 2 minutes, or until heated through. Reheat the waffles in a toaster oven or 350°F oven for 2 minutes, or until heated through and crispy.

(per serving):
calories **352** • fat **34g** • protein **8g** • carbs **6g** • fiber **2g**

Glazed Pumpkin Mini Waffles

MEDIUM option

yield: 8 mini waffles (2 per serving) • prep time: 5 minutes • cook time: 2 minutes per waffle

To make these pumpkin-flavored waffles extra special, use a pumpkin-shaped waffle maker!

1½ cups blanched almond flour

½ teaspoon baking soda

¼ teaspoon fine sea salt

1 teaspoon ground cinnamon

½ teaspoon ground nutmeg

¼ teaspoon ginger powder

⅛ teaspoon ground cloves

2 tablespoons coconut oil or unsalted butter, melted

½ cup confectioners'-style erythritol or equivalent amount of liquid or powdered sweetener (see page 77)

3 large eggs

1 cup fresh or canned pumpkin puree

Avocado or coconut oil spray

CREAM CHEESE GLAZE

4 ounces cream cheese (½ cup) (or Kite Hill brand cream cheese–style spread for dairy-free), softened

¼ cup unsweetened almond milk

3 to 4 tablespoons confectioners'-style erythritol or equivalent amount of liquid or powdered sweetener (see page 77)

1 teaspoon vanilla extract

1. Preheat a mini waffle maker.

2. In a large bowl, use a fork to stir the almond flour, baking soda, salt, and spices until well combined. In another bowl, stir together the coconut oil, sweetener, eggs, and pumpkin puree until smooth. Pour the wet mixture into the dry and stir until well combined.

3. Grease the waffle maker with avocado or coconut oil spray. Spoon 3 tablespoons of the batter into the greased waffle maker and press the lid down. Cook for 2 minutes, or until golden brown and cooked through. Use a fork to gently remove the waffle from the waffle maker or gently flip the waffle maker to release the waffle onto a plate. Repeat with the remaining batter.

4. Make the glaze: Stir the cream cheese with a fork until it is very loose and there are no lumps. Slowly add the almond milk and stir until smooth. Add the sweetener and vanilla and stir until smooth. Taste and adjust the sweetness to your liking. Just before serving, drizzle the glaze over the waffles.

5. Store extras in an airtight container in the refrigerator for up to 4 days. To reheat unglazed waffles, place in a toaster oven or mini waffle maker for 1 minute, or until heated through.

(per serving): calories **245** • fat **21g** • protein **8g** • carbs **8g** • fiber **3g**

Waffle Cone
Mini Waffles

EASY option

yield: 3 mini waffles (1 per serving) • prep time: 5 minutes • cook time: 4 minutes

These sweet waffles taste great with a scoop of my no-churn ice cream (pages 317 to 323) on top!

1 large egg

2 tablespoons unsweetened almond milk or heavy cream

½ cup blanched almond flour

2 teaspoons confectioners'-style erythritol or equivalent amount of liquid or powdered sweetener (see page 77)

1 tablespoon coconut oil or unsalted butter, melted

1 teaspoon vanilla extract

½ teaspoon almond extract (or more vanilla)

Pinch of fine sea salt

Avocado or coconut oil spray

1. Preheat a mini waffle maker.

2. In a large bowl, use a fork to stir together the egg and almond milk. Add the almond flour and sweetener and stir to combine well. Add the melted oil, extracts, and salt and stir well once more.

3. Grease the waffle maker with avocado or coconut oil spray. Spoon half of the batter into the greased waffle maker and press the lid down. Cook for 2 minutes, or until golden brown and cooked through. Use a fork to gently remove the waffle from the hot waffle maker or gently flip the waffle maker to release the waffle onto a plate. Repeat with the remaining batter.

4. Store extras in an airtight container in the fridge for up to 4 days. To reheat, place in a toaster oven or mini waffle maker for 1 minute, or until heated through.

(per serving):
calories **176** • fat **16g** • protein **6g** • carbs **4g** • fiber **2g**

Bacon Cheeseburger
Waffle

EASY

yield: 1 serving • prep time: 5 minutes • cook time: 17 minutes

My boys love bacon cheeseburgers, and they love waffles! They also prefer savory waffles over sweet ones, so I created this recipe for them. I love making these waffles because they are so easy—you can even cook the bacon in a toaster oven. If you like, you can add a drizzle of the nacho cheese sauce from Epic Cheesy Beef Nachos (page 242), as pictured.

2 slices bacon (pork or beef)

Avocado or coconut oil spray

4 ounces ground beef

¼ cup shredded sharp cheddar cheese

2 large eggs

½ teaspoon fine sea salt

FOR SERVING

Sugar-free ketchup, homemade (page 369) or store-bought

Prepared yellow mustard

Ranch dressing, homemade (page 367 or 368) or store-bought

1. Preheat the oven to 400°F. Line a rimmed baking sheet with parchment paper.

2. Place the bacon in a single layer on the parchment and place in the oven (no need for it to be fully preheated). Bake for 8 to 17 minutes, until cooked to your liking.

3. While the bacon cooks, make the waffle: Preheat a waffle maker. When hot, grease it well with avocado or coconut oil spray.

4. Place the beef, cheese, eggs, and salt in a small bowl. Use a fork to stir until well combined.

5. Place the beef mixture in the center of the waffle maker and close the lid. Cook for 2 to 3 minutes, until golden brown and cooked through. Remove from the waffle maker and place on a plate. Top with the bacon and serve with ketchup, ranch, and/or mustard, if desired.

(per serving):
calories **588** • fat **43g** • protein **46g** • carbs **1g** • fiber **0g**

Chocolate
Waffle Sandwich

EASY   option

yield: 1 serving • prep time: 5 minutes • cook time: 4 minutes

This chocolate waffle sandwich reminds me of a giant soft Oreo cookie! If you use black cocoa powder, you get a deeper Oreo-like flavor. You can find black cocoa powder online or at specialty stores.

WAFFLES

1 large egg

2 tablespoons unsweetened almond milk or heavy cream

2 tablespoons blanched almond flour

1 tablespoon unsweetened cocoa powder or black cocoa powder

2 teaspoons confectioners'-style erythritol or equivalent amount of liquid or powdered sweetener (see page 77)

1 tablespoon coconut oil or unsalted butter, melted

1 teaspoon vanilla extract

½ teaspoon almond extract (or more vanilla)

Pinch of fine sea salt

Avocado or coconut oil spray

FILLING

6 tablespoons unsalted butter (or coconut oil for dairy-free), softened

2 ounces cream cheese (¼ cup) (or Kite Hill brand cream cheese–style spread for dairy-free), softened

2 tablespoons heavy cream (or unsweetened coconut or almond milk for dairy-free), room temperature

⅓ cup confectioners'-style erythritol or equivalent amount of liquid or powdered sweetener (see page 77)

⅛ teaspoon fine sea salt

Strawberry, orange, almond, or raspberry extract, or a dash of pumpkin pie spice (optional)

1. Preheat a mini waffle maker.

2. In a large bowl, use a fork to stir together the egg and almond milk. Add the almond flour, cocoa powder, and sweetener and stir to combine well. Add the melted oil, extracts, and salt. Stir to combine well.

3. Grease the waffle maker with avocado or coconut oil spray. Spoon half of the batter into the greased waffle maker and press the lid down. Cook for 2 minutes, or until golden brown and cooked through. Use a fork to gently remove the waffle from the waffle maker or gently flip the waffle maker to release the waffle onto a plate. Repeat with the remaining batter.

4. Meanwhile, make the filling: Place the butter, cream cheese, and heavy cream in a medium bowl and use a hand mixer to combine well. Mix in the sweetener and salt. Add the extract or spice, if using. Taste and adjust the sweetness to your liking.

5. Place one waffle on a plate, top with the filling, and then top with the other waffle.

(per serving):
calories **459** • fat **44g** • protein **11g** • carbs **6g** • fiber **3g**

chapter 11:
basics, sauces & dips

Easy Tartar Sauce / 364

Easiest Mayo Ever / 365

Veggie Dill Dip / 366

Protein-Packed Ranch Dip / 367

Traditional Ranch / 368

Sugar-Free Ketchup / 369

Pizza Sauce / 370

Fruit Dip / 371

Blender Marinara Sauce / 372

Roasted Garlic / 374

Guacamole / 376

Sugar-Free Strawberry Jam / 378

Sugar-Free Chocolate Hazelnut Spread / 380

Soft Tortillas / 382

Sandwich Buns / 384

Easy English Muffins / 386

Taco Seasoning / 388

Easy
Tartar Sauce

EASY

yield: 1 cup (2 tablespoons per serving) • prep time: 4 minutes

Tartar sauce is a must with my Fish Fingers (page 204). Store-bought mayo works best here; I like Primal Kitchen brand.

¾ cup mayonnaise, store-bought

2 tablespoons dill pickle juice

2 tablespoons finely diced dill pickles

¼ teaspoon fine sea salt

1 tablespoon confectioners'-style erythritol or equivalent amount of liquid or powdered sweetener (see page 77) (optional)

Put all the ingredients in a small bowl and stir until smooth. Store in an airtight container in the refrigerator for up to 2 weeks.

(per serving):
calories **135** • fat **15g** • protein **0g** • carbs **0g** • fiber **0g**

Easiest
Mayo Ever

EASY   option

yield: 2 cups (2½ tablespoons per serving) • prep time: 5 minutes, plus 4 hours to chill (not including time to boil eggs)

This is the easiest and highest-in-protein mayo ever, but it's a bit different from traditional mayonnaise. If this version isn't your favorite, I have an easy recipe for classic mayo on my blog, KetoMaria.com. Make sure to chill this mayo in the refrigerator overnight for the best flavor.

6 hard-boiled eggs, peeled

¼ cup beef broth (or vegetable broth for vegetarian)

2 tablespoons dill pickle juice or lemon juice

1½ teaspoons prepared yellow or Dijon mustard

½ teaspoon fine sea salt

Place all the ingredients in a high-powered blender or food processor and puree until smooth. Taste and adjust the seasoning to your liking. Place in the refrigerator to chill for at least 4 hours or overnight for the best flavor. Store in an airtight container in the refrigerator for up to 6 days.

(per serving):
calories **38** • fat **3g** • protein **3g** • carbs **0.2g** • fiber **0g**

Veggie Dill Dip

EASY   option   option

yield: 2½ cups (2½ tablespoons per serving) • prep time: 5 minutes, plus 30 minutes to chill

This herby dip goes great with my Veggie and Savory Fruit Flowers (page 130).

1 cup mayonnaise, homemade (page 365) or store-bought

1 cup sour cream or crème fraîche (or more mayo for dairy-free)

2 tablespoons chopped fresh dill

2 tablespoons finely chopped green onions

½ teaspoon fine sea salt

2 tablespoons chicken broth (optional, to thin the dip; omit for vegetarian)

In a medium bowl, use a fork to mix the mayo, sour cream, dill, green onions, and salt until well combined. Refrigerate for at least 30 minutes to allow the flavors to meld. If the dip is too thick after chilling, stir in the broth 1 tablespoon at a time until the dip reaches your preferred consistency. Taste and adjust the salt to your liking. Store in an airtight container in the refrigerator for up to 4 days.

(per serving):
calories **121** • fat **13g** • protein **1g** • carbs **1g** • fiber **0g**

Protein-Packed
Ranch Dip

EASY · **option**

yield: 2 cups (2½ tablespoons per serving) • prep time: 5 minutes, plus 4 hours to chill (not including time to boil eggs)

This is the easiest and highest-in-protein ranch dip ever, but it is a bit different from traditional ranch. If this version isn't your favorite, I have a more traditional recipe on the next page. Make sure to put this dip in the refrigerator to chill overnight for the best flavor. It works great as a dip for veggies or Kai's Chicken Wings (page 132).

6 hard-boiled eggs

½ cup beef broth (or vegetable broth for vegetarian)

2 tablespoons dill pickle juice

2 tablespoons dried parsley

1 tablespoon onion powder

1 teaspoon garlic powder

1 teaspoon dried chives

1 teaspoon dried dill weed

½ teaspoon fine sea salt

½ teaspoon ground black pepper

Place all the ingredients in a high-powered blender or food processor and puree until smooth. Taste and adjust the seasoning to your liking. Place in the refrigerator to chill for at least 4 hours or overnight for the best flavor. Store in an airtight container in the refrigerator for up to 6 days.

(per serving):
calories **39** • fat **3g** • protein **3g** • carbs **1g** • fiber **0.1g**

Traditional
Ranch

EASY   option   option   option

yield: 2 cups (2 tablespoons per serving) • prep time: 5 minutes, plus 2 hours to chill

Making your own dressing is so easy; all you do is place all the ingredients in a blender and puree until smooth. Simple and delicious! If you eat dairy, you can swap out the mayo in this recipe for softened cream cheese. It makes the most amazing ranch you have ever tasted!

1 cup mayonnaise, store-bought, or 1 (8-ounce) package cream cheese, softened

¾ cup chicken or beef broth (or vegetable broth for vegetarian)

RANCH SEASONING

2 tablespoons dried parsley

1 tablespoon onion powder

2 teaspoons garlic powder

1½ teaspoons dried dill weed

1 teaspoon dried chives

1 teaspoon fine sea salt

1 teaspoon ground black pepper

Place all the ingredients in a 16-ounce (or larger) jar, seal the lid, and shake vigorously until well combined. Cover and refrigerate for 2 hours before serving; it will thicken as it rests. Store in the refrigerator for up to 5 days.

(per serving):
calories **93** • fat **10g** • protein **0.3g** • carbs **0.5g** • fiber **0.1g**

Sugar-Free
Ketchup

EASY   option

yield: 2 cups (1 tablespoon per serving) • prep time: 4 minutes

It is shocking where sugar is hidden—the majority of the sugar we eat isn't even known to us! Most ketchup is filled with corn syrup, sugar, and more sugar. My sugar-free version is so easy yet so delicious and packed with a fresh tomato flavor. Kai puts it on everything, including his scrambled eggs!

1½ cups beef or chicken broth (or vegetable broth for vegetarian)

1 (7-ounce) jar tomato paste

2 tablespoons apple cider vinegar or coconut vinegar

1 tablespoon confectioners'-style erythritol or equivalent amount of liquid or powdered sweetener (see page 77)

1 teaspoon garlic powder

1 teaspoon onion powder

1 teaspoon fine sea salt

Place all the ingredients in a medium bowl and stir until smooth. Taste and adjust the seasoning to your liking. Store in an airtight container in the refrigerator for up to 12 days.

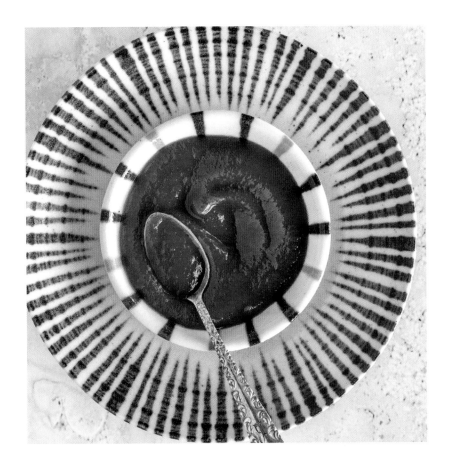

(per serving):
calories 6 • fat 0g • protein 0.3g • carbs 1g • fiber 0.4g

Pizza Sauce

EASY option

yield: 1¼ cups (¼ cup per serving) • prep time: 5 minutes

This sauce tastes great in several recipes in this book, including Pizza Rolls (page 134), Mama Maria's Pizza Chicken Balls (page 208), and Christmas Tree Pizza (page 262). Most pizza sauces are sweetened, so if you prefer a more traditional sauce, feel free to add the sweetener.

1 cup tomato sauce

3 tablespoons grated Parmesan cheese (omit for dairy-free)

2 tablespoons confectioners'-style erythritol or equivalent amount of liquid or powdered sweetener (see page 77) (optional)

2 teaspoons Italian seasoning

1 teaspoon garlic powder

¾ teaspoon onion powder

¼ teaspoon ground black pepper

Place all the ingredients in a small bowl and stir until smooth. Cover and refrigerate until ready to use; it will keep for up to 3 days. Stir before using.

(per serving):
calories **29** • fat **1g** • protein **2g** • carbs **3g** • fiber **0.5g**

Fruit
Dip

EASY   option   yield: 1¼ cups (5 tablespoons per serving) • prep time: 5 minutes

I like to serve this sweet dip with my Fruit Flower Bouquet (page 152). For the yogurt, I like Two Good brand. In this recipe, I also use erythritol brown, which is a natural brown sugar–type sweetener. If you have that option, I highly recommend it.

1 cup plain low-carb yogurt

¼ cup confectioners'-style erythritol or equivalent amount of liquid or powdered sweetener (see page 77) (optional)

1 teaspoon vanilla or almond extract

Place all the ingredients in a small bowl and stir well to combine. Taste and adjust the sweetness to your liking. Store in an airtight container in the refrigerator for up to 4 days.

(per serving):
calories **36** • fat **1g** • protein **5g** • carbs **1g** • fiber **0g**

Blender
Marinara Sauce

yield: 2½ cups (¼ cup per serving) • prep time: 5 minutes • cook time: 20 minutes

MEDIUM   option

Every year, I teach about nutrition while traveling around Italy with the travel agency MilleVie Travel. During our sessions, we often talk about our favorite recipes and how to make a healthy lifestyle easier. One woman named Katya told me about making marinara sauce in a blender. I was so intrigued by this amazing recipe, I made it as soon as I got home. It is now a family staple, and we make it often.

1 pound plum tomatoes, quartered

1 small onion, peeled and quartered

8 cloves garlic, peeled

1 cup packed fresh basil leaves

¼ cup melted coconut oil or lard

2 teaspoons fine sea salt

2 teaspoons stevia glycerite (optional)

1. Preheat the oven to 375°F. Line a rimmed baking sheet with parchment paper.

2. Place the tomatoes, onion, garlic, and basil leaves on the prepared baking sheet. Drizzle the melted coconut oil over the tomato mixture and use your hands to mix. Sprinkle the mixture evenly with the salt.

3. Bake, stirring every 5 minutes, until the garlic is soft and cooked through, about 20 minutes.

4. Remove from the oven and transfer the tomato mixture to a blender. Pulse until you have a sauce with a few chunks remaining, if desired.

5. Store in an airtight container in the refrigerator for up to 3 days, or freeze for up to a month. To reheat, place in a saucepan over medium heat for 3 minutes, or until heated through.

(per serving):
calories 31 • fat 3g • protein 0.3g • carbs 2g • fiber 0.3g

Roasted Garlic

EASY

yield: 12 heads (1 head per serving) • prep time: 5 minutes •
cook time: 25 minutes

Roasted garlic is milder and sweeter than raw garlic, and children often prefer
the taste of roasted garlic over raw. It works great in my homemade pizza
sauce (page 370), Easy Blender Marinara (page 372), or any recipe that calls for
garlic. I keep roasted garlic in my freezer at all times to add a quick punch of
flavor to recipes.

12 heads garlic

¼ cup avocado oil

½ teaspoon fine sea salt

1. Preheat the oven to 400°F. Cut twelve 4-inch squares of
   parchment paper and twelve 4-inch squares of aluminum foil.
   Lay a parchment square on top of each foil square.

2. Slice ⅛ inch off the top of each head of garlic to expose the
   cloves and place the heads in a baking dish. Pour the oil over
   the tops of the heads of garlic, letting it sink down into the
   cloves, then sprinkle the tops with the salt.

3. Put each head of garlic on a square of parchment paper
   placed on a square of foil and wrap the head tightly. Put the
   wrapped garlic in a 9-inch square baking dish.

4. Roast the garlic for 20 minutes, or until soft. Even after it is
   soft, you can continue roasting until it is deeply golden for a
   sweeter, more caramelized flavor—check it every 5 minutes.
   The exact roasting time will depend on the size of your heads
   of garlic, the age of the garlic, and the variety.

5. Allow to cool, then squeeze the garlic cloves from the skin as
   needed. Store extra roasted heads of garlic in the skin in the
   freezer for up to 3 months.

(per serving):
calories **83** • fat **5g** • protein **2g** • carbs **9g** • fiber **1g**

Guacamole

EASY

yield: 3 cups (½ cup per serving) • prep time: 15 minutes, plus 1 hour to chill (optional)

This guacamole tastes great with my Green Eggs and Ham (page 108), Touchdown Tacos (page 192), and Cheese Quesadillas (page 194). I also serve it as a dip with my Veggie and Savory Fruit Flowers (page 130).

3 avocados, peeled and pitted

3 tablespoons lime juice, plus more to taste

½ cup finely diced onions

2 plum tomatoes, diced

2 cloves garlic, smashed to a paste, or ½ head roasted garlic (page 374)

3 tablespoons chopped fresh cilantro

1 teaspoon fine sea salt

½ teaspoon ground cumin

1. Place the avocados and lime juice in a large bowl and mash to the desired consistency. Add the rest of the ingredients and stir until well combined. Taste and add more lime juice, if desired.

2. For the best flavor, cover tightly and refrigerate for 1 hour, or serve immediately.

3. To store, transfer the guacamole to a large resealable plastic bag, squeeze out as much air as you can, and seal the bag. When stored this way, it will keep in the refrigerator for up to 3 days.

(per serving): calories **168** • fat **15g** • protein **2g** • carbs **10g** • fiber **7g**

Sugar-Free
Strawberry Jam

MEDIUM

yield: 2¾ cups (2 tablespoons per serving) • prep time: 10 minutes • cook time: 2 minutes

 I love my mom's sugar-free jam on toasted English Muffins (page 386)! I like to help her make it.

1 pound fresh or frozen strawberries

1 cup cold water

¼ cup confectioners'-style erythritol or equivalent amount of liquid or powdered sweetener (see page 77)

2 tablespoons unflavored gelatin

¼ teaspoon fine sea salt

1. Place the strawberries in a blender and puree until smooth.

2. Put the water and sweetener in a small saucepan. Whisk in the gelatin. Allow to soften for 1 minute, then bring to a simmer over high heat. Add the strawberry puree and salt. Taste and adjust the sweetness to your liking. Lower the heat to medium-high and simmer for 1 minute.

3. Remove from the heat, transfer the jam to clean jars, and allow to cool completely. Cover the jars and store in the refrigerator for up to 10 days, or freeze for up to 6 months (see tip).

tip:

If freezing the jam, leave 1 inch of space at the top of the jar to allow for expansion.

chapter 11: basics, sauces & dips

(per serving):
calories **9** • fat **0g** • protein **1g** • carbs **1g** • fiber **0.3g**

Sugar-Free Chocolate
Hazelnut Spread

MEDIUM

yield: 3 cups (2 tablespoons per serving) • prep time: 10 minutes • cook time: 10 minutes

Nutella, a popular brand of chocolate hazelnut spread, is filled with sugar, so it isn't something I buy at the store. But here is a great sugar-free alternative for Nutella lovers! My recipe testers told me their children loved helping them roll the hazelnuts around to get the skins off. This can be a fun family project!

2 cups raw hazelnuts

½ cup unsweetened cocoa powder

½ cup confectioners'-style erythritol or equivalent amount of liquid or powdered sweetener (see page 77)

½ teaspoon vanilla or hazelnut extract

⅛ teaspoon fine sea salt

3 tablespoons hazelnut oil or melted coconut oil

1. Preheat the oven to 400°F.

2. Put the hazelnuts on a rimmed baking sheet and spread them into a single layer. Place in the oven to toast for 10 minutes, or until the nuts start to darken a little and become fragrant, checking them after 7 minutes to make sure they aren't burning.

3. Remove the pan from the oven, place the toasted hazelnuts in a large clean kitchen towel, and rub to remove the skins.

4. Place the skinless hazelnuts in a food processor or blender and pulse, scraping the sides of the bowl as needed, until you have a smooth nut butter, about 5 minutes.

5. Add the cocoa powder, sweetener, vanilla, salt, and oil to the food processor and process until well blended, about 1 minute. The spread should have the consistency of creamy peanut butter; if it is too dry, add a little more oil and process until the desired consistency is achieved. Taste and adjust the sweetness to your liking.

6. Store in an airtight container in the refrigerator for up to 2 weeks.

(per serving):
calories **73** • fat **6g** • protein **2g** • carbs **3g** • fiber **2g**

Soft Tortillas

MEDIUM

yield: 10 tortillas (2 per serving) • prep time: 5 minutes • cook time: 4 minutes

The texture and flavor of these soft tortillas will remind you of traditional flour tortillas, and they're not difficult to make. Use them for Touchdown Tacos (page 192) and Cheese Quesadillas (page 194).

1½ cups blanched almond flour

5 tablespoons psyllium husk powder

2 teaspoons baking powder

1 teaspoon fine sea salt

2½ tablespoons apple cider vinegar

3 large egg whites

1 cup boiling water

1. Preheat the oven to 325°F. Line 2 rimmed baking sheets with parchment paper.

2. In a medium bowl, whisk together the flour, psyllium husk powder, baking powder, and salt. Stir in the vinegar and egg whites until a thick dough forms. Add the water and mix until well combined. Let sit for 1 to 2 minutes, until the dough firms up.

3. Lightly grease two 8-inch pieces of parchment paper. Separate the dough into 10 balls, about 2 inches in diameter. Place a ball of dough in the center of one of the greased pieces of parchment. Top it with the other greased piece of parchment. Using a rolling pin, roll out the dough into a very thin circle about 4 inches in diameter. This dough is very forgiving, so if you didn't make a perfect circle with the rolling pin, just use your hands to shape the tortilla. Alternatively, if you have a tortilla press, place the dough, sandwiched between the two greased pieces of parchment, in the press and press down to flatten it to the edge of the press.

4. Place the tortilla on one of the prepared baking sheets. Repeat with the remaining balls of dough. Bake for 4 minutes, until the tortillas are cooked through and starting to brown.

5. Store extras in an airtight container in the refrigerator for up to 5 days, or freeze for up to a month.

(per serving): calories **232** • fat **16g** • protein **10g** • carbs **16g** • fiber **10g**

Sandwich
Buns

MEDIUM

yield: 8 buns (1 per serving) • prep time: 5 minutes • cook time: 32 minutes

These buns are made from the exact same ingredients as the tortillas on page 382! You can shape them any way you like—make them into hot dog shapes for Sloppy Kai Dogs (page 190), or form them into sub sandwich shapes and make meatball subs using the meatballs on page 198.

1½ cups blanched almond flour

5 tablespoons psyllium husk powder

2 teaspoons baking powder

1 teaspoon fine sea salt

2½ tablespoons apple cider vinegar

3 large egg whites

1 cup boiling water

1. Preheat the oven to 325°F. Line a rimmed baking sheet with parchment paper.

2. In a medium bowl, whisk together the flour, psyllium husk powder, baking powder, and salt. Stir in the vinegar and egg whites until a thick dough forms. Add the water and mix until well combined. Let sit for 1 to 2 minutes, until the dough firms up.

3. Divide the dough into 8 equal portions and shape each portion into a ball about 2¼ inches in diameter. Place the balls on the prepared baking sheet spaced about 1 inch apart. Bake for 27 to 32 minutes, until the buns are puffed and cooked through.

4. Store extras in an airtight container in the refrigerator for up to 5 days, or freeze for up to a month.

busy family tip:
If your family loves these buns, make extra and store them in the freezer for quick sandwiches.

(per serving):
calories **154** • fat **11g** • protein **6g** • carbs **10g** • fiber **7g**

Easy English Muffins

EASY

yield: 4 muffins (1 per serving) • prep time: 5 minutes (not including time to boil eggs) • cook time: 15 minutes

This recipe makes a very low-carb English muffin that is not only simple to prepare, but so versatile. You can use it for making sandwiches. You can slather each slice with a teaspoon of butter or coconut oil and toast them in a preheated 400°F oven for about 2 minutes. These muffins also make great English Muffin Pizzas (page 178).

3 hard-boiled eggs, peeled

3 large eggs

2 tablespoons coconut flour

1 teaspoon baking powder

½ teaspoon fine sea salt

1. Preheat the oven to 350°F. Grease four 4-ounce ramekins.

2. Place all the ingredients in a blender and puree until smooth. Pour the batter into the ramekins, filling each about two-thirds full.

3. Place the ramekins in the oven and bake for 10 to 15 minutes, until a toothpick comes out clean when inserted in the middle of a muffin.

4. Let cool slightly before removing the muffins from the ramekins. Run a knife around the edges of the muffins to help release them. To serve, cut the muffins in half.

5. Store extras in an airtight container in the refrigerator for up to 4 days, or freeze for up to a month.

(per serving):
calories **116** • fat **8g** • protein **10g** • carbs **2g** • fiber **1g**

Taco Seasoning

EASY

yield: ¼ cup (2 tablespoons per serving) • prep time: 5 minutes • cook time: 5 minutes

There are a few issues with using prepackaged spice mixes. First, caramel coloring, a common ingredient in these mixes, is a food dye that the FDA is in the process of banning due to its links to cancer. Another issue is maltodextrin, also a common ingredient. Sugar has a glycemic index of 52, and maltodextrin is 110! And most brands don't list an actual spice until the fourth ingredient. I'll stick to making my own mixes, like this handy taco seasoning. Use it in my Protein Noodle Taco Lasagna (page 202) and Taco Meatball Holiday Tree (page 272).

2 tablespoons chili powder

1 tablespoon ground cumin

2 teaspoons fine sea salt

2 teaspoons ground black pepper

1 teaspoon paprika

½ teaspoon garlic powder

½ teaspoon onion powder

½ teaspoon ground dried oregano

½ teaspoon red pepper flakes

2 teaspoons confectioners'-style erythritol or equivalent amount of powdered sweetener (see page 77) (optional)

In a bowl, mix together all the ingredients. Store in an airtight container for up to 3 months.

(per serving):
calories **33** • fat **1g** • protein **1g** • carbs **6g** • fiber **3g**

chapter 12:
babies' first foods

Bone Broth / 392

Bone Marrow / 394

Salmon Puree with Salt / 396

Ground Beef with Salt / 398

Salted Egg Yolks / 400

Chicken Pâté / 402

Bone Broth

EASY

yield: 4 quarts (1 cup per serving) • prep time: 10 minutes • cook time: 1 to 3 days

Kai's first food after breast milk (I had a friend pump for me) was my homemade beef bone broth. I would make a pot once a week to put it into his bottle. When he woke up and saw the bottle of broth, his legs would start to kick a mile a minute—he *loved* this stuff! Adults can also drink it as a nourishing beverage, and you can use it to make soups and sauces.

Bone broth is one of the most nourishing foods. If I could bottle it up into a pill, the pharmaceutical companies would be broke! Its medicinal benefits are attributed to its exceptionally high levels of minerals and amino acids. In fact, bone broth can be considered a high-quality multi-mineral and protein supplement. It contains minerals in a form the body can absorb easily—not just calcium but also magnesium, phosphorus, silicone, and sulfur.

Nothing could be easier to make than this broth. Once you get all the ingredients in the slow cooker, it does all the work for you. The longer you cook the broth, the thicker it will get, and the more nutrients will be extracted from the bones. If you roast the bones before making the broth, they will create a darker and more flavorful broth.

4 large beef bones (about 4 pounds), or leftover bones and skin from 1 pastured chicken (ideally with the feet), or 4 pounds fish bones and heads

4 quarts cold water (reverse-osmosis or filtered water is best)

1 medium onion, chopped

2 stalks celery, sliced ¼ inch thick

2 teaspoons finely chopped garlic, or 1 head roasted garlic (page 374)

2 tablespoons coconut vinegar or apple cider vinegar

2 tablespoons fresh rosemary or other herb of choice

2 teaspoons fine sea salt

1 teaspoon fresh or dried thyme leaves

1. Optional: Preheat the oven to 450°F. Place the bones on a rimmed baking sheet. Roast for 35 minutes, or until the bones are browned.

2. Place all the ingredients in a 6-quart slow cooker. Cover and cook on high for 1 hour, then turn the heat to low and continue cooking for a minimum of 1 day and up to 3 days.

3. When the broth is done, pour it through a strainer and discard the solids.

4. Store extras in the fridge for up to 5 days or in the freezer for up to several months.

(per serving):
calories **40** • fat **0g** • protein **10g** • carbs **0g** • fiber **0g**

Bone
Marrow

EASY

yield: 6 servings • prep time: 5 minutes • cook time: 25 minutes

Bone marrow is like a savory Jell-O. It is soft and creamy and oh so delicious! It is also filled with nutrients and helps with bone building. (Most of our bones are built before the age of eighteen.) Sadly, grocery stores often sell these miraculous marrow bones as "dog bones." If you're having a hard time finding marrow bones, just ask the butcher, who will be able to steer you in the right direction.

Now that my children are older, I love to season bone marrow with truffle salt when I make it for us. Adults can spoon it onto scrambled eggs or salmon or smear it on a burger (see page 346).

6 marrow bones

Fine sea salt

1. Preheat the oven to 450°F.

2. Rinse, drain, and pat the bones dry and place in a roasting pan or large ceramic baking dish. If the bones are cut lengthwise, place them cut side up. If they are cut crosswise, stand them up.

3. Roast for 15 to 25 minutes (the roasting time will depend on how large the bones are), until the marrow has puffed slightly and is warm in the center. To test for doneness, insert a metal skewer into the center of a bone. There should be no resistance when it is inserted, and some of the marrow will have started to leak from the bones. Season with salt and serve immediately.

(per serving):
calories **330** • fat **35g** • protein **3g** • carbs **0g** • fiber **0g**

Salmon Puree
with Salt

EASY

yield: 2 servings • prep time: 5 minutes • cook time: 15 minutes

One of the first foods I fed my baby Kai was this salmon puree. He absolutely loved it! I have cute videos of Micah feeding Kai as he scraped the blender clean with a spatula.

1 (4-ounce) salmon fillet, skin and pin bones removed

½ teaspoon fine sea salt

1 teaspoon melted tallow, lard, or coconut oil

¼ cup bone broth (page 392) or bone marrow (page 394) (optional)

1. Preheat the oven to 425°F.

2. Lay a 12-inch square piece of parchment paper on top of a 12-inch square piece of aluminum foil. Place the salmon in the center of the parchment. Season the fish well on all sides with the salt. Drizzle with the melted fat.

3. To form a packet, wrap the ends of the parchment and foil tightly around the fish and fold over twice to secure. Twist the ends and fold them under the fish. Place the packet on a rimmed baking sheet.

4. Bake for 15 minutes, or until the salmon is flaky and no longer translucent in the center. The exact timing will depend on the thickness of the fillet. (Be careful when opening the packet; very hot steam will escape.)

Depending on age:

*   For babies who aren't ready to chew: Place the salmon and ¼ cup of bone broth or melted bone marrow in a blender or food processor and puree until smooth, as shown in the photo. Serve barely warm.

*   For babies who chew: Place the salmon on a plate and smash into very small pieces with a fork. Serve barely warm.

*   Adults can eat the salmon right out of the packet for a super simple dinner.

Store extras in an airtight container in the refrigerator for up to 3 days. To reheat, place the fish in a baking dish in a preheated 350°F oven for 5 minutes, or until warmed through.

(per serving):
calories **198** • fat **16g** • protein **12g** • carbs **0g** • fiber **0g**

Ground Beef
with Salt

EASY   option

yield: 2 servings • prep time: 5 minutes • cook time: 4 minutes

You know we love our beef, which is one of the most nutrient-dense foods! It is richer in nutrients than any fruit or vegetable. When Kai was a baby and I would cook hamburgers or chili for the rest of us, I would make this simple dish for Kai. It is a great recipe for babies who are starting to chew. You can puree the beef mixture for babies who are not yet ready to chew.

1 tablespoon tallow, lard, unsalted butter, or coconut oil

4 ounces ground beef

1 teaspoon fine sea salt

Melt the fat in a small skillet over medium-high heat. Once melted, add the ground beef and season with the salt. Cook, while crumbling the meat into tiny pieces with a wooden spoon, for 4 minutes, or until no longer pink. Remove from the heat and allow to cool until it is barely warm.

Depending on age:

- For babies who aren't ready to chew: Place the ground beef and ¼ cup of bone broth in a blender or food processor and puree until smooth.

- For babies who chew: Serve the beef crumbles on a plate and allow the baby to pick up with their fingers.

Store extras in an airtight container in the refrigerator for up to 3 days. To reheat, place the beef in a baking dish in a preheated 350°F oven for 5 minutes, or until warmed through.

(per serving):
calories **185** • fat **15g** • protein **10g** • carbs **0g** • fiber **0g**

Salted Egg Yolks

EASY

yield: 3 servings • prep time: 5 minutes • cook time: 11 minutes

Egg yolks are a perfect brain food for babies as well as adults. You can add yolks to your baby's diet as early as four months of age; in the slight chance that your baby reacts poorly to them at four months, stop and try again at six months. Why just the yolk? The white is the portion that contains the protein and most often causes allergic reactions. Wait until your baby turns one to feed them egg whites.

Yolks are rich in cholesterol, which is essential for the production of many hormones in an infant. Cholesterol is needed for many functions, including insulating the nerves in the brain and the entire central nervous system. It helps with fat digestion by increasing the formation of bile acids. A baby's brain grows rapidly, and the brain is extremely dependent on cholesterol. Egg yolks are also rich in choline, another vital nutrient for brain development.

The best choice is organic eggs from pasture-fed hens that forage for insects, which contain higher levels of DHA. Don't neglect to put a pinch of salt on the yolk. I save the leftover whites to make my Protein Sparing Pudding, which you can find on KetoMaria.com.

6 large eggs

½ teaspoon fine sea salt

A few tablespoons of bone broth (page 392), as needed

1. Place the eggs in a large saucepan and cover with cold water. Bring to a boil, then immediately cover the pan and remove it from the heat. Allow the eggs to cook in the hot water for 11 minutes. After 11 minutes, drain the water and rinse the eggs with very cold water for a minute or two to stop the cooking process. Peel the eggs.

2. Separate the yolks from the whites and place the yolks in a medium bowl or food processor. Add the salt and a few tablespoons of bone broth and mix until you have a smooth, thick puree, adding more broth if needed to achieve the desired consistency. Serve to your baby with a baby spoon.

3. Store extras in an airtight container in the refrigerator for up to 3 days.

(per serving):
calories **149** • fat **10g** • protein **13g** • carbs **1g** • fiber **0g**

Chicken
Pâté

EASY   option

yield: 8 servings • prep time: 5 minutes, plus 2 hours to chill • cook time: 5 minutes

This chicken pâté is a delicious way to get a large dose of nutrients into your baby. It tastes so good that even adults love it!

½ cup plus 2 tablespoons tallow, lard, or unsalted butter, divided

1 pound chicken livers, thinly sliced

1½ teaspoons fine sea salt

1. Heat 2 tablespoons of the fat in a large cast-iron skillet over medium-high heat. Once hot, add the sliced chicken livers and sauté for 5 minutes, or until the livers are cooked through.

2. Remove the livers from the skillet and transfer to a food processor. Add the remaining ½ cup of fat and the salt and puree until smooth. Taste and adjust the seasoning to your liking. Place in the fridge to chill for at least 2 hours. Serve chilled.

3. Store extras in an airtight container in the refrigerator for up to 4 days.

(per serving):
calories **266** • fat **22g** • protein **14g** • carbs **0g** • fiber **0g**

With Gratitude

I take the little things in life for granted. I think we all do. While I was writing this book, I was still consulting with clients daily. One morning I was brought to tears of gratitude.

I had an early-morning Skype consult before my family was awake. It was a woman who had a very different story from most of my clients. She hired me to help her with her ten-year-old daughter.

Her daughter woke up while we were on the video call and came to sit in her mother's lap. The girl is nonverbal and has epilepsy as well as other conditions. She spends a lot of time in a hospital bed after a bout of seizures.

As I talked with this sweet woman, I noticed something magnificent about her: not once did she complain, despite having slept only four to five hours a night for the past ten years because her daughter struggles with sleep, despite never hearing "I love you" from her child, despite staying in the hospital with her daughter for days at a time, despite battling cancer herself while also taking care of her family. When I feel overwhelmed by life, I will remember this resilient woman who handles more than her share of struggles with grace and love.

I hope this brings feelings of gratitude to all of you and reminds you of your blessings—both big and small. It certainly has for me. This book is in honor of all the families that have children who need to cut sugar out of their diet because their lives depend on it.

This book is also dedicated to my two precious boys, Micah and Kai Emmerich. I had the great opportunity to cook with Halle Berry this past January. After the filming, Micah asked if that experience had been a perfect 10 day (on a 0–10 scale of how spectacular it was). I told him no, but it was a 9 for sure! He asked, "Why not a 10?" I told him, "Adopting you and Kai was a perfect 10, and nothing can come close to that feeling!"

I want to thank the love of my life, Craig Emmerich—my better half! That half doesn't always get recognized or thanked for helping people transform their lives, but in reality, Craig is a huge part of every aspect of my writing and consultation business. He helps me lead my live weekly support group webinars for clients. Not only is he brilliant when it comes to the science of how our bodies function, but he is also my "tech support"! When someone can't find the order they purchased or the meal plans they ordered from keto-adapted.com, Craig responds within minutes with words of kindness and gratitude for their support. He also does all the nutritional info for my recipes. On top of all this, he homeschools our two beautiful children with patience and love. The way my boys adore their father makes my heart burst with joy! Craig is the one who grounds me. When I say yes to everything and have wild adventure ideas that likely won't work, he brings me back to reality. Just ask him about our kayak adventures without a real kayak when we were dating! Here's to Craig, my knight in shining armor despite living with chronic Lyme disease. He truly is my hero!

Thank you to my treasured recipe testers! I am forever grateful to Caroline, who tested every recipe, sometimes three times, to make sure they were perfect. Thank you also to Autumn, Wendy, Erin, Leisa, Serena, and the other recipe testers who prefer to remain nameless. I'm so appreciative of the time and effort you put in daily to test these recipes.

Thank you to Jenny Ross, the most amazing photographer who spent copious amounts of time and effort taking beautiful photos for the book.

To my dear friend Halle Berry, you are a blessing to me and my whole family. I can't thank you enough for helping spread the word of health! I'm so grateful for your kindness and support!

This book wouldn't be what it is without my beloved Victory Belt team! Pam, my sweet editor, helped tremendously. The designers made the amazing graphics and avatars that made this book the most beautiful book! Erich and Lance are the most helpful and responsive leaders an author could ever wish for. I am blessed to have such a supportive team.

And a special thank you to all of you! Yes, YOU! I started writing to help raise money for the adoption of Micah and Kai after Craig lost his job and we could no longer pay our house payment and sold our cars. Writing gave me a reason to wake up, but without you and your support, I wouldn't have my two precious boys. You have changed my life in more ways than you will ever know.

Recipe Quick Reference

• Omits ingredient   O Option

Recipes	page	⌒	🥛	⊘	‰	✗
Protein-Packed Blue Milk	82	E	O	•	O	O
Pizza Eggs	84	E	O		•	•
Strawberry Breakfast Parfait	86	E	O	•		O
Flourless Protein Pizza Crêpes	88	E	O		O	
Easy Baked Bacon and Sausages	90	E	•	•	•	
Breakfast Kabobs	92	E	O	•		O
Ham 'n' Cheese Cupcakes	94	E	O		•	
French Toast Porridge	96	E	O		O	•
Chocolate Minute Muffins	98	E	O		O	•
Chocolate Protein Shake	100	E	•			O
Blender Pancake Snowmen	102	E	O		O	O
Easy Blender Chocolate Donuts	104	E	O			•
Dippy Eggs with Toast Fingers	106	M	O		•	•
Green Eggs and Ham	108	M	O		•	
Micah's Egg Muffin Sandwiches	110	M	O		•	
Crunch Berry Cereal	112	E	O	•		•
Cheeseburger Breakfast Casserole	114	M			•	
Cinnamon Rolls	116	M	O		O	•
Sugar-Free Toaster Pastries (aka Gilmore Girls Breakfast)	118	H				•
Pizza Breakfast Pie	120	M			•	
Blueberry Cheesecake Muffins	122	M	O			•
Monkey Bread	124	H	O		O	•
Eggplant Fries	128	M	O		•	O
Veggie and Savory Fruit Flowers	130	E	O	O	•	O
Kai's Chicken Wings	132	M	O	O	•	
Pizza Rolls	134	M	O		O	O
The Cutest Deviled Eggs Ever	136	M	•		•	O
Pigs in a Blanket	142	M	•			
Cute Mouse Eggs	144	E			•	•
Strawberry Pudding	146	E	O		•	O
Sweet 'n' Sour Turkey Jerky	148	E	•	•	•	
No-Bake Chocolate-Topped Energy Bars	150	E	O	•		•
Fruit Flower Bouquet	152	E	O	•	•	•
Sticks and Dip	154	M		•		
Salmon Jerky Fingers	156	M	•	•	•	
Just Like "Apples" and Dip	158	E	O	•		•
Graham Crackers	160	H	O			•
Swedish Fish (or Gummy Bears)	162	E	•	•	•	
Little Piggy Eggs	164	E	•		•	
Cookie Dough Dip	166	E	O	O	O	•
No-Bake Peanut Butter Lover's Bars	168	E	•	•		•
Iced Animal Crackers	170	M	O	•		•
Sandwich on a Stick	174	E		•	•	
Antipasto on a Stick	176	E		•	•	
English Muffin Pizzas	178	E	O		•	
Chicken Protein Noodle Soup	180	M	O	•	•	
Better Than School Lunch Chicken Patties	184	M	O	O	O	
Bacon Lover's Chicken Nuggets	186	M	O	O	•	
Meat Cookies	188	E	O	O	O	

Recipes	page	⌒	🥛	🍽	⊘	🍴
Sloppy Kai Dogs	190	E	O	O	O	
Touchdown Tacos	192	E	O	O	O	
Cheese Quesadillas	194	E				•
Dinosaur Droppings (aka Meatballs)	198	E	•		•	
Bon Vie Chicken Tenders	200	M	O		•	
Protein Noodle Taco Lasagna	202	M		•	•	
Fish Fingers with Easy Tartar Sauce	204	M	O		•	
Baked Chicken Legs	206	M	O		•	
Mama Maria's Pizza Chicken Balls	208	M	O	•	•	
The Easiest Mac 'n' Cheese	210	E		•	O	
Protein Noodle Pad Thai	212	M	•			
Crispy Baked Ravioli	214	H			O	
Easy Baked BBQ Chicken	216	E	•	•	•	
Cheesy Beef and "Noodle" Casserole	218	E	O	•	•	
Meaty Lasagna Bowls	220	M		•	•	
Protein Noodle Chicken Alfredo	222	M		•	•	
Pizza Party	224	H			O	
Cheese Sticks	227	M			O	O
Breakfast for Dinner	230	M	O			O
Chicken Sloppy Joes	234	E	O	O	•	
Pizza Dog Casserole	236	E	O	•	•	
Cheeseburger Lettuce Wraps	238	E	O		•	
Spaghetti Bolognese	240	E	O	•	•	
Epic Cheesy Beef Nachos	242	E		•	•	
Shredded BBQ Chicken	244	E	•	•	•	
Chicken Enchiladas	246	E	O	•	•	
Sweet 'n' Sour Chicken Wings	248	E	•	•	•	
Egg Roll in a Bowl	250	E	•	•	•	
Fluffy Bunny Scrambled Eggs	254	E			•	
Valentine's Day Breakfast	256	E				
Christmas Tomato Soup with Grilled Cheese Stars and Trees	258	M		•	•	O
Zombie Spaghetti and Eyeballs	260	M	O		•	
Christmas Tree Pizza	262	M			O	O
Heart-Shaped Eggs	264	E	•		•	•
Valentine Deviled Eggs	266	M	•		•	•
Holiday Tree Cheese Ball	268	E		•		•
Halloween Spooky Skeleton with BBQ Riblets	270	M	•	•	•	
Taco Meatball Holiday Tree	272	M	O		•	
Spooky Breadstick Fingers	274	M	O			•
Easy Red, White, and Blueberry Sundaes	276	E	O	•	•	•
Strawberry Cheesecake Santas	278	E	O	•	O	•
Holiday Jigglers	280	E	•	•	•	
Bombdiggity Pops	282	E	O	•	•	•
Shamrock Shake Gummies	284	E	O	•	O	
Pumpkin Pie Gummies	286	E	O	•	O	
Valentine's Day Muffin Pan Ice Cream Cakes	288	E				
No-Bake Strawberry Panna Cotta	292	E	O	•	O	
Just Like Oreos Sandwich Cookies	294	H	O			•
Protein Hot Chocolate	296	M	O		O	
Raspberries and Cream Ice Pops	298	E	O	•	O	•

Recipes	page	⌒	🥛	⊘	%	✗
Extreme Chocolate Blender Birthday Cake	300	M	o			•
Baseball Blender Cupcakes	302	M	o			•
Chocolate Hazelnut Whoopie Pies	304	M	o			•
Kai's Puppy Chow	306	E	o	•		
Crispy Candy	308	E	o	•	•	•
Sugar-Free Chocolate Bars or Chips	310	E	o	•	•	•
The BEST Chocolate Chip Cookies	312	M	o			•
Marshmallows	314	M	•	•	o	
S'mores	316	E	o			
No-Churn Ice Cream Five Ways	317	E		•	o	•
Dairy-Free No-Churn Ice Cream	322	E	•	•	o	
Raspberry Sorbet	324	E	•	•	o	
Truffles Five Ways	326	E	o	o		•
Basic Savory Chaffles or Paffles	334	E	o		•	•
Easy Blender Waffles	336	E	o			•
Chaffle Breakfast Sammie	338	E	o		•	
Cinnamon Roll Chaffles	340	E				•
Blueberry Muffin Chaffles	342	E				•
Chocolate Hazelnut Waffles	344	E	o			•
Drive-Thru Chaffle Burger	346	E	o		•	
Crispy Taco Chaffles	348	E	o		•	
Strawberry Shortcake Chaffle Sandwiches	350	E			o	•
"Apple" Pie Waffles	352	E	o			•
Glazed Pumpkin Mini Waffles	354	M	o			•
Waffle Cone Mini Waffles	356	E	o			•
Bacon Cheeseburger Waffle	358	E			•	
Chocolate Waffle Sandwich	360	E	o			•
Easy Tartar Sauce	364	E	•		•	•
Easiest Mayo Ever	365	E	•		•	o
Veggie Dill Dip	366	E	o		•	o
Protein-Packed Ranch Dip	367	E	•		•	o
Traditional Ranch	368	E	o	o	•	o
Sugar-Free Ketchup	369	E	•	•	•	o
Pizza Sauce	370	E	o	•	•	•
Fruit Dip	371	E		•	o	•
Blender Marinara Sauce	372	M	•	•	•	o
Roasted Garlic	374	E	•	•	•	•
Guacamole	376	E	•	•	•	•
Sugar-Free Strawberry Jam	378	M	•	•	•	
Sugar-Free Chocolate Hazelnut Spread	380	M	•	•		•
Soft Tortillas	382	M	•			•
Sandwich Buns	384	M	•			•
Easy English Muffins	386	E	•		•	•
Taco Seasoning	388	E	•	•	•	•
Bone Broth	392	E	•	•	•	
Bone Marrow	394	E	•	•	•	
Salmon Puree with Salt	396	E	•	•	•	
Ground Beef with Salt	398	E	o	•	•	
Salted Egg Yolks	400	E	•		•	
Chicken Pâté	402	E	o	•	•	

breakfast

82

Protein-Packed
Blue Milk

84

Pizza Eggs

86

Strawberry
Breakfast Parfait

88

Flourless Protein
Pizza Crêpes

90

Easy Baked Bacon
and Sausages

92

Breakfast Kabobs

94

Ham 'n' Cheese
Cupcakes

96

French Toast
Porridge

98

Chocolate
Minute Muffins

100

Chocolate
Protein Shake

102

Blender Pancake
Snowmen

104

Easy Blender
Chocolate Donuts

106

Dippy Eggs with
Toast Fingers

108

Green Eggs
and Ham

110

Micah's
Egg Muffin
Sandwiches

112

Crunch Berry
Cereal

114

Cheeseburger
Breakfast
Casserole

116

Cinnamon Rolls

118

Sugar-Free
Toaster Pastries
(aka Gilmore
Girls Breakfast)

120

Pizza
Breakfast Pie

122

Blueberry
Cheesecake
Muffins

124

Monkey Bread

appetizers & snacks

128
Eggplant Fries

130
Veggie and Savory Fruit Flowers

132
Kai's Chicken Wings

134
Pizza Rolls

136
The Cutest Deviled Eggs Ever

142
Pigs in a Blanket

144
Cute Mouse Eggs

146
Strawberry Pudding

148
Sweet 'n' Sour Turkey Jerky

150
No-Bake Chocolate-Topped Energy Bars

152
Fruit Flower Bouquet

154
Sticks and Dip

156
Salmon Jerky Fingers

158
Just Like "Apples" and Dip

160
Graham Crackers

162
Swedish Fish (or Gummy Bears)

164
Little Piggy Eggs

166
Cookie Dough Dip

168
No-Bake Peanut Butter Lover's Bars

170
Iced Animal Crackers

lunches that rock!

174
Sandwich on a Stick

176
Antipasto on a Stick

178
English Muffin Pizzas

180
Chicken Protein Noodle Soup

184
Better Than School Lunch Chicken Patties

186
Bacon Lover's Chicken Nuggets

188
Meat Cookies

190
Sloppy Kai Dogs

192
Touchdown Tacos

194
Cheese Quesadillas

classic kid meals

198
Dinosaur Droppings (aka Meatballs)

200
Bon Vie Chicken Tenders

202
Protein Noodle Taco Lasagna

204
Fish Fingers with Easy Tartar Sauce

206
Baked Chicken Legs

208
Mama Maria's Pizza Chicken Balls

210
The Easiest Mac 'n' Cheese

212
Protein Noodle Pad Thai

214
Crispy Baked Ravioli

216
Easy Baked BBQ Chicken

218
Cheesy Beef and "Noodle" Casserole

220
Meaty Lasagna Bowls

222
Protein Noodle Chicken Alfredo

224
Pizza Party

230
Breakfast for Dinner

instant pot & slow cooker recipes

234
Chicken Sloppy Joes

236
Pizza Dog Casserole

238
Cheeseburger Lettuce Wraps

240
Spaghetti Bolognese

242
Epic Cheesy Beef Nachos

244
Shredded BBQ Chicken

246
Chicken Enchiladas

248
Sweet 'n' Sour Chicken Wings

250
Egg Roll in a Bowl

holiday fun

254
Fluffy Bunny
Scrambled Eggs

256
Valentine's Day
Breakfast

258
Christmas Tomato
Soup with Grilled
Cheese Stars and Trees

260
Zombie Spaghetti
and Eyeballs

262
Christmas Tree
Pizza

264
Heart-Shaped
Eggs

266
Valentine
Deviled Eggs

268
Holiday Tree
Cheese Ball

270
Halloween
Spooky Skeleton
with BBQ Riblets

272
Taco Meatball
Holiday Tree

274
Spooky
Breadstick
Fingers

276
Easy Red, White,
and Blueberry
Sundaes

278
Strawberry
Cheesecake
Santas

280
Holiday Jigglers

282
Bombdiggity
Pops

284
Shamrock Shake
Gummies

286
Pumpkin Pie
Gummies

288
Valentine's Day
Muffin Pan
Ice Cream Cakes

desserts

292
No-Bake
Strawberry
Panna Cotta

294
Just Like Oreos
Sandwich
Cookies

296
Protein
Hot Chocolate

298
Raspberries and
Cream Ice Pops

300
Extreme Chocolate
Blender
Birthday Cake

302
Baseball Blender
Cupcakes

304
Chocolate
Hazelnut
Whoopie Pies

306
Kai's Puppy Chow

308
Crispy Candy

310
Sugar-Free
Chocolate Bars
or Chips

312
The BEST
Chocolate Chip
Cookies

314
Marshmallows

316
S'mores

317
No-Churn
Ice Cream
Five Ways

Dairy-Free
No-Churn
Ice Cream

Raspberry Sorbet

Truffles
Five Ways

chaffles & waffles

Basic Savory
Chaffles or Paffles

Easy Blender
Waffles

Chaffle Breakfast
Sammie

Cinnamon Roll
Chaffles

Blueberry Muffin
Chaffles

Chocolate
Hazelnut Waffles

Drive-Thru
Chaffle Burger

Crispy Taco
Chaffles

Strawberry
Shortcake Chaffle
Sandwiches

"Apple" Pie
Waffles

Glazed Pumpkin
Mini Waffles

Waffle Cone
Mini Waffles

Bacon
Cheeseburger
Waffle

Chocolate Waffle
Sandwich

basics, sauces & dips

Easy
Tartar Sauce

Easiest
Mayo Ever

Veggie Dill Dip

Protein-Packed
Ranch Dip

Traditional
Ranch

Sugar-Free
Ketchup

Pizza Sauce

Fruit Dip

Blender
Marinara Sauce

Roasted Garlic

Guacamole

Sugar-Free
Strawberry Jam

Sugar-Free
Chocolate
Hazelnut Spread

Soft Tortillas

Sandwich Buns

Easy English
Muffins

Taco Seasoning

babies' first foods

Bone Broth

Bone Marrow

Salmon Puree
with Salt

Ground Beef
with Salt

Salted Egg Yolks

Chicken Pâté

Index

A

acid, using when cooking, 70
adipose cells, 29
adrenaline, 51
advanced glycation end products (AGEs), 75
aldehydes, 24
allulose
    about, 76
    "Apple" Pie Waffles, 352–353
    The BEST Chocolate Chip Cookies, 312–313
    Bombdiggity Pops, 282–283
    Dairy-Free No-Churn Ice Cream, 322–323
    Marshmallows, 314–315
    No-Churn Vanilla Bean Ice Cream, 317
    No-Churn Blue Moon Ice Cream, 318
    No-Churn Chocolate Ice Cream, 319
    No-Churn Strawberries and Cream Ice Cream, 318
    Raspberries and Cream Ice Pops, 298–299
    Raspberry Sorbet, 324–325
almond butter
    Brownie Truffles, 327
    Candy Bar Truffles, 329
    Chocolate Chip Cookie Dough Truffles, 331
    Cinnamon Roll Chaffles, 340–341
    Just Like "Apples" and Dip, 158–159
    Kai's Puppy Chow, 306–307
    No-Bake Chocolate-Topped Energy Bars, 150–151
    Protein Noodle Pad Thai, 212–213
almond flour
    Baseball Blender Cupcakes, 302–303
    The BEST Chocolate Chip Cookies, 312–313
    Blender Pancake Snowmen, 102–103
    Blueberry Cheesecake Muffins, 122–123
    Blueberry Muffin Chaffles, 342–343
    Chocolate Hazelnut Whoopie Pies, 304–305
    Chocolate Waffle Sandwich, 360–361
    Christmas Tree Pizza, 262–263
    Cinnamon Rolls, 116–117
    Crunch Berry Cereal, 112–113
    The Easiest Mac 'n' Cheese, 210–211
    Easy Blender Chocolate Donuts, 104–105
    Easy Blender Waffles, 336–337
    Extreme Chocolate Blender Birthday Cake, 300–301
    Glazed Pumpkin Mini Waffles, 354–355
    Graham Crackers, 160–161
    Iced Animal Crackers, 170–171
    Just Like Oreos Sandwich Cookies, 294–295
    Monkey Bread, 124–125
    Pigs in a Blanket, 142–143
    Pizza Crust, 225
    Pizza Rolls, 134–135
    Sandwich Buns, 384–385
    Soft Tortillas, 382–383
    Sticks and Dip, 154–155
    Sugar-Free Toaster Pastries (aka Gilmore Girls Breakfast), 118–119
    Waffle Cone Mini Waffles, 356–357
almond milk
    Baseball Blender Cupcakes, 302–303
    Chocolate Hazelnut Whoopie Pies, 304–305
    Chocolate Minute Muffins, 98–99
    Chocolate Protein Shake, 100–101
    Chocolate Waffle Sandwich, 360–361
    Cinnamon Roll Chaffles, 340–341
    Cinnamon Rolls, 116–117
    Crunch Berry Cereal, 112–113
    Dairy-Free No-Churn Ice Cream, 322–323
    Easy Blender Chocolate Donuts, 104–105
    Extreme Chocolate Blender Birthday Cake, 300–301
    Flourless Protein Pizza Crêpes, 88–89
    French Toast Porridge, 96–97
    Glazed Pumpkin Mini Waffles, 354–355
    Iced Animal Crackers, 170–171
    Just Like "Apples" and Dip, 158–159
    Just Like Oreos Sandwich Cookies, 294–295
    No-Churn Vanilla Bean Ice Cream, 317
    No-Bake Strawberry Panna Cotta, 292–293
    No-Churn Blue Moon Ice Cream, 318
    No-Churn Chocolate Ice Cream, 319
    No-Churn Strawberries and Cream Ice Cream, 318
    Protein Hot Chocolate, 296–297
    Protein-Packed Blue Milk, 82–83

almond milk (continued)
    Pumpkin Pie Gummies, 286–287
    Raspberries and Cream Ice Pops, 298–299
    Raspberry Sorbet, 324–325
    Shamrock Shake Gummies, 284–285
    Sugar-Free Toaster Pastries (aka Gilmore Girls Breakfast), 118–119
    Waffle Cone Mini Waffles, 356–357
almonds
    Owl Deviled Eggs, 139–141
    Rocky Road Ice Cream recipe, 319
    Spooky Breadstick Fingers, 274–275
    Strawberry Breakfast Parfait, 86–87
alpha-linoleic acid (ALA), 20
amino acids, 20
animal proteins, 18
antacids, bone health and, 46
antioxidants, 16
Antipasto on a Stick recipe, 176–177
"Apple" Pie Waffles recipe, 352–353
Applegate brand, 63
arachidonic acid (ARA), 20
avocado
    Christmas Tomato Soup with Grilled Cheese Stars and Trees, 258–259
    Guacamole, 376–377
    Protein Noodle Taco Lasagna, 202–203
    Shamrock Shake Gummies, 284–285

B

babies
    about, 38
    comparing foods, 39
    first solid foods for, 40–42
    recipes for, 392–403
    rice cereal, 40
baby-led weaning (BLW), 42
bacon
    Bacon Cheeseburger Pizza, 226
    Bacon Cheeseburger Waffle, 358–359
    Bacon Lover's Chicken Nuggets, 186–187
    Breakfast for Dinner, 230–231
    The Easiest Mac 'n' Cheese, 210–211
    Easy Baked Bacon and Sausages, 90–91
    Fluffy Bunny Scrambled Eggs, 254–255
    Football Deviled Eggs, 138–141
    Meat Cookies, 188–189
    Meat Lover's Pizza, 226
    Spaghetti Bolognese, 240–241
    Turkey Cinnamon Rolls, 117

Valentine's Day Breakfast, 256–257
Bacon Cheeseburger Pizza recipe, 226
Bacon Cheeseburger Waffle recipe, 358–359
Bacon Lover's Chicken Nuggets recipe, 186–187
Baked Chicken Legs recipe, 206–207
bananas, 16
bars. See cookies and bars
Baseball Blender Cupcakes recipe, 302–303
Basic Savory Chaffles or Paffles recipe, 334–335
    Chaffle Breakfast Sammie, 338–339
    Chicken Sloppy Joes, 234–235
    Drive-Thru Chaffle Burger, 346–347
basil
    Blender Marinara Sauce, 372–373
    Christmas Tree Pizza, 262–263
    Mama Maria's Pizza Chicken Balls, 208–209
    Owl Deviled Eggs, 139–141
    Pizza Dog Casserole, 236–237
    Pizza Eggs, 84–85
    Veggie and Savory Fruit Flowers, 130–131
    Zombie Spaghetti and Eyeballs, 260–261
batch cooking, 57
beef
    in baby food, 39
    Bacon Cheeseburger Pizza, 226
    Bacon Cheeseburger Waffle, 358–359
    breakdown of, 19
    Cheeseburger Breakfast Casserole, 114–115
    Cheeseburger Lettuce Wraps, 238–239
    Cheesy Beef and "Noodle" Casserole, 218–219
    Chicken Sloppy Joes, 234–235
    Dinosaur Droppings (aka Meatballs), 198–199
    Drive-Thru Chaffle Burger, 346–347
    Epic Cheesy Beef Nachos, 242–243
    Ground Beef with Salt, 398–399
    Halloween Spooky Skeleton with BBQ Riblets, 270–271
    Meat Cookies, 188–189
    Meaty Lasagna Bowls, 220–221
    Pizza Breakfast Pie, 120–121
    Pizza Dog Casserole, 236–237
    Sloppy Kai Dogs, 190–191
    Spaghetti Bolognese, 240–241
    Taco Meatball Holiday Tree, 272–273
    Touchdown Tacos, 192–193
    Zombie Spaghetti and Eyeballs, 260–261
beef bones
    Bone Broth, 392–393
beef broth
    Chicken Enchiladas, 246–247
    Chicken Sloppy Joes, 234–235

Easiest Mayo Ever, 365
The Easiest Mac 'n' Cheese, 210–211
Epic Cheesy Beef Nachos, 242–243
Pizza Breakfast Pie, 120–121
Pizza Rolls, 134–135
Protein Noodle Chicken Alfredo, 222–223
Protein-Packed Ranch Dip, 367
Sloppy Kai Dogs, 190–191
Spaghetti Bolognese, 240–241
Sticks and Dip, 154–155
Sugar-Free Ketchup, 369
Traditional Ranch, 368
beef liver, in baby food, 39
beef sausage
Halloween Spooky Skeleton with BBQ Riblets, 270–271
beef sticks, 67
bell peppers
Christmas Tree Pizza, 262–263
Halloween Spooky Skeleton with BBQ Riblets, 270–271
Holiday Tree Cheese Ball, 268–269
Owl Deviled Eggs, 139–141
Owl Meatballs, 199
Veggie and Savory Fruit Flowers, 130–131
Bento Boxes, 63–66
The BEST Chocolate Chip Cookies recipe, 312–313
Cookie Dough Dip, 166–167
No-Churn Vanilla Bean Ice Cream, 317
Better Than School Lunch Chicken Patties recipe, 184–185
Bibb lettuce
Taco Meatball Holiday Tree, 272–273
big kids, protein needs for, 44
birthday celebrations, 68
Bitter, Zach, 14
blackberries
Fruit Flower Bouquet, 152–153
blender, 73
Blender Marinara Sauce recipe, 372–373
Cheese Sticks, 227–229
Meaty Lasagna Bowls, 220–221
Spaghetti Bolognese, 240–241
Zombie Spaghetti and Eyeballs, 260–261
Blender Pancake Snowmen recipe, 102–103
Breakfast for Dinner, 230–231
blood glucose, 28
blue light, 52
blue spirulina
Protein-Packed Blue Milk, 82–83

blueberries
Blueberry Cheesecake Muffins, 122–123
Blueberry Muffin Chaffles, 342–343
Bombdiggity Pops, 282–283
Breakfast for Dinner, 230–231
Easy Red, White and Blueberry Sundaes, 276–277
Fluffy Bunny Scrambled Eggs, 254–255
Fruit Flower Bouquet, 152–153
Protein-Packed Blue Milk, 82–83
Turkey Cinnamon Rolls, 117
Blueberry Cheesecake Muffins recipe, 122–123
Blueberry Muffin Chaffles recipe, 342–343
bologna, 63
Bombdiggity Pops recipe, 282–283
Bon Vie Chicken Tenders recipe, 200–201
Bone Broth recipe, 392–393
Salmon Puree with Salt, 396–397
Salted Egg Yolks, 400–401
bone health, 46–47
Bone Marrow recipe, 394–395
Salmon Puree with Salt, 396–397
Boston lettuce
Cheeseburger Lettuce Wraps, 238–239
Shredded BBQ Chicken, 244–245
Taco Meatball Holiday Tree, 272–273
Touchdown Tacos, 192–193
breads
Cinnamon Rolls, 116–117
Easy English Muffins, 386–387
English Muffin Pizzas, 178–179
Monkey Bread, 124–125
Pizza Rolls, 134–135
Sandwich Buns, 384–385
Soft Tortillas, 382–383
Sugar-Free Toaster Pastries (aka Gilmore Girls Breakfast), 118–119
Breakfast for Dinner recipe, 230–231
Breakfast Kabobs recipe, 92–93
breakfast sausage
Blender Pancake Snowmen, 102–103
Breakfast for Dinner, 230–231
Easy Baked Bacon and Sausages, 90–91
Flourless Protein Pizza Crêpes, 88–89
breast milk, 38
broccoli, 19
Brownie Truffles recipe, 327
ButcherBox brand, 63
butter lettuce
Chicken Sloppy Joes, 234–235

C

cabbage
    Egg Roll in a Bowl, 250–251
    Veggie and Savory Fruit Flowers, 130–131
cakes and cupcakes
    Baseball Blender Cupcakes, 302–303
    Chocolate Hazelnut Whoopie Pies, 304–305
    Extreme Chocolate Blender Birthday Cake, 300–301
    Ham 'n' Cheese Cupcakes, 94–95
    Valentine's Day Muffin Pan Ice Cream Cakes, 288–289
Canadian bacon
    Christmas Tree Pizza, 262–263
    Meat Lover's Pizza, 226
Candy Bar Truffles recipe, 329
carbohydrates
    about, 13–14
    consumption for kids, 42
    cycle of sugar consumption and, 28–29
    fruits as, 15–17
    sugar-free child athletes, 14–15
    turning to sugar, 12
    vegetables as, 15–17
Carnivore Crisps, 67
cashew milk
    Baseball Blender Cupcakes, 302–303
    Chocolate Protein Shake, 100–101
    Easy Blender Chocolate Donuts, 104–105
cauliflower
    The Easiest Mac 'n' Cheese, 210–211
    Veggie and Savory Fruit Flowers, 130–131
celery
    Bone Broth, 392–393
    Chicken Protein Noodle Soup, 180–183
    Holiday Tree Cheese Ball, 268–269
Chaffle Breakfast Sammie recipe, 338–339
Chaffle or Paffle Sub Sandwich recipe, 334
chayote squash
    Cookie Dough Dip, 166–167
    Just Like "Apples" and Dip, 158–159
cheddar cheese
    Bacon Cheeseburger Pizza, 226
    Bacon Cheeseburger Waffle, 358–359
    Basic Savory Chaffles or Paffles, 334–335
    Chaffle Breakfast Sammie, 338–339
    Cheeseburger Breakfast Casserole, 114–115
    Cheeseburger Lettuce Wraps, 238–239
    Cheesy Beef and "Noodle" Casserole, 218–219
    Chicken Enchiladas, 246–247

    Christmas Tomato Soup with Grilled Cheese Stars and Trees, 258–259
    Crispy Taco Chaffles, 348–349
    Cute Mouse Eggs, 144–145
    Drive-Thru Chaffle Burger, 346–347
    The Easiest Mac 'n' Cheese, 210–211
    Epic Cheesy Beef Nachos, 242–243
    Ham 'n' Cheese Cupcakes, 94–95
    Han 'n' Cheese Chaffle or Paffle Sandwich, 334
    Holiday Tree Cheese Ball, 268–269
    Micah's Egg Muffin Sandwiches, 110–111
    Sandwich on a Stick, 174–175
    Sloppy Kai Dogs, 190–191
    Sticks and Dip, 154–155
    Taco Meatball Holiday Tree, 272–273
    Touchdown Tacos, 192–193
cheese. *See specific types*
Cheese Quesadillas recipe, 194–195
Cheese Sticks recipe, 227–229
Cheeseburger Breakfast Casserole recipe, 114–115
Cheeseburger Lettuce Wraps recipe, 238–239
Cheesy Beef and "Noodle" Casserole recipe, 218–219
chicken
    Bacon Lover's Chicken Nuggets, 186–187
    Baked Chicken Legs, 206–207
    Better Than School Lunch Chicken Patties, 184–185
    Bon Vie Chicken Tenders, 200–201
    Chicken Enchiladas, 246–247
    Chicken Protein Noodle Soup, 180–183
    Chicken Sloppy Joes, 234–235
    Easy Baked BBQ Chicken, 216–217
    Egg Roll in a Bowl, 250–251
    Kai's Chicken Wings, 132–133
    Mama Maria's Pizza Chicken Balls, 208–209
    Meaty Lasagna Bowls, 220–221
    Protein Noodle Chicken Alfredo, 222–223
    Protein Noodle Pad Thai, 212–213
    Protein Noodle Taco Lasagna, 202–203
    Shredded BBQ Chicken, 244–245
    Sweet 'n' Sour Chicken Wings, 248–249
    Sweet 'n' Sour Turkey Jerky, 148–149
chicken bones
    Bone Broth, 392–393
Chicken Breast Carnivore Crisps
    Epic Cheesy Beef Nachos, 242–243
chicken broth
    Chicken Enchiladas, 246–247
    Chicken Protein Noodle Soup, 180–183

Christmas Tomato Soup with Grilled Cheese Stars and Trees, 258–259
Protein Noodle Pad Thai, 212–213
Protein Noodle Taco Lasagna, 202–203
Sugar-Free Ketchup, 369
Sweet 'n' Sour Chicken Wings, 248–249
Traditional Ranch, 368
Veggie Dill Dip, 366
Chicken Enchiladas recipe, 246–247
chicken livers
Chicken Pâté, 402–403
Chicken Pâté recipe, 402–403
Chicken Protein Noodle Soup recipe, 180–183
Chicken Sloppy Joes recipe, 234–235
Chinese 5-Spice Chicken Protein Noodle Soup recipe, 182–183
chives
Cute Mouse Eggs, 144–145
Protein Noodle Pad Thai, 212–213
chocolate
The BEST Chocolate Chip Cookies, 312–313
Blender Pancake Snowmen, 102–103
Brownie Truffles, 327
Candy Bar Truffles, 329
Chocolate Chip Cookie Dough Truffles, 331
Chocolate Hazelnut Whoopie Pies, 304–305
Chocolate Ice Cream Bowls, 310
Coated Marshmallows, 315
Cookie Dough Dip, 166–167
Easy Blender Chocolate Donuts, 104–105
No-Churn Chocolate Ice Cream, 319
Sugar-Free Chocolate Bars or Chips, 310–311
Chocolate Chip Cookie Dough Truffles recipe, 331
Chocolate Hazelnut Waffles recipe, 344–345
Chocolate Hazelnut Whoopie Pies recipe, 304–305
Chocolate Ice Cream Bowls recipe, 310
Chocolate Minute Muffins recipe, 98–99
Chocolate Protein Shake recipe, 100–101
Chocolate Waffle Sandwich recipe, 360–361
cholesterol, 21–23
Christmas Tomato Soup with Grilled Cheese Stars and Trees recipe, 258–259
Christmas Tree Pizza recipe, 262–263
chromium, depletion of, 32
cilantro
Cheese Quesadillas, 194–195
Chicken Enchiladas, 246–247
Crispy Taco Chaffles, 348–349
Green Eggs and Ham, 108–109
Guacamole, 376–377
Holiday Tree Cheese Ball, 268–269

Indian-Spiced Chicken Protein Noodle, 182–183
Protein Noodle Pad Thai, 212–213
Protein Noodle Taco Lasagna, 202–203
Taco Meatball Holiday Tree, 272–273
Touchdown Tacos, 192–193
cinnamon
Cinnamon Roll Chaffles, 340–341
Cinnamon Rolls, 116–117
Graham Crackers, 160–161
Monkey Bread, 124–125
Cinnamon Roll Chaffles recipe, 340–341
Breakfast for Dinner, 230–231
Cinnamon Rolls recipe, 116–117
Breakfast for Dinner, 230–231
citric acid
Holiday Jigglers, 280–281
Swedish Fish (or Gummy Bears), 162–163
cloves
Pizza Breakfast Pie, 120–121
Coated Marshmallows recipe, 315
cocoa butter
Strawberry Cheesecake Truffles, 328
cocoa powder
Baseball Blender Cupcakes, 302–303
Brownie Truffles, 327
Chocolate Hazelnut Waffles, 344–345
Chocolate Hazelnut Whoopie Pies, 304–305
Chocolate Minute Muffins, 98–99
Chocolate Protein Shake, 100–101
Chocolate Waffle Sandwich, 360–361
Dairy-Free No-Churn Ice Cream, 322–323
Easy Blender Chocolate Donuts, 104–105
Extreme Chocolate Blender Birthday Cake, 300–301
Just Like Oreos Sandwich Cookies, 294–295
Kai's Puppy Chow, 306–307
No-Bake Chocolate-Topped Energy Bars, 150–151
No-Bake Peanut Butter Lover's Bars, 168–169
Protein Hot Chocolate, 296–297
Red Velvet Truffles, 330
Strawberry Cheesecake Santas, 278–279
Sugar-Free Chocolate Hazelnut Spread, 380–381
coconut cream
Blender Pancake Snowmen, 102–103
Bombdiggity Pops, 282–283
Breakfast Kabobs, 92–93
Brownie Truffles, 327
Candy Bar Truffles, 329
Chocolate Chip Cookie Dough Truffles, 331
Chocolate Hazelnut Whoopie Pies, 304–305

coconut cream (*continued*)
    Chocolate Waffle Sandwich, 360–361
    Dairy-Free No-Churn Ice Cream, 322–323
    Easy Red, White and Blueberry Sundaes, 276–277
    Protein-Packed Blue Milk, 82–83
    Raspberries and Cream Ice Pops, 298–299
    Red Velvet Truffles, 330
    Strawberry Cheesecake Truffles, 328
    Sugar-Free Chocolate Bars or Chips, 310–311
coconut flour
    Baseball Blender Cupcakes, 302–303
    Blender Pancake Snowmen, 102–103
    Chocolate Hazelnut Whoopie Pies, 304–305
    Chocolate Minute Muffins, 98–99
    Cinnamon Rolls, 116–117
    Easy Blender Chocolate Donuts, 104–105
    Easy English Muffins, 386–387
    Extreme Chocolate Blender Birthday Cake, 300–301
    Iced Animal Crackers, 170–171
    Pizza Rolls, 134–135
coconut milk
    Chocolate Protein Shake, 100–101
    Crunch Berry Cereal, 112–113
    Easy Blender Chocolate Donuts, 104–105
    Just Like Oreos Sandwich Cookies, 294–295
    Raspberry Sorbet, 324–325
    Strawberry Pudding, 146–147
    Thai Chicken Protein Noodle Soup, 182–183
cod
    Fish Fingers with Easy Tartar Sauce, 204–205
collagen peptides
    Protein Hot Chocolate, 296–297
    Shamrock Shake Gummies, 284–285
collagen powder
    Blender Pancake Snowmen, 102–103
    bone health and, 46
    Chocolate Protein Shake, 100–101
    immune health and, 48
    Strawberry Breakfast Parfait, 86–87
    Strawberry Pudding, 146–147
complete proteins, 20
conjugated linoleic acid (CLA), 20
Cookie Dough Dip recipe, 166–167
cookies and bars
    The BEST Chocolate Chip Cookies, 312–313
    Graham Crackers, 160–161
    Just Like Oreos Sandwich Cookies, 294–295
    No-Bake Chocolate-Topped Energy Bars, 150–151

    No-Bake Peanut Butter Lover's Bars, 168–169
cooking tips, 55–56
Cotija cheese
    Protein Noodle Taco Lasagna, 202–203
cottage cheese
    Meaty Lasagna Bowls, 220–221
cream cheese
    Baseball Blender Cupcakes, 302–303
    Blueberry Cheesecake Muffins, 122–123
    Blueberry Muffin Chaffles, 342–343
    Chocolate Waffle Sandwich, 360–361
    Christmas Tree Pizza, 262–263
    Cinnamon Roll Chaffles, 340–341
    Cinnamon Rolls, 116–117
    Cookie Dough Dip, 166–167
    Crispy Baked Ravioli, 214–215
    The Easiest Mac 'n' Cheese, 210–211
    Easy Blender Waffles, 336–337
    Epic Cheesy Beef Nachos, 242–243
    Extreme Chocolate Blender Birthday Cake, 300–301
    Fluffy Bunny Scrambled Eggs, 254–255
    Glazed Pumpkin Mini Waffles, 354–355
    Holiday Tree Cheese Ball, 268–269
    Just Like "Apples" and Dip, 158–159
    Just Like Oreos Sandwich Cookies, 294–295
    Monkey Bread, 124–125
    Owl Meatballs, 199
    Pizza Breakfast Pie, 120–121
    Pizza Crust, 225
    Protein Noodle Chicken Alfredo, 222–223
    Red Velvet Truffles, 330
    Sticks and Dip, 154–155
    Strawberry Cheesecake Santas, 278–279
    Strawberry Cheesecake Truffles, 328
    Strawberry Shortcake Chaffle Sandwiches, 350–351
    Sugar-Free Toaster Pastries (aka Gilmore Girls Breakfast), 118–119
    Traditional Ranch, 368
Cream Cheese Glaze recipe, 354
    Chocolate Hazelnut Waffles, 344–345
crème fraîche
    Veggie Dill Dip, 366
Crispy Baked Ravioli recipe, 214–215
Crispy Candy recipe, 308–309
    Candy Bar Truffles, 329
Crispy Taco Chaffles recipe, 348–349
Crunch Berry Cereal recipe, 112–113
    Strawberry Breakfast Parfait, 86–87

cucumber
    Holiday Tree Cheese Ball, 268–269
    Veggie and Savory Fruit Flowers, 130–131
cupcakes. *See* cakes and cupcakes
Cure Mouse Eggs, 67
Cute Mouse Eggs recipe, 144–145
The Cutest Deviled Eggs Ever recipe, 136–141
    Deviled Egg Flowers, 139–141
    Football Deviled Eggs, 138–141
    Owl Deviled Eggs, 139–141
    Pumpkin Deviled Eggs, 138–141
    Spider Deviled Eggs, 138–141
The Cutest Deviled Eggs Ever, 67
cytokines, 51

D

Dairy-Free No-Churn Ice Cream recipe, 322–323
Deol, Poonamjot, 26
depression, sugar and, 52
Deviled Egg Flowers recipe, 139–141
diabetes, PUFA-driven, 25
dill
    Owl Deviled Eggs, 139–141
    Valentine Deviled Eggs, 266–267
    Veggie Dill Dip, 366
dill pickle juice
    Baked Chicken Legs, 206–207
    Bon Vie Chicken Tenders, 200–201
    Easiest Mayo Ever, 365
    Easy Tartar Sauce, 364
    Protein-Packed Ranch Dip, 367
dill pickles
    Bacon Cheeseburger Pizza, 226
    Cheeseburger Breakfast Casserole, 114–115
    Cheeseburger Lettuce Wraps, 238–239
    Chicken Sloppy Joes, 234–235
    Drive-Thru Chaffle Burger, 346–347
    Easy Tartar Sauce, 364
    Meat Cookies, 188–189
    Sandwich on a Stick, 174–175
    Veggie and Savory Fruit Flowers, 130–131
Dinosaur Droppings (aka Meatballs) recipe, 198–199
Dippy Eggs with Toast Fingers recipe, 106–107
dips
    Cookie Dough Dip, 166–167
    Fruit Dip, 371
    Holiday Tree Cheese Ball, 268–269
    Just Like "Apples" and Dip, 158–159
    Protein-Packed Ranch Dip, 367
    Sticks and Dip, 154–155
    Veggie Dill Dip, 366
docosahexaenoic acid (DHA), 20
dopamine, 45
drinks
    Chocolate Protein Shake, 100–101
    Protein Hot Chocolate, 296–297
    Protein-Packed Blue Milk, 82–83
    Shamrock Shake Gummies, 284–285
Drive-Thru Chaffle Burger recipe, 346–347

E

Easiest Mayo Ever recipe, 365
    Better Than School Lunch Chicken Patties, 184–185
    Cheeseburger Breakfast Casserole, 114–115
    Cheeseburger Lettuce Wraps, 238–239
    The Cutest Deviled Eggs Ever, 136–141
    Easy Tartar Sauce, 364
    Football Deviled Eggs, 138–141
    Meat Cookies, 188–189
    Traditional Ranch, 368
    Valentine Deviled Eggs, 266–267
    Veggie Dill Dip, 366
The Easiest Mac 'n' Cheese recipe, 210–211
Easy Baked Bacon and Sausages recipe, 90–91
Easy Baked BBQ Chicken recipe, 216–217
Easy Blender Chocolate Donuts recipe, 104–105
    Valentine's Day Muffin Pan Ice Cream Cakes, 288–289
Easy Blender Waffles recipe, 336–337
    "Apple" Pie Waffles, 352–353
    Breakfast Kabobs, 92–93
Easy English Muffins recipe, 386–387
    Dippy Eggs with Toast Fingers, 106–107
    English Muffin Pizzas, 178–179
    Micah's Egg Muffin Sandwiches, 110–111
Easy Red, White and Blueberry Sundaes recipe, 276–277
Easy Tartar Sauce recipe, 364
    Fish Fingers with Easy Tartar Sauce, 204–205
Egg Roll in a Bowl recipe, 250–251
eggplant
    Cheesy Beef and "Noodle" Casserole, 218–219
    Eggplant Fries, 128–129
Eggplant Fries recipe, 128–129
eggs
    in baby food, 39
    Bacon Cheeseburger Waffle, 358–359
    Baked Chicken Legs, 206–207

eggs (continued)

Baseball Blender Cupcakes, 302–303

Basic Savory Chaffles or Paffles, 334–335

The BEST Chocolate Chip Cookies, 312–313

Blender Pancake Snowmen, 102–103

Blueberry Cheesecake Muffins, 122–123

Blueberry Muffin Chaffles, 342–343

Bon Vie Chicken Tenders, 200–201

Breakfast for Dinner, 230–231

Chaffle Breakfast Sammie, 338–339

Cheeseburger Breakfast Casserole, 114–115

Chocolate Hazelnut Waffles, 344–345

Chocolate Hazelnut Whoopie Pies, 304–305

Chocolate Minute Muffins, 98–99

Chocolate Protein Shake, 100–101

Chocolate Waffle Sandwich, 360–361

Christmas Tree Pizza, 262–263

Cinnamon Roll Chaffles, 340–341

Cinnamon Rolls, 116–117

Crispy Baked Ravioli, 214–215

Crispy Taco Chaffles, 348–349

Cute Mouse Eggs, 144–145

The Cutest Deviled Eggs Ever, 136–141

Dinosaur Droppings (aka Meatballs), 198–199

Dippy Eggs with Toast Fingers, 106–107

Easiest Mayo Ever, 365

Easy Blender Chocolate Donuts, 104–105

Easy Blender Waffles, 336–337

Easy English Muffins, 386–387

Extreme Chocolate Blender Birthday Cake, 300–301

Fish Fingers with Easy Tartar Sauce, 204–205

Flourless Protein Pizza Crêpes, 88–89

Fluffy Bunny Scrambled Eggs, 254–255

French Toast Porridge, 96–97

Glazed Pumpkin Mini Waffles, 354–355

Graham Crackers, 160–161

Green Eggs and Ham, 108–109

Ham 'n' Cheese Cupcakes, 94–95

Heart-Shaped Eggs, 264–265

Just Like Oreos Sandwich Cookies, 294–295

Little Piggy Eggs, 164–165

Micah's Egg Muffin Sandwiches, 110–111

Monkey Bread, 124–125

Pigs in a Blanket, 142–143

Pizza Breakfast Pie, 120–121

Pizza Crust, 225

Pizza Eggs, 84–85

Pizza Rolls, 134–135

Protein Hot Chocolate, 296–297

Protein Noodle Pad Thai, 212–213

Protein-Packed Ranch Dip, 367

Salted Egg Yolks, 400–401

Sandwich Buns, 384–385

Soft Tortillas, 382–383

Strawberry Pudding, 146–147

Strawberry Shortcake Chaffle Sandwiches, 350–351

Sugar-Free Toaster Pastries (aka Gilmore Girls Breakfast), 118–119

Taco Meatball Holiday Tree, 272–273

Valentine's Day Breakfast, 256–257

Waffle Cone Mini Waffles, 356–357

Zombie Spaghetti and Eyeballs, 260–261

eicosapentaenoic acid (EPA), 20

Emmerich, Maria, contact information for, 7

energy toxicity, 29

English Muffin Pizzas recipe, 178–179

Epic Cheesy Beef Nachos recipe, 242–243

epigenetic changes, 52

epinephrine, 51

erythritol, 75, 78

Everly drink mix

Swedish Fish (or Gummy Bears), 162–163

excitotoxins, 45

Extreme Chocolate Blender Birthday Cake recipe, 300–301

F

families, tips for busy, 57–61

farmer's cheese

The Easiest Mac 'n' Cheese, 210–211

Sandwich on a Stick, 174–175

fats

about, 20

makeup of common, 27

polyunsaturated, 20, 23–26

saturated, 20, 21–23

trans, 20, 23

types, 20

using when cooking, 70

fish and seafood

Fish Fingers with Easy Tartar Sauce, 204–205

Salmon Puree with Salt, 396–397

Fish Fingers with Easy Tartar Sauce recipe, 204–205

fish sauce

about, 75

Cheeseburger Lettuce Wraps, 238–239

Drive-Thru Chaffle Burger, 346–347

Egg Roll in a Bowl, 250–251
Protein Noodle Pad Thai, 212–213
Flourless Protein Pizza Crêpes recipe, 88–89
flu vaccine, 50
Fluffy Bunny Scrambled Eggs recipe, 254–255
Folios cheese wraps, 59
food dyes, 45
Football Deviled Eggs recipe, 138–141
freezing, recipes for, 60–61
French Kids Eat Everything, 67
French Toast Porridge recipe, 96–97
fructose, 75
Fruit Dip recipe, 371
Fruit Flower Bouquet, 152–153
Fruit Flower Bouquet recipe, 152–153
fruits. *See also specific types*
as carbohydrates, 15–17
highest/lowest in sugar, 17
modern vs. ancient, 16

G

gadgets, cooking, 73–74
gamma linoleic acid (GLA), 20
garam masala
Indian-Spiced Chicken Protein Noodle, 182–183
garlic
Blender Marinara Sauce, 372–373
Bone Broth, 392–393
Cheeseburger Breakfast Casserole, 114–115
Cheeseburger Lettuce Wraps, 238–239
Chicken Sloppy Joes, 234–235
Chinese 5-Spice Chicken Protein Noodle Soup, 182–183
Christmas Tomato Soup with Grilled Cheese Stars and Trees, 258–259
Dinosaur Droppings (aka Meatballs), 198–199
Easy Baked BBQ Chicken, 216–217
Egg Roll in a Bowl, 250–251
Guacamole, 376–377
Indian-Spiced Chicken Protein Noodle, 182–183
Mama Maria's Pizza Chicken Balls, 208–209
Meaty Lasagna Bowls, 220–221
Pizza Breakfast Pie, 120–121
Pizza Dog Casserole, 236–237
Protein Noodle Chicken Alfredo, 222–223
Protein Noodle Pad Thai, 212–213
Protein Noodle Taco Lasagna, 202–203
Roasted Garlic, 374–375
Salmon Jerky Fingers, 156–157
Sloppy Kai Dogs, 190–191

Sweet 'n' Sour Chicken Wings, 248–249
Sweet 'n' Sour Turkey Jerky, 148–149
Zombie Spaghetti and Eyeballs, 260–261
gelatin
Dairy-Free No-Churn Ice Cream, 322–323
Holiday Jigglers, 280–281
Marshmallows, 314–315
No-Bake Strawberry Panna Cotta, 292–293
Pumpkin Pie Gummies, 286–287
Raspberry Sorbet, 324–325
Shamrock Shake Gummies, 284–285
Sugar-Free Strawberry Jam, 378–379
Swedish Fish (or Gummy Bears), 162–163
Gerber brand, 39
ginger
Chinese 5-Spice Chicken Protein Noodle Soup, 182–183
Egg Roll in a Bowl, 250–251
Protein Noodle Pad Thai, 212–213
Salmon Jerky Fingers, 156–157
Sweet 'n' Sour Chicken Wings, 248–249
Sweet 'n' Sour Turkey Jerky, 148–149
Thai Chicken Protein Noodle Soup, 182–183
Glazed Pumpkin Mini Waffles recipe, 354–355
gluconeogenesis, 42
glucosamine, 48
glucose, 13–14
Good Chocolate, 59
The Good Chocolate brand, 312, 331
Graham Crackers recipe, 160–161
Cookie Dough Dip, 166–167
Red Velvet Truffles, 330
S'mores recipe, 316
Strawberry Cheesecake Truffles, 328
green chilies
Chicken Enchiladas, 246–247
Green Eggs and Ham recipe, 108–109
green light, 52
green onions
Chinese 5-Spice Chicken Protein Noodle Soup, 182–183
Deviled Egg Flowers, 139–141
Egg Roll in a Bowl, 250–251
Green Eggs and Ham, 108–109
Ham 'n' Cheese Cupcakes, 94–95
Protein Noodle Pad Thai, 212–213
Pumpkin Deviled Eggs, 138–141
Sweet 'n' Sour Chicken Wings, 248–249
Touchdown Tacos, 192–193
Veggie and Savory Fruit Flowers, 130–131
Veggie Dill Dip, 366

Ground Beef with Salt recipe, 398–399
growth charts, 33
Gruyère cheese
    The Easiest Mac 'n' Cheese, 210–211
Guacamole recipe, 376–377
    Cheese Quesadillas, 194–195
    Crispy Taco Chaffles, 348–349
    Green Eggs and Ham, 108–109
    Meat Cookies, 188–189
    Taco Meatball Holiday Tree, 272–273
    Touchdown Tacos, 192–193
gummy molds, 74
gut bacteria, 69–70
gut microbiome, 48

H

Halloumi cheese
    Christmas Tomato Soup with Grilled Cheese
        Stars and Trees, 258–259
Halloween Spooky Skeleton with BBQ Riblets
    recipe, 270–271
ham
    Breakfast Kabobs, 92–93
    Chaffle Breakfast Sammie, 338–339
    Chaffle or Paffle Sub Sandwich, 334
    Green Eggs and Ham, 108–109
    Ham 'n' Cheese Cupcakes, 94–95
    Han 'n' Cheese Chaffle or Paffle Sandwich, 334
    Micah's Egg Muffin Sandwiches, 110–111
    Sandwich on a Stick, 174–175
Ham 'n' Cheese Cupcakes recipe, 94–95
Han 'n' Cheese Chaffle or Paffle Sandwich recipe,
    334
Havarti cheese
    Meat Cookies, 188–189
hazelnut flour
    Chocolate Hazelnut Waffles, 344–345
hazelnuts
    Sugar-Free Chocolate Hazelnut Spread, 380–381
Heart-Shaped Eggs recipe, 264–265
    Valentine Deviled Eggs, 266–267
heavy cream
    Baseball Blender Cupcakes, 302–303
    Blender Pancake Snowmen, 102–103
    Brownie Truffles, 327
    Candy Bar Truffles, 329
    Chocolate Chip Cookie Dough Truffles, 331
    Chocolate Hazelnut Whoopie Pies, 304–305
    Chocolate Minute Muffins, 98–99

Chocolate Waffle Sandwich, 360–361
Cinnamon Roll Chaffles, 340–341
Easy Blender Chocolate Donuts, 104–105
Easy Red, White and Blueberry Sundaes,
    276–277
Extreme Chocolate Blender Birthday Cake,
    300–301
French Toast Porridge, 96–97
Iced Animal Crackers, 170–171
Just Like Oreos Sandwich Cookies, 294–295
No-Churn Vanilla Bean Ice Cream, 317
No-Bake Strawberry Panna Cotta, 292–293
No-Churn Blue Moon Ice Cream, 318
No-Churn Chocolate Ice Cream, 319
No-Churn Strawberries and Cream Ice Cream,
    318
Protein Hot Chocolate, 296–297
Protein-Packed Blue Milk, 82–83
Raspberries and Cream Ice Pops, 298–299
Shamrock Shake Gummies, 284–285
Spaghetti Bolognese, 240–241
Strawberry Pudding, 146–147
Strawberry Shortcake Chaffle Sandwiches,
    350–351
Sugar-Free Chocolate Bars or Chips, 310–311
Sugar-Free Toaster Pastries (aka Gilmore Girls
    Breakfast), 118–119
Waffle Cone Mini Waffles, 356–357
hemp milk
    Dairy-Free No-Churn Ice Cream, 322–323
    Flourless Protein Pizza Crêpes, 88–89
    No-Bake Strawberry Panna Cotta, 292–293
herbs, using when cooking, 70
hibiscus tea
    Swedish Fish (or Gummy Bears), 162–163
high-powered blender, 73
holiday celebrations, 68
Holiday Jigglers recipe, 280–281
Holiday Tree Cheese Ball recipe, 268–269
honeydew melon
    Fruit Flower Bouquet, 152–153
hot dogs
    about, 63
    Little Piggy Eggs, 164–165
    Pizza Dog Casserole, 236–237
    Sloppy Kai Dogs, 190–191
hot sauce
    Pumpkin Deviled Eggs, 138–141

I

ice pops, 74, 283
iceberg lettuce
    Drive-Thru Chaffle Burger, 346–347
Iced Animal Crackers recipe, 170–171
immersion blender, 73
immune health, 48–49
Indian-Spiced Chicken Protein Noodle Soup recipe, 182–183
ingredients, sugar-free, 75–78
Instant Pot, 57, 74
insulin resistant, 29
integrins, 51
Italian sausage
    Meat Lover's Pizza, 226
    Meaty Lasagna Bowls, 220–221
    Spaghetti Bolognese, 240–241

J

jerky, 67
jicama
    Cookie Dough Dip, 166–167
    Just Like "Apples" and Dip, 158–159
    Veggie and Savory Fruit Flowers, 130–131
Just Like "Apples" and Dip recipe, 158–159
Just Like Oreos Sandwich Cookies recipe, 294–295
Just Made Keto cupcakes, 59

K

Kai's Chicken Wings recipe, 132–133
Kai's Puppy Chow recipe, 306–307
Kettle & Fire bone broth, 59
kitchen
    cooking tools/gadgets, 73–74
    picky eaters, 69–72
    planning sugar-free meals, 61–67
    recipes, 79
    sugar-free holidays and birthdays, 68
    sugar-free ingredients, 75–78
    tips for busy families, 57–61
    tips for cooking, 55–56

L

Lakanto, 76
lavender essential oil, 52
leftovers, 63
lemongrass
    Thai Chicken Protein Noodle Soup, 182–183

lemons
    "Apple" Pie Waffles, 352–353
    Raspberry Sorbet, 324–325
lettuce. *See also specific types*
    Chaffle or Paffle Sub Sandwich, 334
    Crispy Taco Chaffles, 348–349
    Epic Cheesy Beef Nachos, 242–243
limes
    Guacamole, 376–377
    Protein Noodle Pad Thai, 212–213
    Sweet 'n' Sour Chicken Wings, 248–249
    Thai Chicken Protein Noodle Soup, 182–183
linoleic acid (LA), 20
little kids, protein needs for, 43–44
Little Piggy Eggs recipe, 164–165

M

macadamia nuts
    Strawberry Breakfast Parfait, 86–87
macronutrients
    carbohydrates, 13–17
    fats, 20–27
    protein, 18–20
magnesium
    bone health and, 46
    depletion of, 31
magnesium glycinate, 52
Mama Maria's Pizza Chicken Balls recipe, 208–209
marrow bones
    Bone Marrow, 394–395
Marshmallows recipe, 314–315
    Protein Hot Chocolate, 296–297
    Rocky Road Ice Cream recipe, 319
    S'mores recipe, 316
meal planning, 57
Meat Cookies recipe, 188–189
Meat Lover's Pizza recipe, 226
meatballs, premade, 63
Meaty Lasagna Bowls recipe, 220–221
mental health, sleep and, 49–52
Micah's Egg Muffin Sandwiches recipe, 110–111
micronutrients, depletion of, 31–32
mini waffle maker, 74
monk fruit, 76
Monkey Bread recipe, 124–125
monounsaturated fats, 20
Monterey Jack cheese
    Cheese Quesadillas, 194–195
    Chicken Enchiladas, 246–247
    Crispy Taco Chaffles, 348–349

Monterey Jack cheese *(continued)*
    Epic Cheesy Beef Nachos, 242–243
    Protein Noodle Taco Lasagna, 202–203
Moon Cheese, 59
mozzarella cheese
    Antipasto on a Stick, 176–177
    Blueberry Muffin Chaffles, 342–343
    Cheese Sticks, 227–229
    Christmas Tree Pizza, 262–263
    Cinnamon Roll Chaffles, 340–341
    The Easiest Mac 'n' Cheese, 210–211
    English Muffin Pizzas, 178–179
    Flourless Protein Pizza Crêpes, 88–89
    Meat Lover's Pizza, 226
    Meaty Lasagna Bowls, 220–221
    Owl Meatballs, 199
    Pepperoni Pizza, 225
    Pizza Breakfast Pie, 120–121
    Pizza Crust, 225
    Pizza Dog Casserole, 236–237
    Pizza Rolls, 134–135
    Sandwich on a Stick, 174–175
    Strawberry Shortcake Chaffle Sandwiches, 350–351
    Sugar-Free Toaster Pastries (aka Gilmore Girls Breakfast), 118–119
    Zombie Spaghetti and Eyeballs, 260–261
Muenster cheese
    Meat Cookies, 188–189
muffins
    Blueberry Cheesecake Muffins, 122–123
    Cheeseburger Breakfast Casserole, 114–115
    Chocolate Minute Muffins, 98–99
    Pizza Breakfast Pie, 120–121
    Valentine's Day Muffin Pan Ice Cream Cakes, 288–289
mushrooms
    Mama Maria's Pizza Chicken Balls, 208–209
    Zombie Spaghetti and Eyeballs, 260–261

N

natural sweeteners, 75–76
Natvia, 76
No-Churn Vanilla Bean Ice Cream recipe, 317
No-Bake Chocolate-Topped Energy Bars recipe, 150–151
No-Bake Peanut Butter Lover's Bar recipe, 168–169
No-Bake Strawberry Panna Cotta recipe, 292–293
No-Churn Blue Moon Ice Cream recipe, 318

No-Churn Chocolate Ice Cream recipe, 319
No-Churn Ice Cream Five Ways recipe, 317–321
No-Churn Strawberries and Cream Ice Cream recipe, 318
    Valentine's Day Muffin Pan Ice Cream Cakes, 288–289
nonalcoholic fatty liver disease (NAFLD), 29
nonstick skillet, 73
noradrenaline, 51
Norbu, 76
norepinephrine, 51
nursing, 38

O

oils, makeup of common, 27
olives
    Antipasto on a Stick, 176–177
    Epic Cheesy Beef Nachos, 242–243
    Halloween Spooky Skeleton with BBQ Riblets, 270–271
    Owl Deviled Eggs, 139–141
    Owl Meatballs, 199
    Spider Deviled Eggs, 138–141
    Touchdown Tacos, 192–193
    Veggie and Savory Fruit Flowers, 130–131
    Zombie Spaghetti and Eyeballs, 260–261
omega-3 fats, 20, 26
omega-6 fats, 20, 26
onions. *See also* green onions
    Bacon Cheeseburger Pizza, 226
    Blender Marinara Sauce, 372–373
    Bone Broth, 392–393
    Cheeseburger Breakfast Casserole, 114–115
    Cheeseburger Lettuce Wraps, 238–239
    Cheesy Beef and "Noodle" Casserole, 218–219
    Chicken Enchiladas, 246–247
    Chicken Protein Noodle Soup, 180–183
    Chicken Sloppy Joes, 234–235
    Christmas Tomato Soup with Grilled Cheese Stars and Trees, 258–259
    Dinosaur Droppings (aka Meatballs), 198–199
    Drive-Thru Chaffle Burger, 346–347
    The Easiest Mac 'n' Cheese, 210–211
    Epic Cheesy Beef Nachos, 242–243
    Guacamole, 376–377
    Meaty Lasagna Bowls, 220–221
    Pizza Breakfast Pie, 120–121
    Pizza Dog Casserole, 236–237
    Protein Noodle Taco Lasagna, 202–203

Shredded BBQ Chicken, 244–245
Sloppy Kai Dogs, 190–191
Spaghetti Bolognese, 240–241
Valentine Deviled Eggs, 266–267
Zombie Spaghetti and Eyeballs, 260–261
oregano
Spaghetti Bolognese, 240–241
Zombie Spaghetti and Eyeballs, 260–261
osteoblasts, 46
osteoclasts, 46
Owl Deviled Eggs recipe, 139–141
Owl Meatballs recipe, 199
oxidative priority, 29

P

packed lunches, recipes for, 62
pancakes
Blender Pancake Snowmen, 102–103
Flourless Protein Pizza Crêpes, 88–89
Parmesan cheese
Baked Chicken Legs, 206–207
Better Than School Lunch Chicken Patties, 184–185
Bon Vie Chicken Tenders, 200–201
Cheese Sticks, 227–229
Eggplant Fries, 128–129
Fish Fingers with Easy Tartar Sauce, 204–205
Flourless Protein Pizza Crêpes, 88–89
Mama Maria's Pizza Chicken Balls, 208–209
Meaty Lasagna Bowls, 220–221
Pizza Breakfast Pie, 120–121
Pizza Dog Casserole, 236–237
Pizza Eggs, 84–85
Pizza Sauce, 370
Protein Noodle Chicken Alfredo, 222–223
Spaghetti Bolognese, 240–241
Sticks and Dip, 154–155
Zombie Spaghetti and Eyeballs, 260–261
Parmesan crostini
Holiday Tree Cheese Ball, 268–269
parsley
Bacon Lover's Chicken Nuggets, 186–187
Cheese Sticks, 227–229
Cheesy Beef and "Noodle" Casserole, 218–219
Crispy Baked Ravioli, 214–215
Spaghetti Bolognese, 240–241
peaches, 16
peanut butter
Candy Bar Truffles, 329
Just Like "Apples" and Dip, 158–159

Kai's Puppy Chow, 306–307
No-Bake Peanut Butter Lover's Bars, 168–169
Protein Noodle Pad Thai, 212–213
peanut flour
Extreme Chocolate Blender Birthday Cake, 300–301
peanuts
No-Bake Peanut Butter Lover's Bars, 168–169
Protein Noodle Pad Thai, 212–213
pecans
No-Bake Chocolate-Topped Energy Bars, 150–151
Turkey Cinnamon Rolls, 117
Pederson Farms brand, 63
pepper jack cheese
Holiday Tree Cheese Ball, 268–269
peppercorns
Cute Mouse Eggs, 144–145
Little Piggy Eggs, 164–165
pepperoni
English Muffin Pizzas, 178–179
Flourless Protein Pizza Crêpes, 88–89
Meat Lover's Pizza, 226
Pepperoni Pizza, 225
Pizza Rolls, 134–135
Pepperoni Pizza recipe, 225
picky eaters, 69–72
Pigs in a Blanket recipe, 142–143
pizza
Christmas Tree Pizza, 262–263
English Muffin Pizzas, 178–179
Pizza Breakfast Pie, 120–121
Pizza Chaffles or Paffles, 334
Pizza Dog Casserole, 236–237
Pizza Eggs, 84–85
Pizza Party, 224–229
Pizza Rolls, 134–135
Pizza Breakfast Pie recipe, 120–121
Pizza Chaffles or Paffles recipe, 334
Pizza Crust recipe, 225
Bacon Cheeseburger Pizza, 226
Cheese Sticks, 227–229
Meat Lover's Pizza, 226
Pepperoni Pizza, 225
Pizza Dog Casserole recipe, 236–237
Pizza Eggs recipe, 84–85
Pizza Party recipe, 224–229
Pizza Rolls recipe, 134–135
Pizza Sauce recipe, 370
Bon Vie Chicken Tenders, 200–201
Cheese Sticks, 227–229

Pizza Sauce recipe *(continued)*
    Christmas Tree Pizza, 262–263
    Crispy Baked Ravioli, 214–215
    English Muffin Pizzas, 178–179
    Flourless Protein Pizza Crêpes, 88–89
    Mama Maria's Pizza Chicken Balls, 208–209
    Meat Lover's Pizza, 226
    Pepperoni Pizza, 225
    Pizza Breakfast Pie, 120–121
    Pizza Dog Casserole, 236–237
    Pizza Eggs, 84–85
    Spooky Breadstick Fingers, 274–275
plain yogurt, 67
planning
    importance of, 53
    sugar-free meals, 61–67
plant proteins, 18
polyunsaturated fats (PUFAs), 20, 23–26
pork
    Chaffle Breakfast Sammie, 338–339
    Halloween Spooky Skeleton with BBQ Riblets, 270–271
pork dust
    Baked Chicken Legs, 206–207
    Basic Savory Chaffles or Paffles, 334–335
    Better Than School Lunch Chicken Patties, 184–185
    Bon Vie Chicken Tenders, 200–201
    Christmas Tree Pizza, 262–263
    Crispy Baked Ravioli, 214–215
    Crispy Taco Chaffles, 348–349
    Dinosaur Droppings (aka Meatballs), 198–199
    The Easiest Mac 'n' Cheese, 210–211
    Egg Roll in a Bowl, 250–251
    Fish Fingers with Easy Tartar Sauce, 204–205
    Pizza Crust, 225
pork panko
    about, 59
    Pizza Breakfast Pie, 120–121
pork rinds
    Epic Cheesy Beef Nachos, 242–243
    Kai's Puppy Chow, 306–307
pork sausage
    Halloween Spooky Skeleton with BBQ Riblets, 270–271
premade meatballs, 63
Primal Kitchen brand, 59
probiotics, 69–70
progesterone, bone health and, 47

prosciutto
    Halloween Spooky Skeleton with BBQ Riblets, 270–271
prostaglandins, 51
protein
    about, 18–20
    for building muscle, 19
    requirements for kids, 43–44
Protein Hot Chocolate recipe, 296–297
Protein Noodle Chicken Alfredo recipe, 222–223
Protein Noodle Pad Thai recipe, 212–213
Protein Noodle Taco Lasagna recipe, 202–203
protein powders, 112
Protein-Packed Blue Milk recipe, 82–83
Protein-Packed Ranch Dip recipe, 367
    Veggie and Savory Fruit Flowers, 130–131
psyllium husk powder
    about, 75
    Cinnamon Rolls, 116–117
    Monkey Bread, 124–125
    Pigs in a Blanket, 142–143
    Pizza Rolls, 134–135
    Sandwich Buns, 384–385
    Soft Tortillas, 382–383
Pumpkin Deviled Eggs recipe, 138–141
Pumpkin Pie Gummies recipe, 286–287
pumpkin puree
    Glazed Pumpkin Mini Waffles, 354–355
    Pumpkin Pie Gummies, 286–287
Pyure, 76

R
radishes
    Cute Mouse Eggs, 144–145
    Veggie and Savory Fruit Flowers, 130–131
Rao's brand, 84, 261
raspberries
    Blender Pancake Snowmen, 102–103
    Bombdiggity Pops, 282–283
    Chocolate Hazelnut Waffles, 344–345
    Fluffy Bunny Scrambled Eggs, 254–255
    Fruit Flower Bouquet, 152–153
    Raspberries and Cream Ice Pops, 298–299
    Raspberry Sorbet, 324–325
    Sugar-Free Toaster Pastries (aka Gilmore Girls Breakfast), 118–119
Raspberries and Cream Ice Pops recipe, 298–299
Raspberry Sorbet recipe, 324–325

recipes
    for freezing, 60–61
    ten-minutes or less, 60
    using, 79
Red Velvet Truffles recipe, 330
rice cereal, 40
ricotta cheese
    Meaty Lasagna Bowls, 220–221
ROAM Snack Sticks, 59
Roasted Garlic recipe, 374–375
    Bone Broth, 392–393
    Christmas Tomato Soup with Grilled Cheese
        Stars and Trees, 258–259
    Easy Baked BBQ Chicken, 216–217
    Guacamole, 376–377
    Mama Maria's Pizza Chicken Balls, 208–209
    Meaty Lasagna Bowls, 220–221
    Protein Noodle Chicken Alfredo, 222–223
    Protein Noodle Pad Thai, 212–213
    Protein Noodle Taco Lasagna, 202–203
    Salmon Jerky Fingers, 156–157
    Spaghetti Bolognese, 240–241
    Sweet 'n' Sour Chicken Wings, 248–249
    Sweet 'n' Sour Turkey Jerky, 148–149
    Zombie Spaghetti and Eyeballs, 260–261
Rocky Road Ice Cream recipe, 319
rosemary
    Bone Broth, 392–393

S

salami
    Antipasto on a Stick, 176–177
    Halloween Spooky Skeleton with BBQ Riblets,
        270–271
salmon
    Salmon Jerky Fingers, 156–157
    Salmon Puree with Salt, 396–397
Salmon Jerky Fingers recipe, 156–157
Salmon Puree with Salt recipe, 396–397
salsa
    Cheese Quesadillas, 194–195
    Chicken Enchiladas, 246–247
    Crispy Taco Chaffles, 348–349
    Holiday Tree Cheese Ball, 268–269
    Taco Meatball Holiday Tree, 272–273
    Touchdown Tacos, 192–193
salt, using when cooking, 70
Salted Egg Yolks recipe, 400–401

Sandwich Buns recipe, 384–385
    Better Than School Lunch Chicken Patties,
        184–185
    Chicken Sloppy Joes, 234–235
    Meat Cookies, 188–189
    Shredded BBQ Chicken, 244–245
    Sloppy Kai Dogs, 190–191
    Spooky Breadstick Fingers, 274–275
Sandwich on a Stick recipe, 174–175
sandwiches
    Chaffle Breakfast Sammie, 338–339
    Chicken Sloppy Joes, 234–235
    Chocolate Waffle Sandwich, 360–361
    Micah's Egg Muffin Sandwiches, 110–111
    Sandwich on a Stick, 174–175
    Strawberry Shortcake Chaffle Sandwiches,
        350–351
sardines, 67
saturated fats, 20, 21–23
sauces
    Blender Marinara Sauce, 372–373
    Easiest Mayo Ever, 365
    Easy Tartar Sauce, 364
    Pizza Sauce, 370
    Sugar-Free Ketchup, 369
    Traditional Ranch, 368
seafood. See fish and seafood
sesame seeds
    Cheeseburger Breakfast Casserole, 114–115
    Cheeseburger Lettuce Wraps, 238–239
    Drive-Thru Chaffle Burger, 346–347
    Sweet 'n' Sour Chicken Wings, 248–249
Shamrock Shake Gummies recipe, 284–285
Shredded BBQ Chicken recipe, 244–245
skillet, 73
sleep
    mental health and, 49–52
    tips for better, 52
Sloppy Kai Dogs recipe, 190–191
slow cooker, 56, 57, 74
smoked cocktail sausages
    Pigs in a Blanket, 142–143
S'mores recipe, 316
snacks, healthy, 67
Soft Tortillas recipe, 382–383
    Cheese Quesadillas, 194–195
    Touchdown Tacos, 192–193
soups
    Bone Broth, 392–393
    Chicken Protein Noodle Soup, 180–183

soups *(continued)*
    Christmas Tomato Soup with Grilled Cheese
        Stars and Trees, 258–259
sour cream
    Cheese Quesadillas, 194–195
    Chicken Enchiladas, 246–247
    Christmas Tomato Soup with Grilled Cheese
        Stars and Trees, 258–259
    Touchdown Tacos, 192–193
    Veggie Dill Dip, 366
Spaghetti Bolognese recipe, 240–241
spices, using when cooking, 70
Spider Deviled Eggs recipe, 138–141
spiral slicer, 74
Spooky Breadstick Fingers recipe, 274–275
spreads
    Chicken Pâté, 402–403
    Sugar-Free Chocolate Hazelnut Spread, 380–381
    Sugar-Free Strawberry Jam, 378–379
starch, 14
stevia glycerite. *See also* sweeteners
    about, 76
    Bacon Cheeseburger Pizza, 226
    Blender Marinara Sauce, 372–373
    Christmas Tomato Soup with Grilled Cheese
        Stars and Trees, 258–259
    Drive-Thru Chaffle Burger, 346–347
    Holiday Jigglers, 280–281
    Spaghetti Bolognese, 240–241
    Strawberry Cheesecake Santas, 278–279
    Strawberry Shortcake Chaffle Sandwiches,
        350–351
    Thai Chicken Protein Noodle Soup, 182–183
    Touchdown Tacos, 192–193
Sticks and Dip recipe, 154–155
strawberries
    Blender Pancake Snowmen, 102–103
    Bombdiggity Pops, 282–283
    Breakfast for Dinner, 230–231
    Breakfast Kabobs, 92–93
    Cookie Dough Dip, 166–167
    Easy Blender Waffles, 336–337
    Easy Red, White and Blueberry Sundaes,
        276–277
    Fruit Flower Bouquet, 152–153
    No-Bake Strawberry Panna Cotta, 292–293
    No-Churn Strawberries and Cream Ice Cream,
        318
    Raspberry Sorbet, 324–325
    Strawberry Breakfast Parfait, 86–87
    Strawberry Cheesecake Santas, 278–279

    Strawberry Cheesecake Truffles, 328
    Strawberry Pudding, 146–147
    Strawberry Shortcake Chaffle Sandwiches,
        350–351
    Sugar-Free Strawberry Jam, 378–379
    Valentine's Day Breakfast, 256–257
    Valentine's Day Muffin Pan Ice Cream Cakes,
        288–289
Strawberry Breakfast Parfait recipe, 86–87
Strawberry Cheesecake Santas recipe, 278–279
Strawberry Cheesecake Truffles recipe, 328
Strawberry Pudding recipe, 146–147
Strawberry Shortcake Chaffle Sandwiches recipe,
    350–351
    Valentine's Day Breakfast, 256–257
string cheese
    Fluffy Bunny Scrambled Eggs, 254–255
sugar
    about, 9–11
    benefits of kids cutting, 32–36
    cycle of consumption, 28–30
    depression and, 52
    harmful effects of eating too much, 30
    micronutrients and, 31–32
    sources of, 11–12
    statistics on, 10
    tips for cutting, 37
sugar-free child athlete, 14–15
Sugar-Free Chocolate Bars or Chips recipe,
    310–311
    Baseball Blender Cupcakes, 302–303
    The BEST Chocolate Chip Cookies, 312–313
    Chocolate Chip Cookie Dough Truffles, 331
    Cookie Dough Dip, 166–167
    No-Bake Chocolate-Topped Energy Bars,
        150–151
    Rocky Road Ice Cream recipe, 319
    S'mores recipe, 316
    Valentine's Day Muffin Pan Ice Cream Cakes,
        288–289
Sugar-Free Chocolate Hazelnut Spread recipe,
    380–381
    Chocolate Hazelnut Waffles, 344–345
    Chocolate Hazelnut Whoopie Pies, 304–305
    No-Bake Chocolate-Topped Energy Bars,
        150–151
sugar-free holidays/birthdays, 68
sugar-free ingredients, 75–78
Sugar-Free Ketchup recipe, 369
    Bacon Cheeseburger Pizza, 226
    Bacon Cheeseburger Waffle, 358–359

Bacon Lover's Chicken Nuggets, 186–187
Better Than School Lunch Chicken Patties, 184–185
Bon Vie Chicken Tenders, 200–201
Cheeseburger Breakfast Casserole, 114–115
Dinosaur Droppings (aka Meatballs), 198–199
Drive-Thru Chaffle Burger, 346–347
Eggplant Fries, 128–129
Meat Cookies, 188–189
sugar-free meals, planning, 61–67
Sugar-Free Strawberry Jam recipe, 378–379
Breakfast for Dinner, 230–231
Easy Blender Waffles, 336–337
Sugar-Free Toaster Pastries (aka Gilmore Girls Breakfast) recipe, 118–119
sunflower seeds
No-Bake Chocolate-Topped Energy Bars, 150–151
Swedish Fish (or Gummy Bears) recipe, 162–163
Sweet 'n' Sour Chicken Wings recipe, 248–249
Sweet 'n' Sour Turkey Jerky recipe, 148–149
sweeteners. *See also* stevia glycerite
blending, 78
natural, 75–76
using in recipes, 77
Swerve, 76
Swiss cheese
Crispy Baked Ravioli, 214–215
Cute Mouse Eggs, 144–145
Ham 'n' Cheese Chaffle or Paffle Sandwich, 334
synthetic dye, 45

T

T cells, 51
Taco Meatball Holiday Tree recipe, 272–273
Taco Seasoning recipe, 388–389
Protein Noodle Taco Lasagna, 202–203
Taco Meatball Holiday Tree, 272–273
tamari
Egg Roll in a Bowl, 250–251
Salmon Jerky Fingers, 156–157
Sweet 'n' Sour Chicken Wings, 248–249
Sweet 'n' Sour Turkey Jerky, 148–149
tea bags
Holiday Jigglers, 280–281
teens, protein needs for, 44
temperature, for sleeping, 52
ten-minutes or less recipes, 60
Teton Waters Ranch brand, 59, 63
Thai Chicken Protein Noodle Soup recipe, 182–183

thyme
Bone Broth, 392–393
Spaghetti Bolognese, 240–241
time-saving food products, 59
tomato paste
Chicken Sloppy Joes, 234–235
Sugar-Free Ketchup, 369
tomato sauce
Cheeseburger Lettuce Wraps, 238–239
Cheesy Beef and "Noodle" Casserole, 218–219
Chicken Enchiladas, 246–247
Chicken Sloppy Joes, 234–235
Christmas Tomato Soup with Grilled Cheese Stars and Trees, 258–259
Dinosaur Droppings (aka Meatballs), 198–199
Drive-Thru Chaffle Burger, 346–347
Easy Baked BBQ Chicken, 216–217
Epic Cheesy Beef Nachos, 242–243
Halloween Spooky Skeleton with BBQ Riblets, 270–271
Pizza Breakfast Pie, 120–121
Pizza Sauce, 370
Shredded BBQ Chicken, 244–245
Sloppy Kai Dogs, 190–191
Sweet 'n' Sour Chicken Wings, 248–249
Touchdown Tacos, 192–193
tomatoes
Antipasto on a Stick, 176–177
Blender Marinara Sauce, 372–373
Chaffle or Paffle Sub Sandwich, 334
Cheeseburger Breakfast Casserole, 114–115
Chicken Sloppy Joes, 234–235
Christmas Tomato Soup with Grilled Cheese Stars and Trees, 258–259
Christmas Tree Pizza, 262–263
Crispy Taco Chaffles, 348–349
Guacamole, 376–377
Protein Noodle Taco Lasagna, 202–203
Sandwich on a Stick, 174–175
Spaghetti Bolognese, 240–241
Veggie and Savory Fruit Flowers, 130–131
tools, cooking, 73–74
Touchdown Tacos recipe, 192–193
Crispy Taco Chaffles, 348–349
Traditional Ranch recipe, 368
Bacon Cheeseburger Waffle, 358–359
Bacon Lover's Chicken Nuggets, 186–187
Better Than School Lunch Chicken Patties, 184–185
Bon Vie Chicken Tenders, 200–201
Crispy Baked Ravioli, 214–215

Traditional Ranch recipe (continued)
    Dinosaur Droppings (aka Meatballs), 198–199
    Kai's Chicken Wings, 132–133
trans fats, 20, 23
Truffles Five Ways recipe, 326–331
turkey
    Chaffle Breakfast Sammie, 338–339
    Chaffle or Paffle Sub Sandwich, 334
    Crispy Baked Ravioli, 214–215
    Micah's Egg Muffin Sandwiches, 110–111
    Sandwich on a Stick, 174–175
    Spaghetti Bolognese, 240–241
    Sweet 'n' Sour Turkey Jerky, 148–149
    Zombie Spaghetti and Eyeballs, 260–261
Turkey Cinnamon Rolls recipe, 117
type 2 diabetes, 29

U

umami, using when cooking, 70
"unwich" wraps, 63
US Wellness Meats brand, 63

V

Valentine Deviled Eggs recipe, 266–267
Valentine's Day Breakfast recipe, 256–257
Valentine's Day Muffin Pan Ice Cream Cakes recipe, 288–289
vegetable broth
    Christmas Tomato Soup with Grilled Cheese Stars and Trees, 258–259
    Easiest Mayo Ever, 365
    Protein-Packed Ranch Dip, 367
    Sugar-Free Ketchup, 369
    Traditional Ranch, 368
vegetable oils, 24
vegetables. See also specific types
    as carbohydrates, 15–17
    highest/lowest in sugar, 17
Veggie and Savory Fruit Flowers recipe, 130–131
Veggie Dill Dip recipe, 366
    Veggie and Savory Fruit Flowers, 130–131
vitamin C, 16, 31
vitamin D, 32, 47
vitamin K2, 47

W

Waffle Cone Mini Waffles recipe, 356–357
waffle maker, 74
watermelon radishes
    Valentine Deviled Eggs, 266–267
whey protein powder
    Crunch Berry Cereal, 112–113
whipped cream
    Breakfast Kabobs, 92–93
    Easy Blender Waffles, 336–337
    Valentine's Day Muffin Pan Ice Cream Cakes, 288–289
Whisps Cheese Crisps, 59

X

xylitol, 76

Y

yogurt
    Bombdiggity Pops, 282–283
    Breakfast for Dinner, 230–231
    Christmas Tomato Soup with Grilled Cheese Stars and Trees, 258–259
    Fruit Dip, 371
    plain, 67
    Protein-Packed Blue Milk, 82–83
    Strawberry Breakfast Parfait, 86–87

Z

Zombie Spaghetti and Eyeballs recipe, 260–261
Zsweet, 76
zucchini
    "Apple" Pie Waffles, 352–353
    Spaghetti Bolognese, 240–241
    Zombie Spaghetti and Eyeballs, 260–261